David Herwald 1982

SCHOONERMAN

SCHOONERMAN

Captain Richard England

Former Master-Owner of *Nellie Bywater*,
Britain's last fully-rigged merchant schooner

With a Foreword by Winston Graham

HOLLIS & CARTER
LONDON SYDNEY
TORONTO

To all who served in schooners
and particularly
to Bill,
with love and gratitude.

British Library Cataloguing
in Publication Data
England, Richard
Schoonerman.
1. Schooners
I. Title
387.5'092'4   HE566.S3
ISBN 0 370 30377 6

© Richard England 1981
Foreword © Winston Graham 1981
Printed in Great Britain for
Hollis & Carter
an associate company of
The Bodley Head Ltd.
9 Bow Street, London WC2E 7AL
by Biddles Ltd, Guildford
Phototypeset in Linotron 202 Sabon by
Western Printing Services Ltd, Bristol
First published 1981

CONTENTS

List of illustrations

The half-title illustrations and the plans of
Nellie Bywater (pp. 282–5) are by the author.

FOREWORD
by Winston Graham

I have never met Richard England, though had events moved more happily for us both—as will be related in this book—we might now be old friends. As it is, I can only recommend *Schoonerman* in the way it should most properly be recommended, without prejudice or personal involvement; and this I most heartily do.

In an age when the amateur sailor, the week-end sailor, the holiday sailor ever proliferates, so that bright new marinas flourish in every little port, and men and women take to the sea for pleasure or to escape from the problems of the land, and vie with each other to pit their varying skills against wind and wave, it is fascinating to read an account written by one of the last true professionals in the harsh world of the coastal schooner trade. For him the sea has indeed been The Cruel Sea. Yet all his vicissitudes in small and vulnerable sailing vessels, his struggles with obstinate, difficult and fractious human beings, his efforts to break through the stifling red tape of the official world, the hardships that constantly beset him, are related with an absence of bitterness and rancour that compel admiration.

There is indeed in this book, although it is a recital of unrelenting struggle, a sense of dedication and happiness, as if Captain England and his wife and daughters achieved a contentment and unity in spite of it all and that, looking back on those days, he finds a real pleasure in the telling and only once the pain.

From any point of view this book must surely be looked on as a valuable record of a time now gone for ever, a vivid yet factual record that carries conviction. It was really like this, one thinks, and it will never come again. As the author remarks at a tragic point in his narrative: *Sic Transit Gloria Mundi.*

WINSTON GRAHAM

AUTHOR'S PREFACE

This book would never have been written but for the patience of a long-suffering wife and the constant encouragement of young friends.

When I began it, I was hopefully relying on old shipmates, ex-schoonermen friends and others in ancillary trades to confirm what I was writing down but, sadly, I discovered they'd all passed on. This brought a sense of urgency to my task.

With only an old man's memories as a guide, I've done my best to portray life in small British schooners during the closing of an era. My story is no different to those of countless past schoonermen; a constant battle against the sea and rapidly changing economic conditions.

I've gone to great pains to make my personal account as faithful and accurate as possible. We all see events through different eyes and the viewpoints in this book are solely my own.

My efforts will not be in vain if I can leave behind, in print, a memorial to the schooners I loved, a tribute to some of the remarkable men who manned them and a record of a British way of life, unchanged for more than a century, which has now gone for ever.

1980

ACKNOWLEDGEMENTS

My grateful thanks for assistance to: D. Houghton, Lloyd's Register of Shipping; Royal National Lifeboat Institution; Gwynedd County Libraries; Charles Jones & Sons, Ltd., Rhyl; James Hughes, Rhyl; J. W. Jones, Rhyl; Michael Powell, London; Cricklade Branch, Wiltshire County Libraries; Family of the late Hugh Jones, Millom; Richard J. Scott, Limerick; Richard Hayward, Litlington; Gilbert Odd, Northiam; Brian Hale, Aldbourne; Eileen Wilkes, Cricklade.

Also to The Society of Authors as the literary representative of the Estate of John Masefield, for permission to quote from that poet's Collected Works.

R.E.
Latton, Wiltshire, 1980

PART ONE

SEA FEVER

'Wouldst thou'—so the helmsman answered,
'Learn the secret of the sea,
Only those who brave its dangers
Comprehend its mystery!'

Longfellow

1

The Beginning: A Raft

I was born in a little town, thirty miles inland from the great seaport of Liverpool. I was the second son of a family of four . . . three boys and a girl. My father and mother were middle class and we were brought up to a comfortable way of life, with good food, clothing and little luxuries that many couldn't afford in those days.

Father was very tall, spare, and heavily moustached. His grey eyes behind pince-nez spectacles were cold and impersonal. His severe expression and aloof, undemonstrative nature discouraged intimacy. An architect and surveyor by profession, he was a pillar of respectability; a sidesman of his church, a Mason and a leading figure in the town's activities.

As children, we'd little contact with him, except when matters of our education or discipline required his attention. In fact, we avoided him as much as possible, for his presence generally spelt punishment or something equally unpleasant. Yet, he was a very good father, provided well for us all and installed in us strict standards of self-discipline, honesty and industry. This was commendable, as I learned through my mother that he came from a family who'd earned for themselves the title of 'the Wild Englands' by their rash behaviour. It was alleged that, between them, the family had broken nearly every bone in the human frame in exploits of horsemanship.

It was from my mother that I gleaned a sparse outline of her family background. She was a complete opposite to Father, small, dark and very much the extrovert. Her father, a talented architect, practised in both Britain and America. The family commuted across the Atlantic in a manner more suitable to this Jet Age than the era they lived in. Before she'd reached her teens, Mother had crossed the ocean in sail and sail-and-steam ships, travelled extensively in the United States and would have remained there but for her mother's ill health and early death. Her marriage to my father, the rearing of her family and constant ill health never succeeded in quenching her roving spirit.

We lived in an ugly, pretentious, red-brick house on the

outskirts of the town. Some people have nostalgic memories of their birthplace but I never liked that draughty, gloomy house and returned there unwillingly only on one occasion after spreading my wings. Even as a child, I regarded it as a temporary home and longed to leave it. Every year, the family spent the month of August on holiday at Rhyl, a small resort on the North Wales coast. To me, the month was pure heaven . . . just to be in sight of the sea. As I grew older, the period between holidays became almost intolerable with my longing for the sea. I'd already decided, when old enough, to become a sailor. Looking back, there's no doubt I was an odd kid to be so strongly motivated, without example, precedent or encouragement.

I was about seven years of age when I made my first positive move by dreaming up the raft.

A favourite play-spot near my home was a large and beautiful country estate, with dense pine woods, wide meadows and over five miles of river winding tortuously through the undulating countryside.

In a secluded bend of the river, I'd an island hideout. Here, over a camp fire, I'd cook all kinds of strange meals, then sit by the fire, eating and drinking and dreaming my dreams of the future. It was here that I planned my escape to the sea. I reasoned that the river must flow to the ocean, so all I had to do was build a raft and let the currents take me to my desired destination. I planned carefully and secretly, not even telling my few chums of the project.

I smuggled a toy carpentry-set saw, a coal hatchet and a few lengths of rope out of the house one weekend, and commenced raft building on the island. Selecting a tall, straight pine tree in the nearby woods, I began felling it with my tiny saw. It was slow work but I persisted all that weekend until the tree toppled over. Cutting the trunk into the desired lengths fully occupied my time for several weekends, but meanwhile, I was saving my tuppence a week pocket money to buy nail fastenings. Gradually, the raft frame was assembled and spiked together. The problem of planking for the deck was solved when I found a sound door of just the right size, in a derelict barn up-river of the island. Dragging it to the river and floating it to the required spot took another day but I was well rewarded for the effort when it was secured on the framework and the raft complete. When launched, the raft had taken over six weeks of my free time, all my pocket money and all the resource I could muster. But, as I gazed at my unwieldy craft afloat off the island, I was justly proud of her. I carefully hid her under the river bank, covered by overhanging willows and sedges which made an effective camouflage, before trudging home with my head full of the great adventure.

The following week seemed interminable and lessons at the little Dame school I attended a terrible drudgery. Someone should have been alerted of something afoot by my strange, preoccupied manner, but it passed un-noticed.

When Saturday, my sailing day arrived, I was in a high pitch of excitement. Early in the morning, I crept from the house to the outside laundry and dressed myself in clothing already hidden there. Clad in an oilskin coat, sou'wester and wellingtons, with my mother's clothes prop and drying line on my shoulders, I set off for the island. The weather was fine, I had a bag of provisions to last me for several days and everything seemed set for a successful start to the enterprise.

The raft was just as I'd left it. I busied myself extricating it from its hiding place and mooring it at a suitable spot for embarking. I was aboard, securing my provisions with cord lashings, when, without any warning, a powerful hand grabbed my collar and hauled me, squirming vigorously, to the safety of the river bank.

Struggling desperately, I slipped like an eel from the restraining hands and fled to a safe distance. Out of breath and very frightened, I turned to face my unexpected assailant.

He was an estate gamekeeper, in a very excitable and angry mood, shouting and waving his arms about, so I kept my distance. After a time, he quietened down and we just glowered at one another. I hoped he'd go away, but instead, he hauled my raft up the river bank and remained guarding it, despite my attempts to draw him away. We both stayed in this position of stalemate until dusk forced me to accept defeat and return home.

A cautious but thorough reconnaissance of the area the following morning failed to reveal a trace of my raft; it had completely vanished. I was absolutely furious and it confirmed my opinion that most 'grown-ups' were potty.

But later on, when I grew old enough to appreciate danger, I realised I'd had a lucky escape. Only a short distance down river from the island was the first of a series of dangerous weirs, all with deep pools below them. I could easily have been drowned but for the gamekeeper's timely intervention.

The setback with the raft prompted me to confine my next ship-building venture to something less ambitious. In a magazine, I saw a picture of an American four-masted schooner which fired my imagination. On the largest sheet of wrapping paper I could obtain, I drew plans of the schooner, using the magazine illustration as a guide. The hull was to be about four feet in length, making a model nearly five feet overall. That I'd neither workshop nor tools didn't deter me. I commandeered a kitchen table and set it up in the laundry, came to an agreement with my brother for the use of his Stripwork tools, 'borrowed' my father's ripsaw and hammer, also various kitchen knives which I converted into chisels by breaking off all but a couple of inches of their blades. The ends of the shortened blades I ground into cutting edges. Our poor kitchen maid got the blame for the missing cutlery.

I obtained a block of pine for the hull of my model at a small timber yard owned by an old, wizened up little Jew. As I walked around the various stacks with the old man, I was very particular about the quality of the timber I needed, rejecting everything with knots or shakes. When I found a suitable piece, I was worried about its cost as all I possessed was a shilling. The price was 1/6d. For a couple of hours I followed the timber merchant round his premises, trying to beat him down to the shilling, until at length, after enjoying his fun, he told me to take the wood and 'make myself scarce'. I think he derived considerable amusement though little profit from our transaction. I felt guilty and very concerned when, shortly afterwards, I heard the kind old man had been made a bankrupt.

The building of the model schooner with such primitive and inadequate tools proved to be a colossal task for such a small boy, but by perseverance I succeeded in turning out a surprisingly fine sailing model, which was to be the first of a fleet of ship models of every rig that I made as a boy. All the information I needed for my models I obtained from books in the town's Free Library. My model shipbuilding gave me dexterity with tools but the most important lesson I learnt from it was the value of books; for I discovered they were the key to knowledge.

During the next few years, I borrowed every book on the sea in the library and read them from cover to cover. Clark Russel, Richard Dana, Morley Roberts, Conrad, Bullen were my light reading but I was equally at home wading through Nicholls's *Seamanship*, Kipping's *Sails and Sailmaking* or Norie's *Navigation*. The number and range of these text books for seafarers suggested a strong link between that inland town and the sea, though this wasn't surprising with Liverpool and its fine ships only thirty miles away attracting a steady stream of adventurous boys and young men away from the locality.

So far, I'd been a 'loner' with no-one to talk to about the sea and ships. None of the boys I knew were the slightest bit interested and quickly sheered off if I mentioned the subject. Then, through my models, I was introduced to an ex-sailorman, Old Dick, and a strange friendship began. Dick, who was about the same age as my father, had served his apprenticeship in the four-masted barque *Kate Thomas*, of the William Thomas Line, Liverpool. He was not overstrong when he went to sea, and the rigours of life in the half-deck of the great steel Cape Horner eventually wrecked his health, ending his seafaring. It was the great disappointment of his life, for he was a natural sailorman, and could never get the sea fever out of his system.

He and his quiet, charming wife made me a welcome visitor at their home. In their living room, redolent of salt water, with pictures of the *Kate Thomas* on the walls, a waterline model of the barque on the sideboard, and a sea chest in a corner, I listened spellbound for hours to the old sailorman's stories of Cape Horn, the nitrate ports of South America, fire, strandings and shipwrecks, the common and frequent happenings of the hard and dangerous West Coast trade. Sometimes, when yarning about a particularly stirring incident, Dick became transformed from a pain-wracked, prematurely old man into the adventurous young sailor of former days. His wife, sitting quietly knitting nearby, would smile indulgently at the momentary change and seemed to approve.

Dick's sea chest fascinated me. Inside the lid was a painting of the *Kate Thomas* under full sail, executed with ship's paints. The barque was professionally correct to the smallest details and flew an oversized house flag at the main truck and her signal letters from the peak of the spanker gaff. She was depicted close hauled on the starboard tack, thrashing to wind'ard through a terrifying sea. Like most sailor's paintings, it had something of the primitive about it which added to its appeal.

The chest contained most of the former sailor's outfit, all neatly stowed. On top of everything was the curiously old-fashioned apprentice's cap, bearing the cap badge of the William Thomas Line, and a brass-bound uniform with buttons tarnished by salt water. Below the uniform were a suit of oilskins, a sou'wester, leather sea boots and other items of clothing. A hand-sewn canvas holdall contained the personal tools of a sailorman ... sheath knife, spike, lignum vitae fids, a serving mallet, palm, sailhook, assorted needles, a hank of flax sailtwine and a lump of beeswax. At the bottom of the chest were Dick's most treasured possessions; the mahogany instrument case containing his sextant, a very old edition of Norie's *Navigation*, parallel rulers, dividers; everything needed by an ambitious young sailor to mug for a 'ticket'. A little drawer was filled with the usual mementoes of a seafarer, bits of coral, a conch shell, shark's skin and teeth and other oddments. One object particularly took my eye. It was a knife lanyard, made up in white cotton. Nearly every kind of ropework used on shipboard was intermingled in a most artistic design. Sinnets, Turk's Heads, footrope, diamond and rose knots, bannister bars and cockscombings were so cunningly blended that the lanyard was a thing of beauty and I never saw its equal in all my later seagoing.

I owed a great deal to this quiet couple, for the old sailor taught me everything that could be learned ashore about ships and his wife made me feel their house was my second home. In my youthful enthusiasm I must have frequently outstayed my welcome. On one occasion in particular I remember causing them acute embarrassment. I persuaded Dick to teach me how to use his sextant, after mugging in Norie's and learning to read the arc and vernier. He rigged up a crude artificial horizon on the lawn at the rear of his house, so I had the great thrill of taking actual star sights on clear nights. I was becoming quite proficient, with practice, until, one night, in the middle of my navigation lesson, we were interrupted by a loud hammering at the front door. Our caller was a neighbour, whose dwelling backed onto Dick's garden. The man was in a violent temper, accusing us of spying through a telescope at his wife undressing and preparing for bed and he threatened us with the direst physical punishment if he caught us at it again. Our explanations to the ignorant neighbour fell on deaf ears, so, to my dismay, navigation instruction in the back garden had to cease.

The absurd incident thoroughly upset Dick and his wife but my enthusiasm and thirst for nautical knowledge remained as strong as ever and I continued to visit them until I left home.

Having lived in the period of two World Wars, I'm amazed at the resilience of children to such tragic events. I remember clearly the outbreak of the First World War and the Sunday lunchtime when my father announced his enlistment in the Royal Engineers. Within a few days, Father disappeared and except for two or three very short leaves, he spent the remainder of the war on active service in France, Belgium and Germany. I scarcely missed him as I'd never seen much of him when he was at home.

When Father returned home from Germany at the end of the War, he was a sick man, confined to bed for many months. Our seaside holidays in 1919 were a convalescence for him, but to me that holiday will be remembered as the first time I went afloat in a sailing vessel.

The railway journey to Chester was quite boring but after that, the train followed the course of the River Dee to the coast. With my nose pressed tightly against the carriage window, I rapturously watched the river widen into a navigable channel. At Connah's Quay I saw what I'd been waiting for . . . the masts and yards of sailings ships, loading at the small port. A little later I caught a fleeting glimpse of two or three more vessels, lying at Mostyn. Past Mostyn, the river fanned out into a wide estuary, guarded by Hilbre Island and there, at the base of the marram-grassed sand-dunes was the Irish Sea, blue and shimmering to the distant horizon. The first sight of it never failed to make me catch my breath.

Rhyl, at the mouth of the River Clwyd owed it's popularity as a holiday resort to it's firm, clean, sandy foreshore. It had all the usual amenities for the summer visitor: theatres, cinemas, pierrot troupes and a fairground, but none of these attracted me. My

19

interests lay in the southern part of the town, near the River Clwyd. Here, on the outskirts of the town, was a large salt-water boating lake which was ideal for sailing my ship models and near to it, my favourite spot, the Foryd, a small tidal harbour formed by a bight of the river, between the toll bridge and the sea. At low water, the harbour nearly dried out, uncovering a large area of mud through which the Clwyd followed a tortuous course before joining the sea in an S bend scoured through the hard sand of Rhyl Flats.

Most of my time was spent at the Foryd, but when the weather suited on Sunday mornings, I carried the big model schooner to the Marine Lake and sailed her across this often choppy expanse of salt water. I chose Sundays, as the lake was then clear of skiffs and pleasure craft and the adjoining fairground closed: the Sabbath was strictly observed in Wales, a stronghold of the Nonconformist faiths.

On a particularly fresh Sunday morning, with the wind causing considerable turbulence on the lake, I was sailing my schooner from one shore to the other and thoroughly enjoying myself. The sails of the schooner had to be carefully adjusted for each passage to ensure that she weathered a kidney-shaped island in the lake's centre. Setting her on course, I then sprinted around the lake to intercept her as she reached the opposite side. She was a swift sailer and the distance I had to run was nearly a quarter of a mile, so it was always a race between us and sometimes I only just arrived in time to prevent her from splintering her jibboom on the battered stone retaining wall surrounding the lake.

Two crossings had been successfully made but, on the third, things went wrong. Either I made an error with the sail trimming or the wind changed. I watched helplessly as the little craft altered course and became trapped on a lee shore of the island. The swells were driving her against the stonework and it was agonising to see the model, which had taken so long to make, being reduced to matchwood. I knew I must get help and charged at breakneck speed for the main gate of the pleasure park. Here I nearly collided with a stallholder in his Sunday best.

'Where can I find the boatman?' I panted, breathlessly.

'Mr Jones will be in the chapel around the corner, Bach,' he answered. 'He sits in the high place, look you.'

I was off again before he'd finished, around the corner as directed and straight into the Methodist Chapel. On a platform at the end of the hall I saw the old boatman with his flowing white whiskers, sitting straight-backed and devout, with his fellow deacons. Down the aisle and onto the platform I careered before an astonished congregation, to gabble an almost incoherent appeal for help.

Heedless of the scandalised looks from all sides and without hesitation, the old man rose from his seat on the rostrum and together we scurried out of the chapel and down to the lake in record time. He launched a skiff, rowed me over to the island and I rescued my model schooner almost unharmed. When we landed at the boat stage, both of us were soaked with salt spray. I couldn't thank the old boatman enough for his kindness but he just stumped off, presumably back to the 'high place'.

Afterwards, I grudgingly decided that there might, perhaps, be something worthwhile in religion in spite of its many disadvantages.

The Foryd harbour fascinated me and I almost lived there during the holidays. From my favourite vantage point, an ancient greenheart mooring pawl on a derelict quay, I watched for hours the life of the little haven. On the far side of the river, there was the timber yard of Charles Jones & Sons with a quay frontage capable of berthing half a dozen small ships; on the town side were the remnants of another quay and a few rotting hulks, the last traces of a former thriving shipyard. Between the old shipyard and the end of the concrete promenade stretched a sloping shingle hard on which a long row of cutter rigged fishing smacks were propped up on 'legs', when the fleet was in port. Handily situated opposite the hard and rising out of the shingle beach, stood the squat, picturesque, Foryd tavern, the place of refreshment for fishermen and sailors.

My time was regulated by the tides, for I liked to be at the Foryd when the fishing fleet was entering or leaving port. Occasional cargoes of cement came to the timber yard quay in home-trade schooners and towards the end of August, timber carriers began arriving from the Baltic; mainly schooners or barquentines with high deck loads of deals. On sighting a vessel standing in for the harbour entrance, I climbed to the top of the sea wall and studied every manoeuvre from when she was boarded by the Rhyl pilot until she was safely berthed alongside the timber yard. Most of these vessels flew the red and white flag of Denmark and hailed from either Marstal or Svendborg and my delight was unbounded when two or three of these smart, well maintained little ships were in the harbour. With the tides full, I'd watch the blonde Norsemen discharging the timber cargoes and at low water, I sometimes rolled my trousers up to my thighs to wade through the mud until I was nearly under the sterns of the dried out schooners where I could examine their hulls, rigging and spars at close quarters.

I frequently returned to my seaside home wet and mudstained but I can't remember my parents complaining. They were puzzled by my lack of interest in all but the harbour and the ships. As long as I kept out of serious mischief and they knew where to find me, they were content. In fact, they seemed relieved that I left them in peace to enjoy their vacation.

The winds and tides brought infinite variety to the Foryd. On days of fresh westerlies and high tides, the smacks made a brave sight entering harbour; clipping along with foaming bows, under a press of sail, each skipper trying to outsail the others. On calm days, the self-same boats, with their useless canvas hanging listlessly from their spars, would be slowly and laboriously poled through the winding channel. I was to become well acquainted with these fine sailing smacks and some of their skippers, too.

One warm, bright Sunday afternoon, I was sitting on my usual pawl, drowsy with the heat and enjoying the peaceful scene. A few yards away, at the old shipyard quay, lay the white painted smack *Lizzie*, tied up as usual away from the rest of the fleet.

I became aware that I wasn't alone on the quay. A summer visitor, out for a Sunday afternoon's stroll, was also enjoying the picturesque view. She was a tall, regal old lady, dressed in rustling, cream alpaca. On her head was an enormous flowered hat and she carried an opened parasol. For some moments she silently contemplated the harbour, the shipping and the fishing boats; a look of perfect bliss on her aristocratic old face. Having taken in all the more distant features of the haven she turned her attentions to the nearby *Lizzie*. As she did so, a brown faced, heavily moustached fisherman, with gold sleepers in his ears, appeared through the smack's forescuttle and, seeing the old lady peering down at him, remarked politely: 'Good afternoon, M'am. It's a lovely day!'

'Good afternoon to you, my good man,' she replied. 'It certainly is. Do you live in that little boat?'

'Aye. That I do, Ma'am. I've a very comfortable little cuddy in the *Lizzie*,' he answered.

The lady beamed: 'How very interesting,' she said. 'It's just like Peggotty in Charles Dickens's *David Copperfield*'.

She prattled on for a few minutes longer, then continued her leisurely and dignified promenading. With a perplexed expression on his tanned face, the fisherman watched her go. Then our eyes met and simultaneously we both burst into uncontrollable laughter.

'It's so funny the things visitors say to us,' he gasped, wiping the tears from his eyes with the back of his hand. 'But I suppose a fisherman's life must seem strange to them. I've seen you about the Foryd for some time, haven't I? Do you like boats? Then come aboard and see over my *Lizzie*.'

I could scarcely believe my good fortune as I accepted the heaven-sent invitation. As I scrambled aboard the smack I thought: this is the real thing, at last!

My new acquaintance, whom I soon called John Henry, conducted me over his boat with obvious pride, explaining all her features in detail. At the end of the tour of inspection, my face must have revealed my desire . . . to go to sea in the *Lizzie*, for, as if reading my thoughts, John Henry invited me to accompany him on a fishing trip the following day.

2

The Smack *Lizzie*

Most of the Rhyl fishing smacks were Lancashire 'Nobbies', a design of boat particularly suitable for West coast fishing. The *Lizzie* was a 'nobby', built by Crossfield's of Arnside, Cumberland. About 38 feet in length, with a beam of 10 feet, she drew 5 feet of water aft. Her lines were exceptionally trim for a working boat, with a nicely curved stem, a rockered keel and a sharply raked sternpost and rudder under the low, overhanging counter.

Rigged as a gaff cutter, with a stout pole mast, she carried a very long tops'l yard which extended nearly 12 feet above the truck when the tops'l was set. Her running bowsprit was 10 feet outboard, and she set a large spread of canvas for sailing speedily to and from the fishing grounds, but could quickly and easily be snugged down to working rig.

For'ard, she had a small forecastle or cuddy, extending to the mast. Entered by means of a lifting hatchway on the fore deck, the cuddy was very snug although it had only sitting headroom. It was painted out in white enamel, with nicely grained seat lockers on each side, a small table in between and a coal bogey stove, for heating and cooking, against the after bulkhead.

From the mast to the counter was a long fishing well, protected by coamings, providing stowage for the nets, dan buoys, fish boxes and other implements of her trade. On one of her narrow side decks lay the trawl beam with its sledge-shaped 'irons'.

From the initial trip in *Lizzie*, I became John Henry's constant companion. Unlike the other smacksmen of the port, who had mates and members of their families to help with the fishing, John Henry worked the *Lizzie* single-handed. All the other fishermen were natives of Rhyl, with homes in the town. John Henry was a 'foreigner' from Chester River and lived alone in his smack, winter and summer, doing his own shopping, cooking, washing and sewing, completely independent in every way. The tall, tough fishermen possessed the same characteristics as his boat; reliability, strength, simplicity and neatness. I believe he was a lonely man for he seemed to enjoy having me for company. During the remainder of my stay at Rhyl and on subsequent visits there, I spent the whole of my time with John Henry in the *Lizzie* and my parents scarcely saw me.

At the beginning, I kept well out of the way, so as not to be a hindrance, helping by stoking up the bogey and keeping a constant supply of hot tea on the brew. The unaccustomed heave of the sea, fortunately, never troubled me and I soon had my sea legs. I kept a watchful eye on everything John Henry did and was soon able to make myself useful about the *Lizzie*, coiling running gear, washing down the decks and even 'spelling' the skipper for short periods at the tiller. The sailing of the boat came to me quite naturally but the intricacies of trawling were another matter. Seeing John Henry at work, I was amazed at the knowledge and skill required of a trawlerman. He seemed to know just where to trawl and when over this chosen 'ground', he'd bring the *Lizzie* head to wind—lying-to, he called it—pay out the net, then heave over the beam before going onto the other tack to tow down wind and tide. The exact adjustments of the trawl warps, the amount of sail to carry, the labour saving tricks for hauling couldn't be learned except by long experience. I never acquired more than the most elementary knowledge of trawling.

My first few trips in the *Lizzie* were during the daytime and the first occasion I went night fishing was a memorable one.

I crept out of a sleeping house and strode along a deserted promenade to the Foryd, with the sound of the breakers in my ears and the channel buoys of Liverpool Bay winking at me out of the darkness.

As I boarded the *Lizzie*, John Henry greeted me with a cheerful: 'Come below, Dick!' through the half opened forescuttle.

In the cosy, lamp-lit cuddy, we enjoyed a mug of tea, toasting ourselves in front of the glowing bogey, as we waited for the tide to make. I could hear it splashing and gurgling on the outside of the pitchpine skin planking of the boat.

When the tide had risen sufficiently in the harbour, we exchanged the fug in the cuddy for the keen salt air on deck.

A nice offshore breeze enabled us to clear the quayside with just the stays'l hoisted. As the *Lizzie* gathered way, we got the mains'l up and headed for the harbour's mouth. In the darkness, we could hear voices, the chirruping of blocks and the creak of gear, as other craft prepared for sea and around us were the vague outlines of several boats already under sail.

Once clear of the channel and other craft, John Henry set the gaff tops'l and flying jib and drove the *Lizzie* towards one of his favourite trawling grounds. I never knew how he found these areas, for a sounding or two with the leadline seemed all he needed to locate them. When over the chosen ground, he lay-to and cleared away the trawl. With the gear overside and the warps satisfactorily adjusted, we settled down in the well with mugs of tea, watching the phosphorescence created by the warps and *Lizzie*'s slow progress down tide. There was something very soothing about her easy motion when towing, for she rode over the swells as naturally as a gull.

John Henry, with his pipe going full blast, steered in silence. Several times, I felt myself nodding off to sleep. After about a couple of hours' towing, John Henry hauled in the trawl, cunningly allowing the tide to do much of the work; though single-handed, it was still a strenuous business. I couldn't do much to help, but when the cod end of the net had been emptied, I gave a hand sorting and boxing the catch, then washed the mud off the *Lizzie*.

The trawling operations continued throughout the night, but although I was determined not to miss anything of the night's fishing, nature took a hand. John Henry noticing I was dozing off, sent me below for a sleep.

'We can't have your Dad blaming me for tiring you out, Dick,' he said. 'Go and have a bit of shuteye.'

I slept like a log for the remainder of the night, until roused by John Henry with a mug of tea.

'You've brought me luck, Dick,' he chuckled. 'We've done well in the night . . . quite a nice haul of dabs and plaice and nearly a box of sole. We won't do much now it's daylight but I'm more than satisfied.'

When we returned to the Foryd, we'd a better catch than any of the local boats.

But it wasn't always like that. Sometimes there was little to show for hours of toil. When trawling became unprofitable and the mackerel were in the bay, John Henry would go after these surface fish with hand lines. I preferred this to trawling as I could handle some of the lines myself and we were under way the whole time. We used up to a dozen lines apiece each with twelve hooks on them, and it was great fun when sailing through a large shoal; hauling in the lines as fast as we could, sometimes with a fish to each hook. Clearing the hooks, rebaiting, hauling; all at breakneck speed. Then, clear of a shoal, a short respite, as *Lizzie* was sailed in quest of another shoal. If we were fortunate, we could fill all our boxes in a few hours and head for home.

When the weather turned too rough for fishing, I helped about the boat, doing a bit of painting, cleaning, passing the ball of marline as John Henry served over a splice; doing things which were to come in useful one day. If we were working together, John Henry sometimes talked about his past life in barges, ketches and schooners, but often there were long periods of silence.

I sensed that something was wrong and one day, he confided in me. The local fishermen resented him using their harbour; that was why the *Lizzie* moored away from the other smacks. They were stirring up trouble and agitating for his expulsion from the Foryd, on the grounds that he was a 'foreigner'. There was only one man he could call a friend at the Foryd; Freddie Harrison, the young skipper of the smack *Three Brothers*.

Not long after hearing this, on a day when strong winds and a heavy sea kept the fishing fleet in port, I was helping John Henry scrub the *Lizzie*'s bottom when she was dried out. Our work finished, we were having a breather and I was admiring the little ship's lines, when he said: 'Aye, she's a grand little boat or I shouldn't be talking to you now! The winter before I met you was a hard time for me with the weather so bad the *Lizzie* was tied up most of the time. It was all I could do to make ends meet.

'Just before Christmas, the weather let up a bit and I chanced my luck and put to sea. For all my trouble, I caught nothing. On my way back, I got caught, proper, though. The wind piped up suddenly about nor'nor'east, with heavy snow squalls. The sea on the flats was something terrible. *Lizzie* was well snugged down when it hit us and she took it well. It went black as pitch and I couldn't see a thing, what with the snow driving into my eyes and all the spray, so I ratched off shore as far as I dare, then reefed the main down to the last band. We ratched off and on, all night; the worst night I can remember a regular blizzard, and the cold was something cruel. I daresn't leave the tiller to get a warm, so just hutched up and had to grin and bear it. *Lizzie* took it all better'n me, though she was all froze up, too. If she hadn't been doing so good, I think I'd have given up. With the first bit of daylight and the tide making, I knew it was my last chance, as I was about done for. I had a go at the Foryd and with luck, made it. As soon as I was in, I'd just enough strength left to heave over the anchor before I passed out.

'Somebody saw us out in the harbour and got help to get me ashore. I was in hospital for a bit with exposure and the frostbite.

'There's not another boat in the Foryd could have come through that night, so now you know why I'm so fond of my *Lizzie*.'

Poor John Henry! As he spun me the yarn, I think he knew that his fight against the local fishermen for the right to remain and work out of the harbour had been lost. The Town Council were now against him and that was the last straw. A week later, he announced his intention of leaving Rhyl for good; sailing the *Lizzie* to Liverpool and laying her up. 'I'll go back on the river, in tugboats,' he said. 'My brother Bob'll help me sail around there, and you can come for a last sail, if you'd like to?'

In due course, Bob, the lighterman, arrived and *Lizzie* was sailed to the Mersey and her laying-up berth in Liverpool's Dukes Dock.

Dukes Dock was a graveyard for Liverpool's unwanted derelicts; a most depressing sight, with mouldering tugs, barges and small craft of every description, slowly dying on it's refuse-laden waters.

The three of us stood on the edge of the dock, gazing down at the gallant little 'nobby', stripped of her sails and gear, but so clean and trim that she was out of place in such surroundings. It was a sad moment for us all, especially John Henry. Without saying a word, we turned our backs on *Lizzie* and walked miserably away.

I was returning to Rhyl by rail from Lime Street station. On the overhead railway and the tram, my two companions barely exchanged a word; it was as if we'd been to a funeral, and, I thought, perhaps we had.

Outside Lime Street, I remembered the money in my pocket,

1. Foryd Harbour, Rhyl, c. 1914, with a 'nobby' similar to *Lizzie* in right foreground. (*J. W. Jones, historian, Rhyl*)

2. Schooner *Via* of Brixham, latterly owned in Kilkeel, Co. Down. Dover in background. (*Nautical Photo Agency*)

3. Windbound schooners, Holyhead Harbour, c. 1914.
(*Gwynedd County Library*)

4. Windbound schooners, Sloyne, River Mersey, c. 1926. *Ryelands* of Lancaster nearest camera. (*K. P. Lewis, Birkenhead*)

enough for the rail fare and a pound I'd saved from my holiday money to buy my fisherman friend some 'baccy'. When I mentioned this, John Henry asked in a voice charged with emotion: 'Got enough for a drink for me'n Bob?' The pound changed hands and with unbecoming haste the two old sailors headed for the nearest pub. 'Won't be long, Dick,' they called over their shoulders, as they disappeared through a door marked 'Public Bar'. It was a remarkably changed couple that emerged in due course; their faces shiny and damp, all traces of the former depression gone. In great good humour, they hustled me into the railway station, found me my train and saw me off.

As my train began to move, John Henry shouted: 'You've got my address, Dick, keep in touch. So-long. So-long!' The two rather unsteady, jersey-clad figures of my friends receded and were lost to view.

Rhyl was never again the same to me. It's only a coincidence, but from the time John Henry and his *Lizzie* were driven out of the Foryd, the fishermen began to suffer bad times. The number of smacks dwindled and, a few years later, the whole fleet had vanished.

I kept in touch with John Henry and was greatly relieved to hear that the *Lizzie* was reprieved from Dukes Dock before she suffered harm. She was sold for conversion to a yacht but I never saw her again.

John Henry spent the remainder of his working life as a Mersey tugmaster, being nearly eighty years of age when he retired. Over the years we met from time to time; on one occasion, with disastrous results which I shall describe later in my story.

3

The Schooner *Via*, 1925

As a small boy, I was very conscious that I had a weak and frail body. My old friend Dick's sad physical condition, caused by the rigour of his early seafaring, was a constant reminder to me that I must toughen-up before attempting to go to sea. So I began training with regular exercising and boxing, and succeeded in improving my muscular development and stamina to a surprising degree.

I tried hard to get my father's blessing to my plans for a seafaring career, but without success. He flatly refused to discuss the subject and the most I ever got out of him was a terse: 'Stuff and nonsense! It's a dog's life!' on one occasion. So, left to my own devices, I prepared the best way I could, saving until I'd a few pounds and collecting together an outfit, the most essential items gifts from old Dick's sea chest. With my outfit packed in a canvas kit bag and sufficient money in my pocket for rail fare and immediate needs, I approached Father for the last time and told him I was off to find a ship the following day. His reaction was the same as before. 'If you're fool enough to go you'll soon come running back home,' he snorted. I then told my mother, but she didn't take it seriously, either.

Next morning, I crept out of the house with my belongings and caught an early train to Liverpool. On arrival, I parked my heavy bag in the 'Left Luggage'. Outside the station, it was raining cats and dogs, the kind of grey, cold, cheerless day that Liverpool is famed for. In a Pierhead café I had a bite to eat and studied the 'Vessels in Dock' columns in a current issue of the *Journal of Commerce*. My luck was out; on the whole of Merseyside I couldn't find more than a dozen vessels with the desired prefix, S.V. for 'sailing vessel', and some of them were lying in distant places such as Weston Point and Runcorn.

Garston seemed my best bet, so I braved the elements again, and soaking wet, boarded a Garston tram outside the Liver Buildings. The tram ride was much longer than I'd expected: through mean, depressing streets full of people of every nationality with one thing in common; they all looked poorly dressed, drab and poverty-stricken. This was my first real glimpse of a big seaport and my heart sank as I gazed through the streaming, steamy windows of the rattling tram. I couldn't help thinking of my father's last words: 'You'll soon come running back home'. When the tram finally stopped in Garston, near the junction of the Stalybridge Dock Road, I was more than glad to exchange the foul stench of wet, dirty clothing and unwashed bodies for the wind and rain outside.

Of the many ships lying in the rain swept docks, only three were sailing vessels; an insignificant little ketch, almost hidden by the coal teaming down on her from the tips; a light barquentine of about three hundred tons, awaiting her loading, and a lovely barque with painted ports, tied up among the timber-laden steamers. The sight of her made me forget my squelching shoes and clammy, wet clothing, for she looked positively regal even in such unlovely surroundings. Her name was *Dagny* and she was under Norwegian registry. Her sails were bent and with everything clean and well cared for, she was in full seagoing order, yet for all that, was strangely quiet. As I walked down the gangway to her wide spacious deck, the only sign of life I could see was a plume of smoke curling from a stove-pipe in a deckhouse amidships. At the door of the deckhouse, I was greeted by a big, blonde, heavily bearded Norseman, who invited me into the shelter and warmth of the ship's galley in the friendliest way. Over mugs of scalding coffee, he told me of *Dagny*'s recent smart twelve days' passage from Canada with a cargo of timber, and poured out his praises of her. But a sad fact emerged from his talk; she would voyage no more, and I was wasting precious time there. The fine little barque was sold, to be shorn of her lofty spars and turned into a coal hulk for bunkering steamers. 'Is bad. Is bad,' the Norseman kept on repeating, sorrowfully, until I left.

I next tried the barquentine across the basin, but fared even worse than before. Her hard-faced captain gave me a terse 'No!' to my request for a job. 'Don't want no truck with runaways!' he spat after me, as I hurriedly retreated shorewards, quite shaken and rapidly losing confidence. It didn't occur to me that my clothes, although soaking wet, were far too good for a lad seeking a job as a ship's boy.

There was no further reason for remaining in Garson, especially as the damp November day was rapidly ending. With the approaching dusk, the dockside lights were coming on, so I took the first tram back to Liverpool Pierhead.

My empty stomach reminded me that I hadn't eaten all day, except for the early morning snack. And, I must have walked miles around the dock basins. No wonder things looked grim!

In a cheap but clean little eating house near the Pierhead, I had a good tuck-in. The food, warmth and rest worked wonders and I decided to have another attempt at finding a ship, but this time in the docks nearest to the Pierhead. In the first I visited, the Canning Half-Tide dock, I saw, to my surprise, the same little ketch I'd seen earlier in the day under the coal tips at Garston. Then she'd been beneath my notice, but the situation had now changed and, small though she was, she had sails. On her stern I read: *Excel* of Poole. In the dim light of the quayside gas-lamps, two men were busy with draw bucket and deck scrubs, removing the last traces of coal from her deck, as I scrambled aboard.

'Can I speak to the Captain?' I asked. One of them grinned and jerked his thumb in the direction of a small caboose that served as the galley. Its tiny doorway was blocked by a huge back and a pair of enormously broad shoulders. At the sound of my hesitant voice, a giant of a man slowly withdrew from the little hutch and turned towards me. He was a frightening sight. His great barrel of a chest, covered in coarse, black, matted hair was exposed where the shirt fronts failed to meet by several inches. His ugly, wide nostrilled face was unshaven, coal blackened and creased with rivulets of sweat. I was so scared by his appearance that, for a moment or two, I was tongue-tied.

In a surprisingly low, pleasant, Irish voice, he asked my business. When I told him I was looking for a job as a ship's boy in a sailing ship, he explained in the most understanding way that his little *Excel* wasn't the ship for me: that I needed a vessel with square rig, where I could learn to go aloft and become a real sailor. He advised me to try the schooner *Via*, in the adjacent Salthouse Dock. 'She's a fine big tops'l schooner, boy, and her captain's a friend of mine. Tell Cap'n Doyle it's Jack Ballance sent you,' he said.

The introduction from big, soft-hearted Captain Ballance did the trick. At the mention of his name, the bluff, white-whiskered old master of the *Via* agreed to take me as 'boy'. Within a few hours I'd collected my kit from the station, shed my wet clothing and, dead tired but triumphant, was lying in a comfortable pipe cot in the *Via*'s clean and roomy fo'c'sle.

The only other occupant of the fo'c'sle was the A.B., John Doyle. He roused me just before daylight, next morning.

As my eyes opened, I became aware of my unusual surroundings by the strong, new exciting odours around me . . . the sailing ship smells of rope, canvas, Stockholm tar and bilgewater.

While dressing in working rig, I took a quick look at the fo'c'sle which was to be my future home. It was a large compartment, shaped to the curves of the schooner's bows, painted out in white. On each side were seat lockers with pipe cots above them, providing sleeping accommodation for four, although only two were ever needed. A massive timber I soon knew as the windlass pawlbitt passed through the forward end of our quarters and against it was a cast iron bogey stove, for warmth in cold weather. A scrubbed deal table, fitted between the pawlbitt and the narrow end of the fo'c'sle, completed the furnishings.

Lighting was provided by an oil lamp on the bulkhead, as it was still dark, but I could see four prismatic decklights in the deckhead for natural lighting.

My first task was to get the galley fire going and help John prepare breakfast. He told me that the preparation and cooking of our meals would be my responsibility, when I'd got the hang of things. That was something I'd not bargained for!

Breakfast was eaten in the smart little after cabin, with the captain presiding at the head of the table. Here I met the fourth member of the schooner's company, Jim Weddock, the mate, an elderly man like the captain. After the meal, I cleared the cabin table, washed up and began cleaning and polishing the cabin and after living accommodation, as instructed by the mate.

The cabin companionway contained a semi-circular stairs with a short alleyway at the bottom. The mate's berth—a tiny room furnished with only a shelf-like wooden bunk—was to port. The alleyway opened into the cabin, which was handsomely appointed. The bulkheads were panelled half-way down in maple and teak. The cabin table occupied the centre space and on three sides of it was a crimson plush settee, the captain's pride and joy.

Above the backrests of the settee was a narrow shelf, edged by a carved teak guardrail. A trim little fireplace with tile surrounds and a brass mantelpiece was set into the fore bulkhead. To starboard, a door led into the Master's quarters. Here, the furnishings consisted of a very comfortable bunk with ample drawer space underneath, a locker seat and a combined desk and dressing table; nothing luxurious but a big improvement on the mate's spartan berth.

What bothered me was the vast amount of brasswork that had to be polished round and about the cabin. Even the companion stairway treads were covered with fretted brass and I saw endless labour ahead. In the midst of all the cleaning and polishing, it was a relief to be told that I was needed on deck to assist with the undocking of the schooner. I was eager to do some sailor's work and so far, had scarcely seen anything of the *Via*'s deck in daylight.

We were ordered to 'single up' and took in all the moorings except for one at the bow and one at the stern. Next, a big hawser, which had been coiled on the mainhatch, was manhandled for'ard, the end taken over the bows and laid out to a massive iron pawl at the dock entrance. As we were dragging it down the quayside John explained that it was a 'grass warp', made of coir fibres, light and buoyant, the most suitable line for moving a ship. Back aboard the schooner, the other end of the warp was taken to a simple hand winch near the mainmast, called the 'dolly', and the remaining moorings cast off. With John and I winding the dolly handles whilst the mate took in the slack warp, the *Via* was hove down into the dock entrance to await a tug. We were all out of breath from our efforts but I was amazed that two men and a boy could move so large a vessel.

Now we were leaving, the Salthouse Dock was deserted except for an old 'wooden wall' Naval Reserve drill ship tied up in a corner. The dock was entirely surrounded by huge warehouses; the upper stories built out over the quays and supported by massive iron columns. John said it was about the oldest dock in Liverpool which, in its heyday, had berthed the finest clipper ships afloat. Now it was obsolete, used only by a few lighters or an occasional schooner. I was rather pleased to know I'd joined my first ship in such an historic dock!

Our tug arrived, a paddle-wheeler named *Troon*, belonging to

Lameys', and we began the tow upriver to Garston. It was a cold, grey day, with a bitter easterly wind blowing across the Mersey, sending the dense black smoke from the tug back over our bows so that we were unable to see ahead. John said the tugmen must be burning their old socks.

The tug sounded a warning blast and rounded to. One of her crew sang out: 'Schooner ahoy! Let-go!' At a nod from Weddock, John slipped the towrope, which splashed overboard and was rapidly hauled back aboard the tug. As the smoke cleared, I could see the stone piers of the Garston Docks entrance just ahead. The *Via*, carrying her way, glided silently towards the entrance, where, in the lee of the watch-house, a group of piermen huddled, ready to take our lines.

The tugmaster leaned out of his wheelhouse window and shouted a farewell to our captain, who waved an acknowledgement. We heard the *Troon*'s telegraph ring, there was a violent thrashing as her paddles churned the brown water into foam, then with a farewell toot of her siren she was away; scurrying at full speed down river in quest of another tow.

A heaving line snaked down from the pier and was hitched to our warp, which we payed out at top speed, until checked by the dockmaster's: 'All fast, Cap'n! Take in the slack! Berth alongside the *Goldseeker!*'

Straining on the dolly handles, we hove the *Via* into the dock. The Old Dock was full of ships, many of them steam colliers, but there must have been at least a dozen sailing vessels where the previous day there had been only a solitary barquentine. The loading berths under the coal tips were all occupied by steamers, for I learned later that the 'windjammers' always took second place to steamers, which I considered a most unfair practice. The waiting sailing vessels lay together at the West Wall and our arrival brought a sprinkling of men and boys to the rails of the moored ships.

'Here's t'at ould coffin, the *Via*,' someone called. 'Would ye look now! They've a new "boy", a foreigner!'

A couple of men scrambled aboard the *Via* to help us on the dolly handles. Greetings from old friends, scraps of news and a deal of good-natured banter were exchanged as the schooner warped to her berth alongside the *Goldseeker*.

Sitting in the galley, cooking supper, after we'd moored up, I was aching in every limb from the unaccustomed heaving and hauling on the dolly and the heavy mooring lines. In the twenty-four hours I'd been in the *Via*, I'd not had a moment's respite: cooking, cleaning, brass-polishing and the extremely heavy work on deck. On thing was clear; it would take all my strength and willpower to adjust to the hard life I'd chosen. There was to be no pay, either, for all this work. A schooner's boy received his keep and a little pocket money which was a matter for the captain's discretion. These conditions applied throughout the schooner fleets.

After the meal, more clearing away, washing up and cleaning. I'd never experienced such utter weariness before. As soon as I was free, I headed straight for my cot in the fo'c'sle and slept like a log.

It was nearly a week before a loading berth was available for the *Via*. The wind and rain had gone and the weather was glorious for late October. Each tide brought new arrivals, until the West Wall was a veritable forest of tall masts. It was a brave sight to see such an array of sailing vessels gathered together, the sun glinting on their spars and paintwork and a pleasant breeze off the river fluttering the windsocks at their trucks.

There were some very fine schooners in the fleet, mostly two-masters, though there were one or two with three masts, and the barquentine. But I thought the *Via* was the equal of any of them, for she had the most handsome appearance, with a good sheer, high flaring bows set off by a beautifully carved figurehead of a young girl, and a sharply raked, wide transom stern. Like most of the other schooners she was rigged as a two-masted double tops'l schooner, but with a particularly heavy rig. I learned from John that her tonnage was 126 tons and she'd been built by Upham of Brixham, Devon, in 1864, specially for the fruit trade, which required both speed and seaworthiness. She originally carried stun's'ls and the boom irons were still on her yards.

Her flush deck was broken by three cargo hatches, all quite small, especially the fore and after ones. In the bows was an up-and-down type windlass for working anchors, and just abaft the mainhatch the dolly winch. The small deckhouse galley and the ship's pumps were near the foot of the mainmast. Right aft, the open wheel was protected by a half-round shelter, containing a lamp locker and a toilet. The cabin companionway and skylight were beautifully constructed in teak, with an abundance of heavy brass fittings. The steering compass in the after end of the skylight was a type known as a tell-tale, which could be read either from the wheel or from below. It was lit at night-time by the cabin lamp.

On a beam, just inside the fo'c'sle scuttle, was a carved inscription: 'Certified to accommodate eight seamen', so perhaps, in the past the *Via* had carried quite a large crew. Her present crew of three men and a boy seemed very small to me, but I discovered it was the same in all the other vessels.

I asked John about the ports of registry on the schooners' sterns. He told me that over half the vessels against the West Wall were Irish-owned. Most of them hailed from either Kilkeel or Annalong. The *Via* belonged to Kilkeel, although she had 'Brixham' on her stern. *Lochranza Castle* of Wick, *Minnie* of Peterhead, *Volant* of Kirkwall and *Goldseeker* of Douglas all belonged to County Down ports. It was a custom of the Down owners to retain the original registration when buying a vessel from abroad. They only changed one schooner to local registry, the *Nellie Bywater* formerly of Whitehaven. When this was altered, to read 'Annalong—Port of Newry', it was very puzzling to port officials everywhere as they'd never heard of Annalong. I didn't dare tell John that I'd never heard of the place, or of Kilkeel either, until then. Now knowing where the *Via* belonged, it didn't occur to me that my parents would have welcomed news of my whereabouts and the ship I was in. I must have been a sore trial to them, but I was too busy for letter writing. Each morning I was up before daylight, lighting the galley fire and helping John and the mate scrub the deck as the kettle boiled. I set the cabin table, cooked the breakfast, and after the meal, did the usual chores of clearing away and washing up. Taking advantage of the fine weather, the mate hoisted me in a bo'sun's chair to the main truck to scrape down the topmast. I scraped both topmasts, then with John's help, did the big lowermasts. The masts received two coats of raw linseed oil from trucks to deck and they looked fine with the sun on them.

It was traditional in schooners for the 'boy' to lay out warps, ferry his captain ashore and do most of the small-boat work, so it was essential to be able to scull a ship's boat with a single oar over the transom. I learned in record time, for old Weddock ordered me into our work boat, known as the 'punt', which was moored under the stern, cast off and gave the boat a hefty push towards the centre of the dock basin. He shouted that I wasn't to return until I could scull. I soon got the hang of it!

I memorised the running gear by the same rough but effective method. Weddock took me on a tour of the pinrails, named the coils, then capsized them on the deck. By the time we'd completed a circuit, the deck was a tangle of ropes.

'Coil them back, nately, boy!' he wheezed. 'All right-haunded.' Re-coiling all that gear was a long job, but as soon as I'd finished, we began another round of the pinrails; this time I had to name the coils and wherever I was wrong, down went the fathoms of manila or hemp, again to be laboriously re-coiled by a tired but more knowledgeable boy. It wasn't long before I could find any coil in the dark.

Errands to the grocer and chandler made a welcome break to my endless work aboard the *Via*. The mate would send me off with a warning growl of: 'Hurry back, boy!' but when I was out of his sight, I made the most of my brief liberty.

There was plenty to interest me in the busy docks. A fine, white-painted three-masted schooner, the Swedish *Isolda*, had arrived in port and lay just beyond the coal staithes discharging a cargo of sweet-smelling timber. I was first drawn to her by her graceful, yacht-like appearance, and then I was intrigued by the sight of two pretty, sun-tanned, flaxen-haired girls, dressed in sailor's dungarees working on her decks. I was told that they were the daughters of the schooner's master, Captain Ahlgren, and that the ship was their home. I thought they were the finest girls I'd ever seen and never passed the *Isolda*, without trying to catch a glimpse of them. Twenty-five years later, I got to know Captain Ahlgren well and a remarkable man he proved to be, with an equally remarkable family, all born in the *Isolda* in different parts of the world and each named appropriately for the country of origin.

The shunting coal trains on the Dock Road crossing were a good excuse for me if Weddock grumbled about me being away too long.

We'd seen little of Captain Doyle since our arrival in Garston. In the mornings, soon after breakfast, he'd come on deck, his white-whiskered, weatherbeaten face glowing from the effects of a vigorous toilet. Clad in a navy-blue serge suit with a heavy gold watchchain across the waistcoat, and wearing a well brushed bowler hat, he'd stump ashore and would be away all day, only returning to the *Via* in time for supper. One evening, at supper time, he informed the mate that he'd bought a cargo of house coal and we were to load it the following day.

The day began an hour earlier than usual, as we had to prepare the *Via* to receive her cargo. The hatches were stripped and the hatch boards laid over the deck and galley roof as protection. Old tarpaulins were draped over the companions and cabin skylight. The booms were guyed out and the yards braced hard against the backstays with the braces unrove on the accosting side of the schooner. After dinner, we were told our loading berth was clear. Feeling very important, I ran a line across the dock and we warped the *Via* under the tips. There were conflicting orders from the quayside and the tips about mooring the schooner, and a gang of trimmers waiting to board us joined in the clamour, but at length we tied up to everybody's satisfaction. The trimmers, armed with spoon-shaped coal shovels and with tallow dips stuck on the peaks of their caps, climbed down into the hold.

As the first ten-ton truck-load of coal teamed down on us from the tip, the *Via* listed over and was enveloped in a choking cloud of coal dust, which turned our spotless little vessel into a shambles. Throughout the afternoon and evening, an avalanche of coal poured down from the tips onto a great heap, which extended from rail to rail over the main hatch, its peak subsiding spasmodically as the invisible trimmers shovelled the cargo into the wings of the hold. How the trimmers could work in the dust-laden, airless conditions below will always remain a mystery to me. The ring of their shovels and the steady disappearance of truck after truck of coal were the only indications of their presence on board.

After nightfall, when all the lights were on, the busy staithes were a fantastic sight. Ships listed drunkenly in all directions; some down by the head, others by the stern; their tall masts reeling and swaying to each fresh onslaught of the teaming coals.

Clouds of choking dust filled the air. The noise was continuous and deafening. It was impossible to sleep with the screech of the tip guides and the thunderous roar of the falling coals. From below in the *Via*, the scrape of the steel shovels added to the din. Into the night and until the early hours of the next morning, loading continued. The last wagon-load teamed down to the welcome shout: 'Here's the one you're looking for!' from the tip foreman. Shortly afterwards, one by one, the trimmers crawled out through a mere rathole in the centre of the filled main hatch and trooped wearily ashore.

It was breaking dawn when we turned to and warped the heavily laden *Via* back to her old berth on the West Wall. As we struggled to start her moving, the mate found fault with everything we did. He was like a bear with a sore head. Even John, who was usually bubbling over with good humour, barely spoke a civil word. Moored up again, with the surplus coal cleared from the deck and the hatches battened down, things were not so bad. Clad in oilskins and seaboots we gradually got rid of the coal dust, beginning on the booms, house tops and rails, and finishing with the deck. Every drop of water we used had to be lifted from the dock in a draw bucket. How I envied the steamboatmen their powerful deck hoses for washing down! The worst had been done before I was allowed to prepare breakfast.

A terrible thing happened to me during the meal. I sat down to breakfast wearing a sticky pair of oilskin pants. To my utter dismay, when I tried to move, I found I was stuck fast and although I tried to hide the fact, and wriggled about in an attempt to get free, it was all to no avail. In a panic I stood up quickly, there was a nasty rending sound as I did so. The seat of my pants had lifted the pile right out of the settee, leaving a bare, black imprint of my buttocks in the plush.

The captain was speechless for a moment or two but he quickly found his voice. Mealtimes were embarrassing to me for some time afterwards. At the end of a long, trying day, it was a relief to get cleaned up and changed for a few hours ashore.

I saw John for the first time out of his working rig, refreshed by a tub down and a change of clothes, and I realised he was a fine looking man. He was about twenty years old, with broad shoulders and a strong fit body, all bone and muscle. His face was handsome in a dark Irish way and he had a mop of black curly hair. With his strong sense of humour, generous nature and his complete reliability under any conditions he was a grand shipmate who, despite the big difference in our ages, always treated me as an equal.

I'd no idea how we would spend our few hours' shore leave as neither of us had any money, but we found plenty of amusement in watching others get rid of theirs. At the top of the Stalybridge Dock Road there was a little pleasure fair and the crew of a Norwegian freighter, well fortified with liquor, had taken over the rides for the evening. In typical sailor fashion they were enjoying themselves with their girl friends of the evening and a chair-o-plane ride was the main attraction. The antics of the big, blonde Norsemen in their elegant suits, kid gloves and silver grey trilby hats were better than any picture show. Whirling around in mid-air with their girls they courted them in mime, kissing, embracing, posturing and posing, so shamelessly, so ridiculously, that we were helpless with laughter. The fairground proprietor was ringing his hands but didn't dare interfere. I expect he knew how things would end. We left rather hurriedly just in time to avoid getting involved in a violent free-for-all which turned the show-ground into a battlefield. I'd never before seen sailors on the spree and it was an experience for me. Back aboard *Via*, we turned in early, expecting to sail the following morning, but thick fog and an absence of wind kept us in dock. I was cleaning out the punt when the master of a steamer which was leaving the dock hailed me: 'Will you run some wires out for me, boy?'

Glad of the opportunity to practise my newly acquired skill with an oar, I laid out the wires as directed. When I'd finished, he shouted for me to scull under the wing of his bridge.

'Hold your cap out, son,' he said. 'Here's something to go to the pictures with.' I couldn't believe my good luck when I saw two half-crowns in my outstretched cap. I hastened back to the *Via* and tumbled aboard: 'Look what he's given me, John. Here! you have one of them.'

Before John could take the proferred coin, a great, hairy paw came swiftly from behind me and grabbed both half-crowns. In a twinkling of an eye, they disappeared into the mate's trouser pocket without so much as a word being spoken. I've never

41

forgotten this incident: the first money I'd earned and the astonishing speed with which it had gone. How we hated Weddock for such mean behaviour, but looking back over the years, I believe he was an amusing and likeable character, apart from the occasional stinginess. He was a short, very fat and almost bald man in his early sixties, with a ragged grey walrus moustache and shaggy eyebrows. We rarely saw him dressed in anything but a shirt and trousers with the braces showing. It was our little joke that he never changed or took off his shirt, for we never saw him do so. Some of his oddities were very trying to us. His small berth at the foot of the cabin companion would sometimes be so crammed with old magazines and periodicals that he could barely squeeze into it. Yet, whenever a Mission padre brought us some reading matter he confiscated the lot. Our share, when it came for'ard, consisted solely of religious tracts. We never saw Weddock read anything, so goodness only knows what he did with all those magazines.

He didn't believe in shore leave and we wouldn't have had a break if he'd had anything to do with it. He never stepped ashore himself except to go home when we were in Kilkeel, and expected us to do the same. 'Might be tempted to spend a penny or two,' John sneered, when we were talking it over. But whatever our personal grievances might be, we respected him as a sailorman. He was one of the best schooner mates I ever sailed under.

The next day dawned fine but chilly. As I lit the galley fire the captain came on deck, squinting aloft to the main truck, where the windsock fluttered gently now and again in the light early morning airs. It gave every indication of a fair south-easterly breeze later on. Weddock rolled up to the galley door. 'Hurry with the breakfast, Dick,' he said, 'we're sailing at high water.' After a quick meal, the *Via* was warped down the dock, close to the entrance. We hoisted the punt with the burtons, stowing it on its chocks on the main hatch and then flaked all the running gear in readiness for making sail. When the gates began opening I helped John loose the headsails then climbed after him up the shrouds to the topsail yards. The sun was now fully up, rapidly clearing the early morning mist from the river. From the topsail yard footropes, I could see far down the Mersey, past the Woodside Stage and the *Conway* training ship. A nice steady south-easterly breeze ballooned the clewed-up topsails as we freed them from the gaskets. Regaining the deck, we hoisted the headsails and upper tops'l yard and sheeted home the sails as a pierman let-go our singled-up moorings. The canvas filled, *Via* slowly gathered steerage way and we glided through the entrance into the brown swirling waters of the Mersey.

Puffing and panting from his exertions, Weddock led us to the boom foresail halyards. 'Boom fores'l next—then the main,' he wheezed. First one fore-an'-after, then the other, rose slowly and jerkily up the tall masts and filled with wind. We were all out of breath by the time the mainsail was set. A Woodside ferry, packed with city workers, swept under our stern. As she passed, I caught a brief glimpse of the white faces of her passengers as they leaned over the rails to watch us go by. I felt sorry for them. What an existence! to be shut up, day after day, in their stuffy factories, shops and offices—though I doubted if any of them would have changed their way of life for ours if they'd had the choice.

Liverpool Landing Stage, with its liners, packets and ferry boats, dropped astern. We had the *Via* under full sail by the time New Brighton lighthouse was abeam. The first of the ebb tide began to lend us its powerful aid as the *Via* joined the long procession of outward-bounders making for the open sea. Strung out between the channel buoys were ships of every description and nationality, ranging from great cargo liners and tankers to little coasting steamers and even a few schooners like ourselves. As soon as we cleared the Bar, it was surprising how quickly they all vanished over the horizon.

As I sat in the swaying galley, preparing our dinner of salt beef and vegetable, I realised how naturally I was fitting into my new life. The first couple of days had been really tough, but now I was gradually getting hardened to it and hadn't any regrets about being a sailor.

After the meal and the usual chores, Weddock sent me over the bows with a can of linseed oil to oil the bowsprit. Out on the footropes, hidden from sight by the square fores'l, I took my time over the job. It was very pleasant there, watching the little blue and white lady on our stem curtseying to the swells. Now and again, a dash of spray flew into the air, the drops sparkling like

43

jewels in the sunshine. From the extreme end of the bowsprit, I had a grand view of the schooner sailing towards me. 'Thought you'd fallen overboard,' grumbled Weddock, as I put my gear away in the lamplocker aft. But even the cross-grained old mate was in good humour at the prospect of a quick and pleasant passage home. The fair wind held until after dusk, then began to take off.

Watches were set after supper, John and the mate going below until midnight. The captain told me to keep a good look-out but the sea around us was deserted. Gradually a mist closed in reducing visibility to under half a mile.

'Better get the foghorn out of the locker, Dick!' called Captain Doyle from the wheel, as a blanket of thick fog drifted down like smoke and shut us in completely. From aloft, there was a rattle of gear and the low thunder of slatting canvas, as the breeze failed us altogether.

The watch passed slowly, with the *Via* rolling to the swells without steerage way. I sounded the foghorn at regular intervals and listened for other ships. I was very cold and drowsy. The fog saturated the sails and rigging and big drops of moisture pattered down on deck. Beads of it formed on my eyebrows and nose. The booms kept up a monotonous creaking as they chafed against their saddles to the movements of the ship.

It must have been nearing midnight when the captain suddenly asked: 'Can you hear anything, boy?' We both listened intently for some moments but I could only hear the usual noises of the ship and the sea. 'Sound the horn again,' he said. As I began turning the handle, the bows of a large vessel loomed out of the fog and bore swiftly down on us. Absolutely petrified, I saw her great side, agleam with lighted ports, towering above us and she surged by, so close it was a miracle she didn't foul our yards. As quickly as she'd appeared, she was gone again, swallowed up by the clammy fog. Her wash set the *Via* rolling so violently that the sea splashed and gurgled through the washports and John and the mate rushed on deck alarmed by the sudden commotion.

'It was the bloody mailboat. Mother o'God! They never even saw us,' raved the Old Man, startled out of his habitual calm by the narrow escape. We'd missed being cut down by the steamer by a hair's breadth. It was the end of my watch, however, and I was determined not to lose any sleep. Relieved by John, I hurried below and within seconds was dead to the world.

As a growing youngster, my greatest difficulty in adjusting to sea life was the 'four on, four off' watch system. During my night watches, especially the twelve-to-four 'middles', I constantly found myself dozing off, although still on my feet. My sleeping time was never enough.

It seemed no time at all before I was awakened by John's cry of 'Rise and shine! Rise and shine!' Pulling on my outer garments, I enquired, sleepily: 'What's the weather like, John?'

'Fog's gone and there's a nice s'utherly breeze,' he answered. 'Picked it up after rounding the Chickens. Should see Slieve Donard soon after breakfast, if it holds.'

When it was light, we turned to with the usual deck scrubbing and a short spell on the pumps. By the time I'd cooked the breakfast of bacon and eggs, with lashings of potatoes and onions, I was ravenous. There was always plenty of good food in the *Via* and we could eat our fill.

When first sighted, the vague, shadowy outlines of the Mourne mountains were barely distinguishable from the banks of cloud. As we closed the land, it revealed itself as a vividly coloured patchwork of mountain, fields and bog, dotted here and there with tiny white cottages. A mile or two from the land, we put about and ratched off and on, awaiting the tide. *Via* jogged along under two lowers and headsails. The other five sails had been taken in but we left the double tops'ls in the buntlines. Everything was readied for entering harbour; warps flaked down, fenders out and the starboard anchor at the cathead.

'Should be enough water for us now, Jim,' observed Captain Doyle. 'Ready about . . . Lee-ho!'

Answering her helm, *Via* rounded to, her headsails backed and when round on the new tack, we hauled them over for the final board towards the harbour. We could see the entrance, with a cluster of ship's masts behind it and as we closed the piers, a crowd of men and boys, laughing and whooping like wild Indians, put off to the schooner in small boats. They swarmed over our rails and took possession of our deck. It was great fun to see the boisterous, yelling mob warp the *Via* into Kilkeel harbour, turning the labour into a lighthearted frolic.

We weren't allowed to do anything but make a harbour stow of the tops'ls aloft. By the time we'd regained the deck, *Via* was snugly moored, the sails furled and coated and everything coiled down and shipshape. Our numerous helpers had even ranged the port cable in the waterways and guyed out the mainboom to list the *Via* towards the stone quayside.

'That'll do, Jim,' said the captain as he stepped ashore. 'Be down to start at eight in the morning.'

Not long afterwards, I watched my other two shipmates hurrying up the harbour road, bound for their homes.

4

Strongholds of Sail

Kilkeel, the *Via*'s home port, was a pleasing contrast to the bustling, grimy docks of Merseyside. Situated on the unspoilt green coastal strip at the foot of the Mourne mountains, the sleepy little harbour had a small outer basin enclosed by granite piers and a larger inner harbour with a stone quay on one side only. There were no dockside buildings or cranes. A narrow macadam road wound through fields and bog from the harbour to the small town, about a quarter of a mile away.

The *Minnie*, another fine schooner, was berthed astern of the *Via* at the inner harbour quay. She was easily recognisable, being the last Down schooner to have the old-fashioned headgear of bowsprit, running jibboom and dolphin striker. Ahead of us were two little ketches, *Excel* and *Henrietta* and a few tarred ñickey' fishing boats.

With the exception of the cook of the *Minnie*, who was a bit of a recluse and a 'foreigner' like myself, the crews of the other vessels were all local men who went home when the day's work was done. After dark, the harbour was completely deserted and I felt very lonely by myself in the *Via*. My first night in solitude was a disturbed one, for although I was dead tired, I was kept awake by alarming creaks and groans from the *Via*'s timbers as the water level dropped in the tidal harbour and the schooner settled on the bottom. It was my first experience of a heavily laden wooden vessel taking the ground and, from the noises, I thought she was suffering severe damage. I wasn't much better off when these sounds ceased. The captain's warning 'to look out for thieves' caused me further uneasiness during the night. Several times I imagined someone was on deck and turned out to investigate but it was only the swish and slat of the running gear and the soughing of the wind aloft.

John was the first aboard in the morning and I helped him set up the cargo 'dolly', a simple hand winch which could be put together or taken apart very quickly. It had few components: a pair of A brackets, an axled drum which fitted into bearings at the tops of the brackets, and a couple of cranked iron handles socketting on the axle ends. It was assembled on the shore side of the deck, abreast of the foremast, and kept in position by a few fathoms of anchor cable ranged across the feet of the brackets. Most 'dollies' had wooden drums, about six inches in diameter, but the *Via*'s was different. It was a heavy metal one about eighteen inches across, and worked on the principle of a flywheel, easing considerably the labour on the handles. This was Captain Doyle's innovation.

Weddock and the captain arrived and, under the mate's direction, we rigged the derrick, a gaff we carried lashed to the rails. A single whip from the 'dolly' led through a large gin block on the peak of the spar and had a cargo hook on its end. To control the swing of the derrick, we bent on two manila guys, one leading through a block high in the outboard shrouds, with a weight known as a 'dead-man' at its end, the other taken ashore. When rigged, the derrick was hoisted up the foremast with the boom fores'l halyards.

John stripped off his shirt, rubbed a few drops of oil into the palms of his hands and I followed his example. As we did so, a number of horse-drawn carts rattled down the quay and from the leading one jumped two local men engaged by Captain Doyle as 'fillers'.

John and I stationed ourselves at the 'dolly' handles, Weddock took the end of the quayside guy and the fillers, armed with shovels, clambered into the open mainhatch. We were ready to begin discharging our cargo of 210 tons of coal.

Tim, the filler, and his big, rawboned son shovelled the coal into a wicker-work skip of about 2 to 3 cwts. capacity, until it was full, then hooked on the whip, with a shout of 'Heave away!'

We bent our backs and hove round the dolly handles at top speed. The basket of coal whipped up from the hatch and as the derrick swung towards the quay with the list of the schooner, Weddock steadied it with his guy so that the skip came to rest above a waiting cart. Capsizing the coals into his cart, the carter gave the empty basket a swing inboard. Aided by the pull of the 'deadman' and the weight of the cargo hook, it returned to its former position in the hatch. Another filled basket was hooked on in place of the empty one and the operation began again, to be repeated over and over again throughout the day. It was hard work but we made a sport of it, singing and shouting as we hove at the winch. If the pace slackened, Weddock 'spelled' one or the other of us on the handles. I knocked off work half an hour before the others to cook dinner. For working up a healthy appetite, dollying took some beating. We did full justice to the lashings of ham and eggs, potatoes and fried onions, washed down with pints of strong, well sweetened tea. I was hardening to the life and was quite proud of my strength and endurance.

It took us about a week to ten days to discharge, depending on local conditions and the weather. This was the way sailing ships had been discharged for centuries, and as one of the last men to have participated in 'dollying', I've described it in detail. By the late 20's, most schooners had been fitted with motor winches and 'dollying' was quickly forgotten.

We worked from eight to six each day except Sundays, which were free.

On my first Sunday I determined to visit the oddly named Annalong, which seemed complementary to Kilkeel. I borrowed an old boneshaker of a bike from John and pedalled the few miles north on the coast road which wound its way along the shoreline, with the wild slopes of Slieve Donard on one hand and the Irish Sea the other. I passed neither habitation nor traffic on the road. It was a scene of peace, beauty and tranquillity.

Annalong proved to be even smaller than Kilkeel. The harbour was at the bottom of a little side road that dipped steeply down to sea level and it consisted of a small basin, built of granite at the mouth of a narrow river whose source was somewhere up in the Mournes. It was obviously a difficult place of entry, even in fine weather, for a vessel of any size. To negotiate the entrance, it was necessary to make a very sharp turn to port in what was scarcely more than a large stream. There were no dock gates, but in bad weather the basin could be closed by lowering heavy timber baulks into slots in the stone knuckles with a small hand crane. About half a dozen of the fine schooners I'd already seen in Garston were moored in the basin, all spotlessly clean and shipshape but deserted. I was to find the Sabbath was as strictly observed here as in Wales. Cycling back to Kilkeel, I never encountered a soul on the road.

When the coal cargo was out of the *Via*, we loaded her with the captain's bagged potatoes. In addition to being master-owner of the *Via*, Captain Doyle had a coal and potato business in Kilkeel and a nice little hotel at nearby Warrenpoint. He was a very respected and prosperous member of the small community. Carrying his own goods most of the time, he kept the *Via* in constant employment and reaped the full benefit of her trading. The potatoes were discharged in Liverpool and we returned to Kilkeel with another coal cargo from Garston.

I was soon known in Kilkeel as the 'boy from the *Via*'. People passed the time of day to me in the streets and I became a regular customer at the grocer's shop where I spent my few shillings' pocket money on either cake or jam, for I've always had a sweet tooth and sweet things weren't eaten in the Down schooners. It seemed to amuse them in the little shop.

Captain Doyle treated me very kindly. I had a standing invitation to spend the evenings whenever I wished at his home, where he and his two charming daughters always made me welcome. The girls were about my own age, one a good pianist and the other a violinist, and our happy musical evenings together helped me to forget my loneliness and shortened the nights in the schooner. But our conversations were limited by my painful shyness with the girls and their father's strong Ulster accent, which was often incomprehensible to me. Oddly enough, my clearest recollections of those occasions were of the simple suppers provided by the girls before I returned to the *Via*. They were only bread and butter with a glass of milk, but the bread had just been baked in the home, the butter newly churned and the milk was fresh from the cow. Never have I enjoyed anything better!

So far my seafaring had been without incident, as our captain was very skilful at choosing his weather and our crossings of the Irish Sea seemed almost a routine. I'd always imagined life in sailing ships to be full of exciting happenings but in the *Via* everything went quietly and smoothly, as it should in an efficiently run ship. Then the unexpected happened.

We loaded coal at Garston for Kilkeel and brought up in the Sloyne anchorage, the wind a dead muzzler. It slowly veered to about nor'-east and settled into a brave wind, giving us a good slant from Liverpool Bar to the Chickens. I enjoyed that grand sail. Gradually the wind took off, but we carried enough of it to make the land. We were ahead of our tide with the fast sail, so as usual, we ratched about, just jogging along at about three knots. There was quite a big swell left over from the fresh breeze of the previous night.

We were standing in towards the shore for the third or fourth time when the *Via* suddenly brought up with a sickening crunch. I was knocked off my feet by the collision and badly frightened. Instinctively, I looked at Captain Doyle, who was at the wheel. He was frozen with shock; his usually florid face drained of colour.

The swells lifted the heavily laden schooner off the obstruction then dropped her down again with a fearful thump, making the deck jump and causing her tall topmasts to whip about like fishing rods.

Weddock was the first to recover from the initial shock of grounding and reacted quickly and decisively.

'Over with the punt, lads. Aisy now. Let her go with a run! In you go, boy, and drop her under the bow. Man, Man . . . hould her off!' The tubby old mate issued orders, one after the other, moving with an astonishing speed for a man of his age and bulk.

Under the schooner's bows, in the soaring, diving punt, I struggled to fend her off as the mate, John and the captain unshackled the port anchor and bent on a brand new warp. John dropped into the punt and helped me hold her as the captain and mate lowered the big, heavy bower anchor into our frail craft. By the time it was balanced across the punt's gunnels, we were up to our knees in water, but there wasn't time for baling. Coils of warp followed.

With an oar apiece, we pulled desperately to seaward over swells which seemed very high from our little boat, for in the troughs, we lost sight of the *Via* completely. The last coil of warp slipped over the punt's transom and John gasped: 'Way enough, Dick! Grab that haundspike!'

Getting the huge anchor clear of the waterlogged boat without capsizing was the toughest part of the job, but we somehow managed it. Heartened by our success, we pulled with a will back to the schooner, where the captain and mate had already taken up the slack of the warp with the windlass.

Doubling up on the brakes, we all four hove away for dear life, spurred on by the schooner's violent bumping on the hard seabed.

Thankfully we felt her slide clear into deep water. Captain

Doyle dashed back to the wheel to head us away from the dangerous reef which had nearly been our undoing.

It says much for the *Via's* builders, Uphams of Brixham, that after such a severe bumping on the hard rocks, the schooner was only making a small amount of water which we were easily able to contain with our pumps. When we moored up in Kilkeel harbour, we were told our plight had been observed from the shore and those who saw it thought we were 'goners'.

I'd had more than enough excitement but our close call made me suddenly grow up.

As well as I can remember, at that time, nine schooners and two ketches were owned in Annalong and Kilkeel. They were the schooners *Via*, *Minnie*, *Goldseeker*, *Alpha*, *Bengullion*, *Nellie Bywater*, *Volant*, *Lochranza Castle* and *Ellie Park*. The ketches were *Henrietta* and *Excel*. Some of the vessels were master-owned but others had their sixty-four shares spread between several families. Schoolmasters, publicans, fish merchants and other men of substance had shares in schooners. The Annalong quarry owners, Gordon and Robinson, had interests in several vessels. Generally, the masters were the principal shareholders. Most of them were dour, bewhiskered, middle-aged men with an air of dignity and authority which greatly impressed me. After nearly a lifetime I can still vividly recall the Carens, McKibbins, Chambers, Doyles, McVeighs, Purdys and Campbells, courageous seamen who were respected wherever they went. Only men of nerve and experience could trade regularly to such difficult ports as Kilkeel and Annalong, situated on the rockbound Down coast with Carlingford Lough the sole refuge in bad weather.

The only young master was Captain Caren of the *Goldseeker*, who'd served from boy to mate with his father and succeeded the grey-bearded old patriarch when still in his twenties.

The vessels were manned almost exclusively by local men and boys, some of them sons and near relatives of the masters. Instead of wages, masters and crews received shares of their vessel's earnings, a system which suited these independent people.

Potato cargoes to Liverpool, with coal homeward to Down, were often the owner's private ventures. In addition, all the vessels carried 'stone' cargoes, a few loaded in Kilkeel though most were exported from Annalong. The 'stones' were Mourne granite setts and kerbs, quickly loaded down wooden shutes, consigned to Liverpool and discharged there at the Corporation Depot, Canning Half-Tide Dock.

They were bad cargoes in rough weather and we rarely carried more than a hundred tons, for a schooner with a kerb cargo sailed as if in a straight-jacket and, in a seaway, she had a most uncomfortable roll, the dead weight in the bottom of her half-filled hold acting like a pendulum. I was always glad when a 'stone' cargo had been landed.

After a few stays in Kilkeel, I became aware that times were bad for many of the people. Fishing was at a very low ebb and the small farms were sadly run down. On every hand there was unemployment and extreme poverty. Partisan feelings from the recent 'troubles' were still very strong, with the border between Ulster and the new Free State only five miles away. I was constantly hearing stories of violence and I sensed an undercurrent of lawlessness abroad which often frightened me. This was brought home to me one night when I was alone in the *Via* in Kilkeel harbour.

Tired out with a day's hard dollying, I was fast asleep in the fo'c'sle when I awoke with a start. A scraping sound, followed by a few bumps and a faint murmur of voices seemed to come from the hold, separated from the fo'c'sle by a wooden bulkhead.

At first, when only half awake, I thought it must be my imagination as the hatches had been re-covered at the end of the previous day's work. But again I heard the sounds, more distinctly.

Slipping from beneath the warm blankets, I quickly pulled on my pants and guernsey and crept barefooted up the companion ladder. It was a very dark night; at first I couldn't see a thing as I peered out of the open scuttle, but as my eyes became accustomed to the darkness I made out several shadowy forms moving stealthily around the main hatch.

Feeling far from brave, I stepped out on deck and with an assumed boldness, confronted the intruders.

'What are you doing here, at this time of night?' I demanded.

For a moment or two there was silence. They were a wild looking lot and they just stood staring at me until a tall, gaunt scarecrow of a man who appeared to be their leader, muttered something to his companions in a strong brogue which I didn't understand. There was a burst of laughter and they renewed their activities, completely ignoring my existence.

The covered hatch had been opened up and from below I could hear the ring of shovels. A dozen or more well filled sacks of coal were hauled up from the hold on the end of a coil of running gear. The intruders worked quietly, speedily and efficiently but I was powerless to stop them. As the last bag reached the deck, I watched helplessly as each of the gang shouldered a sack of coal and filed ashore. The darkness swallowed them up and a little later I heard, very faintly in the distance, the sounds of a cart receding up the harbour road.

Captain Doyle and the mate took things very calmly when I reported the thieving to them the following morning. Apparently, such incidents were commonplace, so that no-one ever complained to the unpopular R.U.C. But, from then on, I disliked my long, lonely nights aboard the *Via* even more.

Meanwhile, I was gaining the most valuable experience in the *Via*. Under Weddock's rough and ready schooling, I'd changed from a soft greenhorn of a boy into a tough, handy young seaman. I could handle the punt with the best, could furl a tops'l in fair weather or foul, stand a trick at the wheel and pull my weight at any task in the schooner. In addition, I'd learned to prepare and cook food properly. I kept my eyes and ears wide open and let nothing of value escape me. The hard, manual labour, especially the dollying, together with a diet of plain, wholesome food had worked wonders to my physique. I was as fit and strong as any boy in the Down schooners. But I was getting restless. I'd seen the fine West-country schooners in the Mersey and heard talk of voyages around the 'Land', which aroused my curiosity. I thought it would be good experience to serve in one of these vessels which brought China clay from Cornwall and returned with coal. In spite of the kindness of the people of Kilkeel and Annalong, I knew I'd always be a foreigner in these two closely knit communities. It was a great privilege to work in one of their finest schooners, with the ideal conditions of a fatherly old captain, excellent accommodation and a plentiful supply of good food. I believe that Little Arthur, cook of the *Minnie*, and I were the only English nationals ever to serve in the Down schooner fleet.

Little Arthur's reason for being there, however, was different to mine. All this mild, inoffensive, scholarly man needed was a sanctuary from a world which had proved too much for him. His life before he was befriended by the big-hearted Down schooner-men will always be conjecture, but from my few meetings with him, he appeared to be a well educated and cultured man. He wasn't much of a cook and was nearly useless as a sailor, being so close sighted he was unable to stand a watch or lookout. His only interest in life was reading. Although we were the only two foreigners in the Down fleet, the few times I spoke to him were when he was doing the rounds of the ships in quest of books and magazines. The more highbrow the book, the better, and his special delight was a classic or a book of poetry. His shipmates of the *Minnie* said he spent half the night reading with a small oil lamp or a candle for light. No wonder his spectacles had lenses as thick as pebbles!

I can still see him now . . . sitting in the *Minnie*'s galley cooking dinner . . . a little shrimp of a man under five feet, clad in baggy, ill-fitting clothes, totally absorbed in a book and paying scant attention to the food frizzling on the hot range. There must have been plenty of burnt offerings served up where Arthur was cook but I never heard of him being 'fired' and he remained in Down schooners to the end of his life. Many years later, in 1938, I heard how Little Arthur met his death. He was in the Annalong schooner *Lochranza Castle* during a November gale, when she was driven on the revetment wall in the Mersey estuary. All hands were rescued by the New Brighton lifeboat before the schooner broke up and sank but Arthur died in hospital from pneumonia, caused by exposure suffered whilst clinging in the rigging of the stranded vessel.

One evening, at Annalong, I witnessed an unforgettable gather-ing of sailing vessels. Most of the local vessels were home and with a few foreigners there, too, over a dozen schooners and ketches nearly filled the small basin so that it was possible to walk across them from one side of the dock to the other.

I was never again to see such a large, well cared for fleet of sailing vessels in more perfect surroundings. Their decks and paintwork glistened from the evening wet-down; gear neatly coiled and stowed. Aloft was the same fine order; rigging taut, spars bright with oil, and sails furled to a nicety. Set against a background of ancient stone cottages and the steep, rocky slopes of the Mournes, the schooners were a beautiful sight.

They stirred me so that I vowed, there and then, that one day I'd command my own schooner. For a ship's boy it was like reaching for the moon but, inexplicably, in the future I was to be firmly linked to Annalong and one of her finest schooners.

Twenty eventful years were to pass before I saw again that small Down port, but when I returned it was with my vow accomplished.

5

The Sea's Toll

Via became due for survey, so Captain Doyle arranged for me to sail in Jack Ballance's *Excel* for a time. I misunderstood his instructions and the *Excel* sailed without me. With the china clay traders in mind, I said goodbye to my friends of the *Via* and returned to Liverpool.

My first call was at the Dingle home of John Henry, but he was away in his tug. Chatting to his daughter in their living room which overlooked the Herculanean Dock, I glanced through the window and saw below me in the basin a beautiful full-rigged ship, painted light grey with white masts and yards, deep loaded and ready for sea. She attracted me like a magnet and I forgot my plans for schoonering. I fell for the ship like falling for a girl and determined to seek a berth in her.

She was the *Fortuna* of Buenos Aires and flew Norwegian colours. An old seaman on the dockside told me she'd formerly been one of James Nurse's fleet of fast 'coolie carriers' but now belonged to a Norwegian whaling company based in South Georgia. She'd just loaded the season's stores for the whalemen.

I tackled the *Fortuna*'s 'styrman' for a job, but unbelievably, he couldn't speak English. He was the only Norwegian ship's officer I've ever met without a knowledge of the language. As we struggled to communicate with one another on the ship's poop, I noticed some of the crew lashing a number of red-painted drums marked 'Carbide' to the taffrail. Our efforts to talk were a complete failure and I gave up in disgust.

From the dockside, I took a last look at the lovely ship, before heading for the Sailor's Home and a night's rest. Next day I found myself a seaman's berth in a Chester River schooner lying coal-laden in Garston and bound 'round the Land' to Truro, Cornwall. We were held up in dock for a few days by severe gales and one evening, ashore in Garston, I saw on a newsagent's billboard a caption: GALE HAVOC. HARROWING STORIES OF THE SEA. I bought a paper and read of the tragic losses of the *Fortuna* and the *Excel*. Both vessels had left the Mersey on the same tide and within hours of clearing the Bar were caught in violent sou'-westerly gales.

The *Fortuna* had towed to a good offing and made sail. Abeam of Point Lynas the wind increased to gale strength. During the stormy night, the poop deck blew up and two men were killed by the explosion. The ship was on fire aft and settling fast as the crew launched their two lifeboats. It was a difficult operation with the ship in flames and a heavy sea running but both boats got away from the stricken *Fortuna*, miraculously survived a terrible night and made the Welsh coast.

The loss of the *Excel* was reported more fully. Captain Ballance told the reporters: 'We were from the Mersey with coal for Carlingford when the gale struck us. The seas were very high and the *Excel* began making water. Getting by Carmel Head, some of the bulwarks went. We tried to get her into Moelfre but more of the bulwarks went and so did the main gaff, leaving us out of control. We did her as well as we could and I told the mate to put up a distress signal. By this time the seas were running right over us. The pilot cutter came up and said something I didn't understand. The weather was fit to kill anybody. Then a German steamer came and stood by us but couldn't come near enough to take us off, because of the seas. The mate got hit on the head when the gaff carried away and I was trying to save my little dog from going overboard and all we could do was hang on. Then the Moelfre lifeboat came and took us off. They were splendid!'

The rescuers' versions of that terrible night are epics in the annals of the Royal National Lifeboat Institution.

At 3 p.m. Friday, 28 October, 1927, the Moelfre, Anglesey, pulling and sailing lifeboat *Charles & Eliza Laura* was called out in the teeth of a sou'-westerly gale and heavy seas, to search for a vessel reported in distress off Carmel Point. The vessel hadn't been located when darkness set in; the weather was rapidly getting worse and it seemed hopeless to continue to look for her. Just as the search was about to be called off, the wreck was sighted.

As the lifeboat soared on the crests of the big seas, her crew saw a little ketch, low in the water, half her bulwarks gone and her sails in ribbons, wallowing helplessly. Through the spray and spindrift, three men could be seen on her signalling to be taken off. The wreck was awash with the angry waves piling over her and it was obvious she might founder any moment.

Second Coxswain William Roberts, prompted by Captain

Owen Jones with the approval of all the crew, decided to sail the lifeboat directly on top of the ketch amidships, hoping a big wave would carry her aboard, as it seemed impossible to get alongside in time to make a rescue.

William Roberts steered on the crest of a huge wave straight at the wreck and the lifeboat struck the mainhatch coamings of the *Excel* with terrific force, 'grounding' on her deck. For a few moments the lifeboat lay on top of the wreck, just long enough for the three men to be hauled into her. One of the rescued men had a small dog in his arms as he was being pulled into the lifeboat but the animal struggled free and was swept away. When the water-logged ketch dropped sickeningly into a trough, the *Charles & Eliza Laura*, badly holed in three places, slid clear.

The gale increased to hurricane force and it was hopeless to attempt sailing back to Moelfre. Throughout a long, dark night, the damaged lifeboat beat about in the raging seas. She was full of water and had lost most of her buoyancy. The waves broke over her continuously. Rescuers and rescued alike had to hold on grimly to the lifelines to save themselves from being washed overboard.

Sixty-five year old William Roberts, who, like his mates had been tumbled aft time and time again by the seas, had injured his head and was getting very feeble. He was washed right out of the boat on one occasion but still had the presence of mind to retain his grip on a lifeline. Two of his mates hauled him back aboard but he became very weak. The incessant battering of the waves, as the small craft plunged through, rather than over them; the blinding, choking brine in eyes, throat and nostrils and the stupefying effects of constant immersion in the icy water was as much as the strongest man could bear. Will Roberts died during the night. He talked to his friend Tom Williams right to the end. His last words were a request for a chew of tobacco.

Tom Williams said: 'The worst trouble was brine in the eyes. I closed my eyes and tried to brush the salt away but it blinded me for a time. Coxswain William Roberts had his sou'-wester blown away just after launching. From 3 o'clock on Friday afternoon until nine the following morning, he stood bareheaded at the tiller until his eyes were nearly closed with the salt.

The *Excel*'s mate, Henry McGuiness, was lying aft with one of our crew holding his head above the water. He was quiet for a long time, then it was found that he was dead, too!'

Ashore there was great anxiety about the Moelfre lifeboat being overdue at her station and word was sent by road to Beaumaris. The Beaumaris lifeboat immediately put to sea to search for her and at 5.30 in the morning, distress signals were sighted near Puffin Island. Coxswain Matthews steered in that direction and found the stricken *Charles & Eliza Laura* in the nick of time, for her crew were almost beyond further effort. The Moelfre boat was taken in tow and made Beaumaris at nine in the morning.

Subsequently, the badly holed *Charles & Eliza Laura* was transported to London and put on view to the public by the Royal National Lifeboat Institution. Second Coxswain William Roberts and Captain Owen Jones received the Institution's Gold Medal. Bronze Medals were awarded to the twelve surviving crew members and to the widow of William Roberts in addition to a Memorial Certificate.

Big, kind-hearted Jack Ballance never fully recovered from his ordeal and was a broken man to the end of his days.

At the time, I only heard the bare facts of the disasters. I was truly thankful that fate had prevented me from sailing in either of these unfortunate ships. I'd been lucky, but the tragic shipwrecks made a deep impression on me for some time afterwards.

During the course of a lifetime, I've witnessed many acts of gallantry both afloat and ashore but for sheer unselfish heroism I award first place to the men who manned the open sailing and pulling lifeboats such as the *Charles & Eliza Laura*. To pull or sail out to sea in a raging gale, unable to communicate with the shore and depending solely on their own skill, strength and endurance for survival, all in the hopes of saving lives, required a special breed of men.

In schooners carrying coal to the West Country and china clay back to the Mersey, I found my true vocation. Although none of these vessels was superior to the *Via*—I believe she was the finest schooner I ever served in—the voyages were of far longer duration and I got in plenty of sea time. We were never less than a week on passage and sometimes, in bad weather or calm conditions, this

5. Barquentine *Francis & Jane* of Plymouth. (*Nautical Photo Agency*)

6. Crew of *Francis & Jane*. Davey Jones, cook; Pilot Petersen, A. B.; Bill Roberts, A. B.; Mou'zle, boy; Pilot Ted Spence, A. B., with Toby the dog; George Cort, mate; and Captain W. F. Cort, master. (*Author*)

7. Schooner *Alert* of Falmouth entering a West Country port under sail. (*The late Captain Peter Mortensen*)

8. Crew of schooner *Alert*. Captain Peter Mortensen, master, centre front. (*The late Captain Peter Mortensen*)

could increase to five or six weeks. I rounded the 'Land' in fair
weather and foul and savoured the sailorman's satisfaction of
seeing the Longship's light receding astern after battling against
stiff sou'-westerlies and big Atlantic seas to double the grim, most
sou'-westerly corner of Britain. Some of our coal cargoes were
consigned to the most unlikely, out-of-the way spots, which were
reached by long tows up winding, tree-lined rivers, with our yards
often brushing the dense foliage. The china clay was generally
loaded at the small ports of Charlestown and Par and although
the white dust of the clay was everywhere, the tiny harbours
possessed a great appeal. Since those days, I've never lost my
nostalgia for the West Country.

But even in the smallest ports, I began to notice an ever increasing number of small, modern Dutch motor vessels. Holland was
building a huge fleet of these subsidised ships for the Home Trade
and schoonermen, quite rightly, feared and hated the Dutchmen
for their competition was ruthless at a time when freights were
scarce. It was obvious that the Dutchmen were a great danger to
the schooner trades.

To combat the difficult times, many schooners had small auxiliary engines installed. I saw the introduction of engines as a
disaster and still don't believe it helped much in the survival
of schooners. For passage-making the engines were totally
inadequate, the fuel too costly and few schoonermen made
good engineers. Many of the older masters refused to have their
schooner's sailing qualities spoiled with a motor. It was generally
the sons, anxious to move with the time, who were responsible
for the changes.

I'd already seen a few motor schooners about, such as the
North Barrule and *Solway Lass*, and took them for granted. But
when I saw the *Goldseeker* in Garston with her tops'l yards gone
and her smart little cabin gutted to make way for an engine, I was
horrified. And what an engine! A semi-diesel of only 30 h.p., it
required heating with a blowlamp before starting. When it was
judged hot enough for combustion, the huge flywheel was rocked
a few times and then given a sudden heave, when it was supposed
to commence running! When I viewed this contraption, I said to
Captain Caren: 'It's a pity to spoil a fine schooner in this way!' He
retorted: 'It had to be done. Dad was against it but I don't care. I

hate the sea, anyway!' A remark which was difficult to swallow, from a man who continued to command the *Goldseeker* for a further twenty-five years.

The main advantages of power were gained in the vicinities of harbours. An auxiliary cut out the ever-increasing cost of tugs, gave a master the right to enter or leave dock and load in turn with steam or motor vessels, and ended the slow hand warping in dock basins. In every other respect, a schooner depended on her sails, especially in bad weather.

In December, 1928, four coal-laden schooners, the *Goldseeker, Ellie Park, Nellie Bywater* and *Bengullion* left the Mersey together, all homeward bound. When they passed the Bar lightship, the wind was a moderate west-sou'-westerly but freshening. Just before darkness set in, Captain Caren of the *Goldseeker* saw *Bengullion* under shortened canvas, heading for the Chicken Rock, Isle of Man. He was probably the last man to see the vessel before she vanished for ever.

The *Goldseeker* and the other two schooners tried to make the shelter of Holyhead in rapidly worsening conditions but the wind backed southerly and increased in strength, picking up a very high sea. Before the *Goldseeker* was round the Skerries, the little engine packed up and shortly afterwards the standing jib blew away.

Rounding to off the South Stack in an attempt to make Holyhead bay, her bulwarks were stove in, then the mainsail split from head to foot and to save the spars, the flogging remnants had to be cut away.

Captain Caren ran his schooner off before the wind and took all the canvas off her until she was under bare poles. Throughout the night the *Goldseeker* drove down wind without any canvas set but at dawn her exhausted crew managed to hoist a reefed fore-stays'l which made her more manageable. Under this scrap of sail, she made the land off Carlingford Lough and eventually anchored in Rostrevor Bay.

The crews of the *Ellie Park* and *Nellie Bywater* had similar ordeals and the schooners suffered storm damage but they also survived.

It was thought that the ill-fated *Bengullion* successfully rounded the Chicken Rock and made the Down coast too far north to find shelter. Either ratching off and on or, perhaps, running for Belfast Lough, she was overwhelmed by the seas and foundered, taking with her the master, James Campbell, his son James and the seaman Henry Hughes. But no-one could say exactly how she met her end.

The value of auxiliary engines remained a moot point with schoonermen but even the most conservative sailormen saw the great advantages of a motor winch for cargo handling. With their introduction, discharging with a dolly winch became a thing of the past. I never disliked dollying out a cargo with good shipmates. If a rival vessel was working out a cargo at the same time as ourselves, we often had wagers with her crew to see who would land the greatest tonnage in a stated time. Although the victor's prize was seldom more than a few 'Woodbines', then tuppence a packet, it turned hard labour into a sport.

I chose my ships by their appearance for I could never resist a fine looking vessel, so my working conditions varied. After the *Via* I served in schooners owned in Wales, Eire, Lancashire, Devon and Cornwall, but I never found a vessel where I was so well treated and fed or with such a comfortable, dry and roomy fo'c'sle as that first Down schooner. Whenever I was in the Mersey, I kept a sharp look-out for her and tried to get news of my Down friends. I saw her only once, briefly, in Garston. She was as spic and span as usual, a pleasure to look at, but I was disappointed to find only Weddock aboard. He made me very welcome and we had a good yarn together in the cabin.

He explained that the others had gone to Mass as it was St Patrick's Day. When I asked after Captain Doyle's family, the old mate chuckled: 'Be Jasus, Dick! The cap'n's little daughter says you were a sad disappointment to her. "Never even asked me to go for a walk", says she.' After a bit of leg pulling, I shook hands with Weddock and left the *Via*. I was never to see her again. On 5 June, 1931, homeward bound with coal from the Mersey, she struck the Hellyhunter Rock, Carlingford Lough in thick weather. She was badly holed by the sharp reef and Captain Doyle and his crew barely had time to swing out their punt and jump in before the schooner sank. They landed safely at Cranfield Point. When I heard the news, I was thankful all my friends were safe, but the loss of the *Via* saddened me. A former 'fruiter', she was a beauty and sailed like a witch. She was Captain Doyle's pride and joy and he denied her nothing, so that she was always a pleasure to a sailor's eyes—clean, shipshape alow and aloft, with never a ropeyarn out of place.

Describing a little fruit schooner like the *Via*, John Masefield the sailor poet wrote:

> Very fair, if not divinely tall;
> With the scent of oranges and lemons in her wake.

6

'Old Horse'

Poor pay and hard conditions never bothered true sailormen and they were quite content with their lot if they were properly fed. Most of the master-owned schooners were well victualled but some that were shore-owned were run at starvation levels.

Day and night, I was always ravenous, due to the sea air, hard manual work and a fast developing body.

In the *Via* I'd been able to eat my fill of good quality, nourishing food. I soon discovered that she was an exception, not the rule. On their usual short sea-passages, the Down schooners' mainstays were bacon and eggs, with plenty of potatoes, onions, baker's bread, best quality butter, tea, sugar and tinned full-cream milk. For a change, we had hand-salted beef. Nothing was ever stinted.

In other trades where we could be at sea for lengthy periods, food was the same as in deepwatermen; salt fish, salt beef, rice, potatoes, split peas, 'hard tack' biscuit, margarine, tea, coffee, sugar, tinned skimmed milk. The quality and quantity of these items varied considerably from one schooner to another. Traditionally, in properly run vessels, Sunday was 'duff' day.

A standard breakfast at sea was salt fish; Newfoundland cod, split, salted and dried until it resembled leather. It needed twenty-four hours of steeping before boiling, otherwise it was so full of brine it was uneatable. Good-quality salt fish, properly prepared and cooked, was very tasty but the cheap grades had little to recommend them.

Some captains were very particular about their beef. They personally selected good cuts of prime meat at a butcher's and had it sent aboard for salting. It still makes my mouth water to think of the enormous pieces of prime quality beef I helped pickle.

We did the salting on the cabin table, rubbing coarse block salt into the meat until it couldn't absorb any more. It was a common belief that the beef would go bad if one of the salters had recently been with a woman, so the captains were very careful whom they chose for this task. When salted, the meat was submerged in brine of a density that would float a potato. Salt would be stirred into the brine until this was achieved. It was essential to cover the meat completely with brine in the harness cask, otherwise it became tainted. Well steeped beforehand and then properly cooked, this hand-salted beef was very good, either hot or cold.

In many schooners, however, the beef was the commercial variety, pickled with saltpetre and bought in the cask. It was supposed to keep much longer than the hand-salted meat. But, opening a cask was always a gamble. Sometimes the contents were tainted and the stench terrible; neither steeping nor cooking could alter it. If we were unfortunate enough to get a bad cask, we always swore it was condemned ex-Admiralty stores bought cheaply at the Naval Dockyard sales, though probably it was a leaking cask that had turned the beef bad. It was highly dangerous to eat it but the alternative was to starve. As the age-old shanty goes:

Old horse! Old horse! What's brought you here
That's carted bricks for many a year,
And now grown old with sad abuse?
They salt you down for sailors' use.

Even when faced with hunger, a sailorman's strong sense of humour asserted itself. In schooners, the best safeguard against bad or insufficient food was the custom of all hands eating together in the cabin. The captain sat at the after end of the table and had first choice, followed by the mate, seaman and boy. All shared the same food, good or bad. I recall with amusement 'duff' days in a Cornishman where the grub was good and plentiful. Our tough mate carefully marked the portions of suet pudding with his knife, before cutting and serving, always leaving a generous piece in reserve. Gobbling up his share with evident enjoyment, he'd glared aggressively at us, with his knife and fork poised over the remaining duff and demanded: 'Anybody want any more?' None of us had sufficient courage to say 'Yes', although the selfsame charade was repeated every duff day. We then enviously watched him consume the extra plateful of pudding, pat his ample stomach and observe, quite unnecessarily: 'I likes duff!'

Baker's bread was eaten in port but at sea it was always hard-tack. This biscuit was supplied in two qualities, 'Cabin' and 'Crews'. Cabin biscuit was very good and on the rare occasions when we had it I thoroughly enjoyed it. The more usual Crews biscuit was very different. It was so hard it would have broken the teeth of a bulldog. After eating it for a week or two, the jawbones became so tender and sore, it seemed impossible to take another bite. We then softened the biscuit in our tea or powdered it with a belaying pin but eating it either way upset the stomach and caused acute indigestion. After feeling like a balloon for a few days, I'd soon be back to using my teeth and jaws again. Being young, with strong teeth and jaws, it was only a minor inconvenience to me, but for the old men it must have been a great problem, though little was said.

Fresh water, taken for granted and freely wasted ashore, was carefully conserved in sailing vessels. No sailorman wasted fresh water. Most schooners carried about four or five hundred gallons in a metal tank on deck and one of the mate's most important duties before leaving port was to see that the tank was filled. The tank tap had a detachable handle which was always in the mate's keeping, but at the filler cap, a cylindrical dipper on a chain could be lowered into the tank to obtain sufficient water for a drink at any time during the day or night. Otherwise, supplies for other purposes were issued by the mate.

In a little barquentine, with six men in the fo'c'sle, the water ration for washing ourselves and our clothing per day was a two-gallon bucket shared between all six. We washed in strict rota, so that over a period, each in turn could be first. On days when I was last to wash, I only did my hands, for by then the water resembled thick soup.

As things were at the time, we fared pretty well in schooners, much better than the men on weekly articles in Home-Trade steamers who had to feed themselves. I've watched seamen in these ships going aboard just before sailing with only a loaf of bread and a bottle of beer to see them through a passage of several days.

Before I went to sea, nobody told me that a schooner's boy was also the cook. In many vessels, good food was often spoiled by boys who were unable to prepare or cook the simplest meal. Salt fish and beef was cooked without a proper steep beforehand, which not only made it unpalatable but could result in a crew suffering from boils. Salt-water boils, we called them, a common complaint among sailormen and they mainly appeared wherever there was chafe from clothing or oilskins. Immersion in sea water contributed to the complaint but the real cause was the food.

When I first took over in the *Via*'s galley, I was totally ignorant of cooking. I'd no wish to become a sea cook but decided to do my best and learn all I could. As the meals in the Down schooners were mainly 'fry-ups', with John's initial help I was soon able to cope. I kept the galley and everything in it spotlessly clean and tried to make the food more appetising by dishing it up properly on a neatly laid cabin table.

During later voyaging to and from the West Country, there was a lot more scope for a cook. As the galleys were only big enough for a cast-iron range at one end and bench seat with coal bunker underneath at the other, the preparation of dishes had to be done below on the cabin table.

Salt fish and beef were usually just boiled but I tried my hand at making fish cakes, hashes and other alternative ways of serving up these staple foods. It was a bit more trouble but worth the effort. And a few suet dumplings added to the traditional boiled beef and spuds were greatly appreciated, especially in bad weather. They were easily made; just two parts self-raising flour to one of Atora suet, with a pinch of salt and pepper, mixed dry. Then a little water added to make a stiff dough. Small balls of this dough were dropped into the pan with the beef for the last ten minutes boiling.

A sailor's idea of good feeding was to have plum duff served once a week. The ingredients for this highly regarded treat were the same as for the dumplings, except that sugar was substituted for the condiments and currants and sultanas were liberally added. The dough was made into a roll, wrapped in a well floured cloth, then boiled for about three hours. The mate of the *Ryelands* gave me a useful tip about improving the duff. Instead of boiling it in a cloth he kept a large cylindrical sweet tin, obtained from most sweet shops for the asking, and put the duff into this for cooking, after greasing it's inside. The result was a very much lighter pudding which had been steamed instead of boiled.

Curry and rice and Dogsbody—boiled rice with currants and sultanas added—were the usual rice dishes on shipboard. To make a change, if there was a little tinned milk to spare, I diluted it and made a tolerable rice milk-pudding. Many of the schooner-men were first rate sea cooks and I was always on the lookout for useful hints. 'God sends the food; the Devil the cooks' would do for some, but I hated to see food ruined. In bad weather this was sometimes unavoidable. It required great care to carry the prepared dishes from the cabin to the galley. With both the galley doors closed to keep out the seas and spray, a cook had a difficult time trying to keep his pans on the reeling range without being burned or scalded. The high temperature in a closed-up galley was uncomfortable enough but the downdraught from the sails could fill the little deckhouse with sulphur fumes and smoke which was a trial even for those immune to seasickness. When the food was successfully prepared and cooked, there was always the danger of losing the lot when carrying it back to the cabin. I always reckoned the cook had the worst job in a schooner during bad weather.

Old schoonermen knew which vessels to serve in and which to avoid, to be sure of a full stomach. The captain's name was the guarantee. Captain W. F. Cort, of Polruan, Cornwall, was one of the best masters to serve with, for under his command a sailorman received good and sufficient food at all times. When master of Westcott's barquentine *Francis & Jane*, his interest went as far as posting a weekly menu in the cabin companionway.

We had a full-time cook, appropriately named Davey Jones. A quiet, reserved man with white hair and a tobacco-stained walrus moustache, he'd served for over fifty years in sailing ships and his discharge book read like a roll of honour of tall ships. The Lochs, the Shires, the Garths and the ships of William and Robert Thomas were all there. He was badly ruptured—an occupational complaint common to sailormen who, in times of stress, were obliged to exert themselves beyond reason—but continued at sea, although confined to a galley. During his long service, he must have suffered from the efforts of many 'hash spoilers' who called themselves cooks, for he saw to it that we'd nothing to complain about. The worse the weather, the better was his food. On one occasion when we were shipping it green, he baked us an enormous jam tart and delivered it to the cabin table intact and still piping hot, after negotiating a very hazardous course from the galley to the cabin companionway.

Although seemingly engrossed in his culinary duties, nothing escaped his notice in the everyday working of the ship. I'd been having a bit of friendly rivalry with another young sailor of about my own age. The two of us were responsible for the loosing and furling of the barquentine's fore t'gallant, each taking a yardarm. For some time, Mou'zle, as he was nicknamed, always beat me to the yard, picking up his part of the sail and regaining the deck well ahead of me. But, after a time, I learned to read the signs when the t'gallant would come in—the vessel being overpressed, with the captain or mate taking a keen interest in the sky to wind'ard and the canvas aloft. I immediately stationed myself near the weather foremast shrouds. Almost before the order to reduce sail was spoken, I was over the sheerpole and 'way aloft. The first to the yard had choice of the weather yardarm, which was very important. When braced up, the footrope on the lee side became shortened, so that instead of the yard being at normal waist height it was at an uncomfortable knee level.

The first time I was able to claim the weather yardarm, the race was mine. I'd picked up the sail to the bunt, passed the gaskets and slid down a backstay to the deck before Mou'zle had half finished. As I paused to recover my breath, old Davey poked his head and shoulders through the galley door and said: 'Good for you, lad! Knew you could beat him,' then bobbed back again. The approval of the old shellback completed my happiness.

Shortly afterwards, the *Francis & Jane* became due for survey and was laid up, never to sail again. I wonder what happened to Davey Jones?

Food shortages in schooners were usually caused by lengthy passages. One of the hungriest times I ever had was in *Emma & Esther*, just before the thirties depression. A nice two-master of 108 tons gross, she was beginning to show the signs of hard times; paintwork flaking, spars in need of linseed oil and the standing rigging grey for the want of tar. The crew of four consisted of her captain, a tall rawboned A. B. named Pough from Bideford, Sam, a pleasant, well spoken South African A. B. and myself. For reasons unknown there was no mate. But we all knew our work and did it without supervision, although there was little maintenance done for our paint locker was bare of the necessary paints, oils and tar.

We loaded coal under the tips at Garston for Gweek, Cornwall and had a good slant from the Mersey to Wicklow Head. From there to the Smalls the wind took off until we barely had steerage way down the coast of North Cornwall. The Longships in sight, even the light airs deserted us and we lay completely becalmed between St Ives bay and Land's End, in blazing hot weather.

We'd been at sea three weeks and the food situation was becoming serious. Our salt beef, in a harness cask on deck, was tainted before we left the Mersey and the hot sun made it stink to high heaven. And there had been a blunder with our bread, though well intentioned. Shore bakers were beginning to wrap bread, claiming it would keep indefinitely. Our captain substituted it for the usual hardtack and we thoroughly enjoyed the luxury of soft bread for the first week at sea, then paid dearly for the pleasure when the loaves turned mouldy under their grease-proof paper wrappings.

Although potatoes, margarine, tea, sugar and tinned milk had been most meagrely rationed, almost everything had gone.

On the first day of the calm, we were at dinner in the small, horseshoe-shaped cabin. The captain was on deck, mooning about near the useless wheel. He scarcely ever touched any food at mealtimes and seemed to be able to exist on fresh air. It was stifling hot below and we were half naked. On the table was our dinner; an evil smelling lump of salt beef and half a loaf of mouldy bread.

Sam and I watched with loathing, tinged with envy, as Pough cut a small slice of the putrid meat and regardless of it's awful smell, slowly chewed it. Unable to stand either the sight or the smell of the meat any longer, Sam burst out, explosively: 'For Christ's sake, Pough! If you've done with the stinking stuff, heave it overboard. It's a wonder it doesn't kill you!'

Without a word, Pough took the meat to the top of the companion stairs and flung it into the sea. This had become a daily routine. We dined on a frugal meal of mouldy bread, margarine and weak tea. Until the wind had died, we'd been looking forward to our arrival in the Helford River, where the captain would be obliged to replenish our stores and end our misery. But the weather had now put an end to our hopes.

'What'll we do if this calm lasts?' I asked my mates. 'We'll be out of everything but salt junk in a couple more days. If we eat that bloody meat, it'll poison us.'

71

'Best thing we can do is make some fishing lines and try to catch a few fish,' suggested Pough. 'The Old Man doesn't seem to care if we all starve. Beats me what he lives on. It's goodbye from me to that bloody old skinflint, when this cargo's out, I can tell you!'

Sam and I exchanged glances. We'd heard this before. It was easier said than done with berths in other schooners difficult to find, especially when hard up, as we all were.

'That's a good idea about trying our hand at fishing, Pough,' said Sam. 'Let's make up a couple of lines and see if there are any mackerel about. I could polish off a dozen myself, right now.'

Encouraged by thoughts of a meal of delicious fresh fish, we got busy. Using a ball of sailtwine for lines, we fashioned hooks with suitable wire I found in the lamp locker and soon had some very crude lines hanging over the schooner's counter. But it was disheartening work, with only bits of rag for lures and the lines straight up and down in the glassy water. We'd not had a bite by sundown.

'Can't expect much in daylight with these lines. We'll do better when it's dark,' said Pough, the optimist. 'We need a fish for bait then we'd pull 'em, in lads!'

During the night we diligently tended the fishing lines but without success. After daybreak the sun rose like a fiery ball in a cloudless sky, blazing down on a sea of burnished silver undisturbed by the slightest ripple. As we wet down the deck, it dried instantly. Our old, patched sails hung limply from the spars, looking very dingy and ill-fitting. Towards midday, the heat was intense, making the pitch in the deck seams bubble and the planking uncomfortably hot to our bare feet.

During the full heat of the day, we didn't work. We tried to find a bit of shade somewhere on deck for the fo'c'sle was like an oven. It was almost too much trouble to move from one bit of shade to another as the sun crossed the heavens. We felt as lifeless as the becalmed *Emma & Esther*. Our fishing lines were neglected and forgotten.

In the cool of the evening, we roused ourselves enough to sluice the sun-scorched deck. The gnawing pangs of hunger returned and we made another frugal meal from what was left in the food locker. So little remained, we were forcibly reminded of the need to persist with our fishing. As a glorious sunset brought the day to a close, we renewed our efforts with the lines but the night's fishing was again unrewarded.

The third day was again fiercely hot, without a breath of wind. Several times I imagined the *Emma & Esther* was closer to the land but put it down to the clear visibility. After nightfall, it became obvious to us all that the schooner was in the grip of a tidal stream which was gradually setting her, broadside on, towards the steep-to shore.

The captain was up and down the cabin companionway like a cat on hot bricks and his uneasiness was infectious. Slowly but surely we drifted in the darkness towards the black, menacing bulk of the towering cliffs, seemingly only a stone's throw away. The sea sounded alarmingly turbulent at their base, despite its lake-like surface offshore. The results of stranding at such an inhospitable spot were too horrible to contemplate.

I saw the captain's face in the light from the cabin skylight, as he peered at the compass. His anxiety was painful to watch. Leaving the compass, he strode to the rail and gazed irresolutely at the cliff face. To our relief, he gave us the order to ship the sweep to try to turn the schooner's head to the tide.

With the long, heavy oar in the fore rigging and all hands straining on its loom, we did our utmost to swing the heavily laden *Emma & Esther* in the required direction, but although we pulled until we were fit to drop, there wasn't any appreciable improvement from our efforts. Too exhausted to continue, we gave up the hopeless struggle. It was then that we noticed an extraordinary thing . . . the cliffs seemed to be further away and were gradually receding. In the nick of time, the tide had turned and was now setting us offshore again.

By breakfast-time, we were back in approximately our old position lying motionless under a fierce sun. It seemed as if the calm would never end. We made a pot of tea which finished the tea and cut into our last mouldy loaf, rationing ourselves to one slice apiece although we were desperately hungry. It was an unbelievable situation, to be nearly starving, yet within sight of the land; and the captain didn't seem the least bit concerned at our plight.

A shout from the deck interrupted my gloomy thoughts. Pough, who'd taken his mug of tea on deck, was excitedly waving a silvery object at us through the open skylight.

'We've caught a fish . . . we've got some bait!' he yelled. 'Now we'll get some grub, lads.'

The very small mackerel in his hand filled us with renewed hope. We baited our home-made hooks with tempting slivers from the little fish and gave our full attention to the angling, ignoring the heat, though, during the day, we had little encouragement. After dusk, Pough caught another mackerel, a beauty this time.

'That's one for a start,' he shouted triumphantly. 'Hurry up, you two, and catch some more and we'll have decent breakfast for a change.'

Overnight, the *Emma & Esther* was again set shorewards but not enough to cause anxiety or interrupt our fishing and our catch was four fat mackerel and a smaller one which we kept for bait. Our breakfast of boiled mackerel, small slices of mouldy bread and a weak tea made from the previous day's tea leaves, seemed a banquet. It was the last time we bothered to eat at the cabin table. The calm continued for a further four days and we lived solely on the few fish we were able to catch at night. As they were caught, we gutted them, dropped them into a bucket of boiling water for a few minutes, then consumed them on the spot. Things looked really desperate when we lost two of our fishing lines which unaccountably parted and couldn't be replaced as we were out of twine and wire. Then the heavens relented and breathed again, ruffling the polished surface of the sea with the gentlest catspaws, ghosting us round the Land and the Lizard to an anchorage in Falmouth Bay.

Shortly after bringing up, a smart, white-painted motor quay-punt filled with summer visitors ranged alongside the *Emma & Esther*. The boatman swarmed aboard and disappeared below with our captain to haggle over the price of a tow into the Helford River. Meanwhile, we leaned over the schooner's rail in the hopes of a chat with the holiday makers. In gay, light summer clothing, they seemed so fresh and clean to our sailor's eyes, people from a different world. Several pretty girls of about my own age were in the boat and impulsively, I asked one of them if she and her friends would like to come aboard to see over the schooner.

She completely ignored me, turned to another girl and in a voice we could all hear, said: 'Isn't it a horrible, dirty little ship and aren't they awful men on her?'

Shamefaced, we slunk away from the schooner's rail, aware for the first time of our wild appearance; half naked, gaunt, unshaven and burnt nearly black by the sun.

Having struck a satisfactory bargain for the tow, the captain ordered us to heave up. The quay-punt took us up the Helford River as far as Passage, where we again anchored. Only one thought was in our minds: a square meal. Before the captain's lips had framed the order, we'd launched the punt. Sam and I pulled him across to Helford village and lay off. Our visions of a good tuck-in abruptly faded when he returned to the beach with two small paper bags of food. Stunned, we pulled back to the *Emma & Esther* and as we slid alongside her shabby, work-scarred side, Pough's head and shoulders appeared above the rail. The eager anticipation on his face died when he saw the pitifully small bags in the stern sheets, to be replaced by mingled rage, astonishment and dismay.

I was the last to board the schooner. My two shipmates were gazing at the brown paper bags which the captain had left on the galley seat locker, as if unable to believe their own eyes. Then Pough burst out with a torrent of abuse of the captain, which for sheer descriptive invective I've never heard equalled.

'Let's see what we've got, anyway,' said Sam, practically. The bags contained a couple of loaves, two small tins of corned beef, a quarter of tea, sugar, skimmed milk and a small pat of margarine. I could have wolfed the lot myself, in my starved condition. 'Make some tea, Sam. I'll open the bully.' I grabbed a can to open it as the captain arrived on the scene.

'Who told you to open the corned beef?' he demanded. 'Hand it over! You and Sam take the punt down to the beach below Passage and gather a bucket of mussels for tea.'

He scooped up the provisions and before we could say anything, had retreated to the cabin.

'Blast him!' I exploded. 'He can fetch his own bloody mussels and eat 'em. He must be crazy, expecting us to eat mussels after living on mackerel for over a week.'

'It's no good, Dick. We've got to obey orders. Grab that draw bucket. The sooner we're done, the sooner we eat.' Sam dropped back into the punt and I followed with the bucket but I was seething with rage.

'There's a bit of breeze and the tide's ebbing,' said Sam. 'We'll step the mast and sail down the river. I'm too bloody done in to scull.'

Under the dirty old lug, we part sailed, part drifted with the tide, more concerned with discussing our situation than with the course we were taking. Too late to avoid her, we saw the gleaming white topsides of a large, anchored steam yacht right ahead. Our heavy, tarred punt struck her with a resounding thump. As I fended off, a brassbound officer leaned over the yacht's rail and in a hoarse whisper, told us what he thought of us. We gave him a surprise. All our pent-up feelings of the past week were released in a flood of the foulest language we could muster between us and we fully described his antecedents, his guests and the yacht. And we made certain that the expensively dressed, pampered throng, dancing under the stern awning, heard us too.

Letting off steam did us both good and in a far better mood, we gathered the mussels and returned to the *Emma & Esther*.

Our first meal in port was bread and margarine and tea, for excepting the captain, none of us would touch the mussels.

I lay awake in my bunk half the night, trying to think of a way to escape from the *Emma & Esther* but the draw-back was lack of money. I was determined, however, not to help dolly the cargo out on a diet of bread and margarine.

Next day, the problem solved itself. Pough and I had to pull the captain up to Gweek in the punt, to collect the mail. During a long, hard row up the lovely, tree lined river, I was agreeably surprised to find how fit I was, although as thin as a skeleton. Pough, who was in his fifties, was in poor shape and was about all in when we reached Gweek.

The captain was away for a couple of hours and Pough lay down in the boat to recover, so I had a stroll around the quiet little village, not meeting a soul, yet conscious that curious eyes were peeping at me from behind the curtained, cottage windows.

When, at length, the captain returned to the boat, he pitched me a letter. After glancing at the familiar writing and postmark, I stuffed it in my pocket. It was rare for a schoonerman to have mail and this was totally unexpected.

Half a mile down river, we picked up a fair breeze which enabled us to ship our oars and sail back to the schooner.

Curled up in the bows and hidden by the billowing lug, I opened my letter. Folded inside the writing paper were five pound notes: the money may come in handy, in the hard life you have chosen, wrote the understanding sender.

That night, I took Sam aside and told him I was leaving the *Emma & Esther* before daylight and asked him to accompany me.

'We'll go to Falmouth and after a good feed, try to ship together in another vessel. I've enough money to see us right for a bit,' I explained.

'Wish I could leave with you, Dick,' he replied. 'Thanks for the offer but I've reasons for staying here. I don't blame you for clearing out. Good luck to you!'

Just before dawn, I quietly lowered my bag into the punt and Sam landed me on the beach. A firm handgrip, then he pushed off to scull back to the sleeping schooner.

Tramping along the leafy country lanes to Falmouth, I felt as free as a lark. When I arrived in the port, my first stop was at a little waterside eating house frequented by sailors. Here I polished off three enormous breakfasts, one after the other, to the amazement of the waitress who served me. It was some weeks before I fully recovered from the effects of that hungry Chester Riverman.

7

Windbound

Freezing on a bleak North Sea in bitter nor'-easterlies straight from North Cape; sweltering under the blazing sun, becalmed on seas of glass; pumping for dear life in Atlantic gales; peering sightlessly into dense fogs and seafrets, conscious of danger from invisible steamer traffic or the land: plenty of variety and three pounds a month—that was our lives.

I saw the coastlines of Britain and the Continent through hail, rain, snow and sunshine, sometimes too close for comfort, for I now recognised the land as a hazard as great as the sea. Mentally and physically I thrived on the tough apprenticeship. It sounds crazy, yet at times I had a feeling I'd done it all and seen it all before.

Lying windbound was a common occurrence. A fresh and persistent headwind could force the most stubborn schooner captain to an anchorage. There were traditional spots with good holding ground for windbound sailing vessels to bring up, on all coasts. To the west and south, Holyhead, Milford Haven, Falmouth, Plymouth Sound, the Solent and Dover provided excellent shelter, but the east coast offered little more than open roadsteads protected by sandbanks, or wide bays where sudden shifts of wind could be extremely perilous.

I experienced the joys of rolling scuppers under in Yarmouth Roads, lying to an uneasy anchor under the Spurn or Flamborough, and was thankful, especially in winter time, that many of the remaining schooner trades were concentrated on the Irish Sea, Atlantic and English Channel seaboards.

When a deadmuzzler set in, we only gave in after a battle. Close-hauled, tack after tack, we'd punch away, only to lose hard-won miles until our captain finally decided to make for the nearest anchorage. We were rarely alone when windbound. A headwind usually brought a goodly number of schooners together. One after the other, they'd give up the long, tiresome beat to wind'ard and like a flock of sheep following a leader, they'd come trailing in to let-go.

As each vessel hove in sight, standing towards the anchorage, the crews of the brought-up schooners would try to identify her. The old hands, who knew the slight difference in individual rigs, could recognize nearly every schooner on the coast from a silhouette in the distance. As she worked in closer, we'd criticise her appearance, her handling and everything about her with great professional enjoyment.

Although our ships were idle when windbound, the crews were kept fully occupied with the never-ending maintenance work. If the headwind persisted, punts would be swung out to ferry the captains between the neighbouring schooners. We all tried to be included in a boat's crew and felt aggrieved if left behind even if it meant a hard pull. A good long yarn with another vessel's crew made a welcome break to our ordered routine and no doubt the captains were the better for letting off steam to one another during those trying periods of delay.

Ship visiting was good for our morale. To see new faces and to enjoy talking with others of our kind was a pleasure and a safety valve after being cooped up in our little ships for long periods— three or four weeks at sea were commonplace and forty and fifty days' passages not unknown. Yet I can't ever recall any quarrels or serious bickerings in the small companies of three of four men and a boy. A captain and mate sometimes exchanged a few sharp words but that was the only evidence of tension I ever saw.

Except for the intermittent trickle of business letters to the masters, little if any correspondence was received. Even in port we rarely saw a newspaper. Few of the schooners had wireless sets. Yarning was about our only means of communication. By word of mouth we passed round the happenings on the coast; news of shipmates, strandings and ship losses, the idiosyncrasies of captains and all the lore of our little ships. When the latest gossip had been exchanged, if time allowed, we'd be entertained by shipmates' reminiscences, very personal and professional accounts of past ships, captains and shipmates, told in a humorous fashion, with the humour strongly slanted against the teller. There was little scope for 'Jeremias' and from our laughter at these fo'c'sle gams, it sounded as if we hadn't a care in the world.

Contrary to popular beliefs, the topics of the yarns were rarely of woman or smut. Perhaps it was because we had so little contact with women that we held them in more respect, for the yarns mirrored our outlooks and our lives. A certain degree of exaggeration was allowable, even expected in a yarn.

One of the best yarn-spinners I ever listened to was an old A.B., Bill Roberts. He was reputed to be in his eighties and was the oldest seaman I ever encountered afloat, yet he was still remarkably strong and active both on deck and aloft. He'd spent the whole of his life in sail and was full of the ancient superstitions of the sea and had both the best and the worst habits of the deepsea shellback, including heavy drinking. At the end of a long ocean voyage, hard drinking was natural and allowable, but in the shortsea trades, it was undesirable and, fortunately, uncommon, as it required money to go on a spree. Lack of money never worried Bill. He could go ashore penniless and return to his ship 'half-seas-over', for few could resist buying him a drink in return for his stories. I was shipmates with him in the schooner *Ryelands* and, later in the barquentine *Francis & Jane*.

When I joined the *Ryelands*, Bill greeted me with: 'This ship's a home from home. The cap'n and mate are both young men so I'm a father to the lot of you!'

There was some truth in his remark, for at sea he was the best practical sailorman I ever came across, but in port he was a thorough nuisance with his drinking. Sailing time drawing near and Bill missing, I was often sent by the mate to find him. He was easily traced to some waterside bar, where I'd find the tall, gaunt old man in dungarees and a battered felt hat, dipping his grizzled whiskers into a foaming tankard and entertaining an open-mouthed audience of longshoremen with one of his yarns. To get him away from a pub and back to the *Ryelands* taxed my ingenuity and patience to the full. At sea again, all would be forgiven as he was a tower of strength. He was a splendid helmsman and it was a treat to see him at the wheel of a schooner. For his fine-weather 'tricks' he kept a special clean suit of dungarees, the best in his outfit. Clad in these, he'd stand as erect as a guardsman, grasping the wheel spokes, with his faded blue eyes alert for the slightest variation of the breeze. No-one else could make a schooner so responsive. Under his sensitive hands she would point higher when on a wind, would be drier in bad weather and when there were but the lightest of airs, she would still ghost along.

Bill was chock full of strange notions and taboos. For some

reason, he refused to use the schooner's lavatory or 'heads', although it was scrubbed out thoroughly each morning. Instead, every evening after dusk he'd perch precariously on a cathead over the bows to relieve himself, looking like an old gannet gone to roost and providing us with great amusement. There was an excuse for his behaviour during bad weather with a heavy sea running, for then a user of a wheelshelter 'heads' was liable to be lifted violently off the toilet seat by a column of water forced up the straight-through discharge pipe as the vessel's counter slammed down in the troughs. But even during the calmest conditions Bill stubbornly used a cathead.

He knew the ports of the world like the back of his hand and in addition, had the most astonishing knowledge of Britain, particularly of the pubs. We often had a game trying to catch him out by mentioning little known 'boozers' at small inland towns and villages well off the beaten track, but he always convinced us he'd been there at some time or another. I once asked him how he knew about places so far from the coast. He explained that after long voyages to foreign parts, he'd sometimes tire of the sea. Paying off, he'd go on the tramp, loafing quietly and happily along the highways and byways of Britain anywhere between Land's End and John-o'-Groats, sleeping in barns, haystacks or under hedges, without a care in the world. One day, the sea fever would return and he'd go back to the Seven Seas in one of the ever diminishing fleet of tall ships.

His yarn of how he nearly 'retired' was a favourite with schoonermen. On the strength of his fifty years' service in Liverpool owned sailing ships, some well-meaning people used their influence to get him into the Aged Mariner's Home at Wallasey. When he arrived at the Home for an interview with the Matron, poor Bill was overawed by the fine buildings and beautiful surroundings, but his chief worries were about the restrictions of the new life ahead.

Knowing old sailors and their ways, the Matron made a big point of the daily allowance of a pint of beer, hoping to reassure him. Bill was absolutely dumbfounded at the news.

At this point of his story, he'd have us all in stitches with the righteous indignation on his face as he demanded: 'What good's a single pint to a feller like me?'

A few days after entering the Home, Bill was out for a walk when he met some old shipmates who'd just paid off a barque lying in the West Float. A glorious spree followed.

'Next day, when I come to, I found a berth in a nice little schooner,' he'd end off his story, deep satisfaction in his voice. 'No more of that soddin' Home for me. Just fancy . . . only a bleedin' pint a day for life. Might as well be in "chokey"!'

I left the *Ryelands* in a hurry because of Bill's drinking. We were held up in Runcorn Lay-by through a coal strike, so the captain and mate took a few days off to go home. Bill went on the 'blind' and after three days of it, I'd had enough. I packed my bag and departed in such haste that I forgot my watch, a big old-fashioned silver lever, once my father's, which I left hanging on a nail over my bunk.

I joined another schooner bound to Falmouth with coal for the Gas Works. When we arrived, I learned that the *Ryelands* had towed up to Truro a day or two before. At the first opportunity I took a bus to Truro to recover my watch.

From the bridge, I saw the *Ryelands* discharging at the coal wharf. As luck would have it, the captain, in shore rig, was just leaving the schooner, so I waited until he'd emerged from the covered archway and walked some way up the street towards his Agents before boarding the *Ryelands*.

Bill and the mate were heaving away on the dolly winch. At my 'Hullo, Bill! I've come for my watch', the old shellback's face registered the most comical expression of surprise and alarm.

'Have you seen the "Old Man" an' told him about it, Dick?' he enquired anxiously. Guessing that something was wrong, I answered: 'Not yet. But if I don't get my watch back at once, I'll speak to him alright.'

'Oh, no! Don't do that, Dick, or I'll be fired. Wait a minute and I'll get it for you . . . Ginger!' he bawled down the hold. 'Come on deck. I want to speak to you.'

A tough-looking, carroty-headed lad, who was filling baskets in the hold, threw down his shovel and climbed the ladder to the deck. He vanished with Bill behind the galley where they had a very heated argument if the sounds of the angry voices were anything to go by.

'What's the trouble?' I asked the grinning mate.

'Bill sold a watch to Ginger, just before we left Runcorn. It must have been yours. I wouldn't care to be in his shoes, now. Ginger's a regular fire-eater,' was the reply.

A moment or two later, a very haggard Bill reappeared with my watch. Thrusting it into my hand, he begged me to go before the captain returned. On my way back to Falmouth, I couldn't help speculating on the consequences of my visit to the *Ryelands*. One thing was certain . . . Bill was in for a stormy time.

Twelve months or so later, I was again shipmates with Bill, this time in the barquentine *Francis & Jane* under Captain Cort. He never mentioned the *Ryelands* or the Truro incident to me, so I never heard what happened after I left. But, to my amazement, Bill was a reformed character. In port and at sea, his behaviour was exemplary. No-one took liberties with W. F. Cort and well he knew it.

In sailing vessels a man's background or past was regarded as private and was never pried into by any of his mates. But sometimes during our yarning, a sailor would speak of his home life and how he came into schooners.

A good yarn we heard when windbound was spun by the big, truculent mate of a smart West-Country schooner. A Cornishman in his early thirties, he'd been a ship's boy, then seaman and finally mate in vessels commanded by his father. This was the time-honoured way to an eventual command in families whose men had followed the sea in schooners for generations. It was a long, hard apprenticeship under a captain who expected more from a son than from anyone else. His story was about the first time he left his father to sail in the *Alert* under 'Mad' Mortensen.

''Twas forced 'pon me, so to speak,' he began, in his broad West-Country dialect. 'Me and Dad had a reg'lar di-do 'bout shore leave an' a maid I were courting. I bain't particular no-ways 'bout what I says an' gets fired. I were in the boozer all night 'til chucking out time an'fair mazed I be. I come to wi' Peter the Dane shaking me. "Turn to, me 'andsome!" says 'e; "you'm mate o' the *Alert*, bound to Methil. Rouse up the lads to get under way." Oh, my dear soul! What a trip! Tack an'tack up Channel, then no sooner round the Foreland, the wind come away s'utherly, strong to gale. Mortensen cracked on, wild as a fitcher. Flamborough abeam, taups'ls an' flying jib were scat asunder by a hard squall. Fair jawner! It were wet backsi'es up along to Methil. I knows now why they calls 'e "Mad" Mortensen! I were soon back wi' me ol' Dad, I can tell 'ee!'

That anyone could scare the hard-case Cornishman was good for a laugh anytime. Stories of Captain Mortensen and his *Alert*, of reckless sail-carrying, incredibly fast passages and the Dane's fiery temper, were to be heard all around the coast. None of the stories lost anything in the telling but undoubtedly the *Alert*'s master was the most colourful, daring and successful schooner captain of the period between the Wars.

The first time I met him, he was in his early thirties, unusually young for a command when most captains were nearer sixty. His appearance was in keeping with the stories. Lean and athletic, with dynamic energy, he was a strikingly handsome man. A tight-lipped mouth under a well kept moustache and a determined chin revealed something of his character, but the dominant features of his tanned face were his eyes: brilliant, mocking and for ever gleaming with a strange, devil-may-care light.

Peter Mortensen was born 1893 in Faaborg, Denmark. He arrived here during the First World War in a Danish schooner. For a time, he was a seaman in the *Pearl* of Falmouth and other West-Country schooners. After only a few years on the coast, his outstanding ability earned him a command. At first he was known as Peter the Dane but later, when in command of the *Alert*, he was nicknamed 'Mad' Mortensen because of his daring exploits with the schooner. He and the *Alert* were the subjects of so many yarns that they were inseparable and became almost a legend with schoonermen.

The *Alert* was one of the finest looking vessels on the coast. Built by Brundritt of Runcorn in 1885, she was a three-masted tops'l schooner of 163 tons gross with a beautifully modelled hull and a lofty rig. Under Peter's command she was always smart and spotlessly clean and there was no room for shirkers in her crew. He sailed her so hard she gained the reputation of being the fleetest schooner on the coast.

In later years when schooners were just a memory, Peter and I were close friends and we had many a good yarn together about our past lives. I once remarked about the *Alert*: 'She must have been a fine schooner for you to make such fast passages, Peter!'

He chuckled: 'She was as rotten as a pear but nobody knew it,' he answered.

Looking back, it's a fact that the speediest vessels were always those that were on their last legs. A schooner working and leaking to an alarming degree in rough weather generally sailed like a witch. But with pump drill the order of the day, it required a master of Peter Mortensen's calibre, with nerve and skill, to get the best from such a vessel . . . and her crew, for continuous pumping was an exhausting, heartbreaking task.

After relinquishing command of the *Alert*, Captain Mortensen bought the three-masted tops'l schooner *Mary Barrow* of Falmouth, another fine vessel of 163 tons gross, built by Lean of Falmouth in 1891. He traded with her until 1938, when she was driven ashore on the Isle of Man and became a total loss. The same week that he lost his ship, his little son was drowned bathing from a Cornish beach. His sad losses were almost a parallel to my own and were a common bond between us.

For some time after visiting other vessels, we'd have new topics to discuss and laugh about. I remember an occasion when we of the *Francis & Jane* had been aboard the rival barquentine *Waterwitch*. For the first time we'd seen the very superior quarters of her crew but what impressed us most about their fo'c'sle was the colour scheme—a tasteful shade of pale blue.

Bill Roberts was dumbfounded when he saw such an unusual setting for our yarning and scarcely uttered until we were back aboard our own vessel. Then, spitting disgustedly over the rail, he said: 'Did you ever see the likes of it? That's no sailor's fo'c'sle . . . it's a bleeding lady's boodwor!' The 'boudoir' kept us amused for some time afterwards.

I always enjoyed the anchor watches when brought up in a windbound anchorage. Pacing the deck in solitude, keeping well clear of the cabin and fo'c'sle so I didn't disturb the sleepers below, it was a time for thought and contemplation. If we had the company of other schooners, I specially liked the first watch, as before the light failed, I could study their rig and appearance at leisure. I was often stirred by the sight of some particularly handsome craft floating proudly on the gleaming water, the dying sun glinting on her well oiled spars and her taut rigging silhouetted black against the sky. And then came the sunset, sometimes spectacular in its beauty, followed by the enveloping darkness in which the twinkling riding lights on the forestays of the anchored schooners were the only indications of their presence. For those of us who had receptive eyes, our calling had its compensations.

But anchor watches weren't always so peaceful. I experienced all the usual hazards of dragging anchors, steamers bearing down on our helpless vessels in thick fog, and the difficult situations brought about by sudden changes of wind and weather. My most vivid memory, however, was an occasion in the late twenties, when I witnessed a gathering of windbound sailing vessels as impressive as any in the days when sail was supreme. Bound 'round the Land', we were forced by a vicious s'utherly gale into the shelter of Holyhead. Two or three schooners were already brought up there when we arrived, and we were followed by what seemed to be every remaining sailing vessel on the coast. As each additional schooner battled around the breakwater the anchorage became so congested that it became a matter of concern to the masters in the assembling fleet. The whole of the harbour in the lee of the breakwater was dotted with windbound schooners and ketches with scarcely enough room for them to swing.

For three anxious days and nights we carefully tended our anchors and cables at each change of tide, to avoid fouling with other vessels.

Then the wind took off, slowly veered to the nor'-west and settled there. The sound of the first windlass pawls was the signal for all to heave up. It was most exciting, with every captain trying to be the first away. Although we hove like madmen on our windlass, we were almost the last schooner to clear the breakwater as we'd been anchored too far from the entrance. It says much for the seamanship of the captains that there were no collisions or fouled ground tackle as the vast fleet got under way. Within an hour every vessel had cleared the harbour.

I've always regretted not counting the ships and taking their names, but so it is that history goes unrecorded. Yet, perversely, on another quite unremarkable occasion I noted the vessels around us. We were in the Sloyne anchorage, River Mersey, midway between the Dingle and Newferry. Here inward bounders brought up to await their tugs for the tows to Garston, Weston Point or Runcorn. With inclement weather or unfavourable winds, outward schooners patiently bided their time in the Sloyne. At one time or another, I'd seen most of the schooners of my day in this anchorage which was a good spot to view them to advantage as they were generally down to their marks and free of dockside grime.

This time, we had for company two barquentines, *Waterwitch* and *Francis & Jane*; four three-masted tops'l schooners, *Jane Banks, Mountblairy, Emily Warbrick* and *Shoal Fisher*; also two two-masters, *Snowflake* and *My Lady*. Of these fine vessels, I thought *Jane Banks* the most handsome although the light-grey-painted steel *Shoal Fisher* came a good second for looks and the tiny *My Lady* well deserved her name.

Although it was well over fifty years ago, the beautiful pictures of those little ships proudly riding to their anchors in the Mersey will never fade from my memory.

8

Armstrong's Patent.

A wooden schooner required constant attention from her crew. Excepting when we were working cargo, a day began with a routine scrubbing of deck, galley and 'heads'—the galley and 'heads' receiving particular care—even the toilet seat was scrubbed white. Then the pumps were manned until they sucked, a very necessary precaution in all wooden ships, however tight they might be.

After breakfast, if we weren't occupied with the sailing of our vessel we were detailed by the mate to tasks of maintenance; chipping, scraping, painting, varnishing, tarring, splicing, serving or sewing—the endless work of keeping a schooner smart and seaworthy. If the weather was too bad for work about the deck or rigging, we were given old rope to unlay and make into sennits or chafing gear in the shelter of the fo'c'sle. In my time, I've made miles of sennit rovings and bag-o'-wrinkle chafing gear.

Masts were kept clean and bright by scraping periodically from trucks to deck, then oiled with raw linseed. Some captains had auger holes bored in the centres of the lowermast heads, closed with wooden stoppers. When swabbing down with oil, the holes were filled several times with the raw linseed then re-plugged. The oil seeped down the hearts of the spars to their heels and we could always tell when masts had been treated this way as they scraped as easily as butter. Well kept masts were not only protected from rot but as old Weddock once said to me as I was swabbing down the *Via*'s mast: 'That'll lighten our work when hoisting sail!'

At least once a year, the wire standing rigging, which was parcelled and served over, had to be tarred down with either Stockholm tar or a 'blacking'. We were continually renewing worn or damaged servings and replacing ratlines. If a sailor saw a rotten ratline aloft, it was a rule that he cut it with his knife to prevent an accident.

Keeping the standing rigging taut and shipshape was another job which kept us busy. The shrouds and backstays of a wooden schooner were tensioned with deadeyes and lanyards. The operations of 'setting up' rigging was where a good mate showed his mettle.

First of all, the seizings on the Italian hemp lanyards were removed and the lanyards overhauled through the deadeyes. The mate then examined them for wear, especially at the 'nips'. If satisfactory, they received a liberal dressing of Stockholm tar. A strop would be racked on the shroud or stay being set up, about ten feet above the sheerpole and a tackle hooked onto it with its fall at the lower block. The end of the lanyard was bent to the hook of this block with a double Blackwall hitch. The tackle was finally Blackwall-hitched to the hook of a heavy purchase—usually the freed throat halyards—and all was ready for setting up.

As we hauled on the halyard fall, in one operation the shroud or stay was tightened and its lanyard hove taut. The mate carefully watched the lanyard, well lubricated with tar, rendering through the deadeyes and with his marline spike eased it so that all parts shared an equal strain. 'All taut', there was a pause as he aligned the spars, squinting aloft from various positions. When he was satisfied, we replaced the seizings, removed our gear and cowhitched the lanyard just above the sheerpole. Its end was seized neatly alongside one of its parts. In all such jobs of practical sailorising, mates each had their own ways of improving or simplifying the work.

Which reminds me of the time a very capable mate experienced unexpected difficulties when setting up the rigging of the Irish three-master *Mount Blairy* in Garston. The captain was ashore when we tackled the job. We set up the fore rigging, then started on the main. Jim, our tall, lean, Lancashire mate, kept sighting the masts from every angle, becoming increasingly worried as the work progressed. For some reason, although we made several attempts, we couldn't line up the masts.

'The 'Old Man'll play hell with me if we don't get 'em right,' he complained. 'Can't think what's wrong with the bitch!'

For a few moments he gazed at the offending 'sticks', a puzzled frown creasing his tar-stained face. Suddenly, he slapped his thigh . . . 'I've got it!' he exclaimed. 'Cutty had her ashore off Wicklow, last year. I'll bet she's got a twist in her somewhere. Come on, look lively! Get those seizings on again before he comes back or we'll be at the job all night.'

Just as the last seizing was completed, we saw the captain on the dockside, squinting at the masts. From his black looks, we knew there was trouble ahead. As he stepped aboard, he pitched into the mate, finding fault with everything we'd done. Jim soon lost his temper and in the middle of a first-class slanging match I made things even worse by stepping backwards into the tar pot which upset over a spotless deck. With the captain supervising, we began again the impossible task of lining up the three masts. It was quite dark by the time we were done and the results were no better, though the 'Old Man' wouldn't admit it. The others knocked off, leaving me on my knees scrubbing away with sand and canvas, trying to remove the tar stains from the deck.

The smartness of a schooner was often judged by the condition of her paintwork. We were for ever cleaning and painting the white ventilators, deckhouses and insides of bulwarks, so we were rarely without a paint-brush in our hands.

To ease the pully-hauly of a schooner's crew, an efficient mate would systematically overhaul the running rigging blocks until every block had received attention. Each block would have its pin knocked out and the sheaves removed. After cleaning and greasing, they were replaced. If obtainable, graphite grease was the best lubricant for the pins and sheaves. When the blocks had received this treatment, it was surprising how much labour was saved by reducing friction to a minimum. The introduction of patent sheaved blocks for sailing vessels was a great labour saver but, unfortunately they were expensive. Second-hand blocks of this type were widely sought after by schoonermen to replace the usual lower priced 'dumb' blocks.

Twice a year, or more often if it were possible, we scrubbed, scraped and painted the bottoms of our vessels. The work was done when dried out in suitable harbours. When cleaned off, a hull was carefully examined for weeping seams and trunnel heads and defects remedied by hardening up or recaulking. Caulking irons and mallet were essential tools in wooden ships and schoonermen were obliged to be skilful caulkers. With minor repairs completed, the bottom and topsides were tarred with two coats of black varnish. I always heaved a sigh of relief when bottom cleaning was finished as a hundred tonner was more than enough work for three men and a boy, working between tides.

Our sails, a major expense to a schooner owner, received constant care and attention. At every opportunity when at anchor or in port, we hoisted and dried our heavy flax canvas. Restitching and patching were done aboard, for sailormen were expected to be handy with a palm and needle. Only extensive repairs were done by shore sailmakers. We also repaired hatch tarpaulins and made all the small covers for skylights, ventilators, wheel, etc., ourselves. I'd a natural aptitude for sailmaking which I turned to good account in the last working years of my life.

Whenever possible, our captains assisted with the maintenance work. It was a subtle reminder to us that they'd reached their commands by way of the hawse pipe. James Doyle of the *Via* always re-packed the plungers of the 'Deluge' bilge pumps and I never saw him allow anyone else to do this job. It was his way of knowing the pumps were in perfect order. W. F. Cort's favourite tool was a paint brush and the small, 'tiddly' work, such as lettering the lifebuoys, punt or wheelcover were his speciality. Something of an artist with a marline spike, Peter Mortensen liked nothing better than an intricate job with rope or wire. They believed in the simple rule of good leadership—never order a subordinate to do anything you can't do well yourself.

Our machinery, the permanent dolly winch and the windlass, required little maintenance beyond painting and an occasional oiling and greasing. Powered by our strong arms and backs, their efficiency and reliability were taken for granted. But it required skill and experience to get full advantage from these aids. Working anchors with an up-and-down windlass was an art in itself. The slow action of the windlass—each stroke of the handles or 'brakes' heaved up only about a foot of cable—was a factor of the utmost importance in times of stress and danger. Trapped on a lee shore, with a heavy sea causing a vessel to snub violently, heaving up was an operation requiring plenty of nerve and skilled judgement, for an error could so easily lose a fine schooner and all in her.

The up-and-down windlass evolved from the ancient hand-spike windlass of the earliest sea-going ships. The massive bitts and twin barrels remained. The iron axle with whelps and three ratchets had wedge-shaped oak leaves fitted between the whelps to form the barrels. Oak warping drums were fitted at the ends of the axle. For'ard of the central main ratchet, a stout pawlbitt stepped on the keelson and passing through the fo'c'sle, rose to a height of about four feet above the deck. To' this was bolted the heavy iron pawlplate with the main pawls which engaged in the central ratchet and prevented the barrels revolving in the wrong direction. Mounted on top of the pawl-bitt was the rockerarm with sockets each side to take the levers or 'brakes' used to operate the windlass. Metal rods connected the ends of the rockerarm to the driving pawls which slid on the rimmed edges of the two side ratchets, a most ingenious arrangement.

A downward stroke of a brake caused the opposite driving pawl to engage in its ratchet, revolving the barrels in an upward movement. When the same brake was raised, the pawl disengaged and slid down the ratchet to its former position.

The alternate action of the driving pawls continuously rotated the windlass barrels. It's sad that the inventor of this simple, effective and trouble-free device should be anonymous, for it combined the mechanical advantages of the lever and gearwheel to perfection.

Anchors and cables for merchant vessels are regulated by Lloyd's Rules and are in accordance with the equipment number in the register. Sailing vessels' ground tackle was heavier than for steamers of a corresponding size. An average sized schooner's bower anchors each weighed roughly 15 cwts: her cables about 1¼-inch diameter stud link with approximately eight 15-fathom shackles for each anchor. When not in use, the anchors were catted and fished on either bow. Here the bulwarks were reinforced with stout, sheet-iron covered billboards and the rail cappings protected with half-round iron to save them from damage when working anchors.

Except in the very oldest vessels, a schooner's catheads were of iron, fitted with 'tumbler' quick releases for the chain catstoppers.

Cables led from the anchors through the deck-level hawsepipes, over the tops of the windlass barrels and round them three turns. From the windlass, they led to cable mangers on either side of the fore hatch, thence through spurling pipes to the chain lockers underneath the after end of the fo'c'sle.

Anchors were kept in readiness for instant use by ranging a few

9. Foredeck of schooner *Nellie Bywater*. Up-and-down windlass and ground tackle clearly shown. (*Author*)

10. Schooner's roller reefing gear, *Nellie Bywater*. (*Author*)

11. Schooner's permanent dolly winch and galley, *Mary Barrow*. (*The late Captain Peter Mortensen*)

12. Figurehead of schooner *Volant* of Kirkwall. The ultimate adornment. (*Author*)

shackles of cable forward of the windlass and having another two or three shackles in the mangers. Claw shaped stoppers called 'dogs', which fitted between a cable's links and were secured to the windlass bitts by lengths of chain, were used to prevent the ranged cables flying through the hawsepipes by their own weight.

When not being worked, the second bower anchor cable was disengaged from the windlass by loosely hanging off its three turns from a strongback above the windlass barrel.

Preparing to anchor, we cast off the shank painter and lowered the crown of the working anchor down the billboard until the anchor was 'apeak'—suspended from the cathead by the cat-stopper through its ring. The dog was knocked off the cable and a safety-pin removed from the release tumbler. The mate stood by with a crowbar, ready for the order to 'let-go!'

When the order was given, he released the catstopper tumbler with his crowbar and the anchor plunged down, taking with it the ranged out cable which roared through the hawsepipe. If extra scope was needed, we surged the cable over the windlass barrel by throwing its last turn over the barrel and the weight on the cable did the rest. It was as well to look after your fingers when veering out cable on a rough, dark night. Anchor work could be very difficult under wintery conditions, with a schooner rearing and plunging about like a wild stallion on a lunge, freezing spray flying over the bows. Fleeting extra shackles of heavy cable from the mangers to the windlass and surging it out could be very trying, and there was always that nagging fear that we would 'drag' in spite of the extra scope.

After riding to a full scope, getting underway was a long, laborious operation for two men and a boy, for most of the captains were elderly men who but rarely provided 'muscle'.

To heave up an anchor, the brakes were shipped in the rocker-arm and the 'dog' knocked off the cable. As we pumped the brakes up and down, the cable came in and heaped itself on the after side of the windlass. From time to time this had to be cleared by dragging it along the deck to its manger with a chain hook.

When all but the minimum cable to hold us was hove in, we hoisted enough canvas to suit the situation, wind, weather and tide. As the unsheeted sails slatted and banged, we again short-ened the cable until it was 'up and down'. To help break out the anchor the captain sheeted home some of the canvas and canted the schooner's head to the desired tack. Meanwhile, we were heaving away with might and main until the stock of the anchor appeared above the water. When we were free of the ground, the remaining sails were sheeted and trimmed. Under way, the anchor was catted—hoisted to its cathead with a burton which had a U-shaped hook on its end, so that the chain catstopper could be passed through the anchor ring and secured—then fished, by transferring the tackle's hook to the anchor's crown and heaving up until the shank was snugly on the rail where it was secured with the shank painter.

These are but the barest details of working anchors. It requires little imagination to picture the varied and sometimes difficult situations which could arise for a schooner's small crew coping with both anchors and sails together. Quick thinking and smart seamanship were needed to keep out of trouble. But, whatever the conditions, it was always strenuous work which toughened our arms and backs. The degree of muscular development resulting from our hard manual labour is illustrated by this amusing anecdote.

During the thirties depression, a friend of mine, Harry, was out of a berth owing to so many schooners having to lay-up. Looking around for something to keep the wolf from the door, he heard that a champion boxer was in urgent need of sparring partners during preparations for a title fight. Fancying himself with his fists, Harry applied for a job, although not very hopefully. To his delight, he was taken on. It seems that the Champ was a bit rough in the workouts and applicants were getting scarce but my friend only discovered this later.

The punishment dealt out to sparring partners by the Champ during training sessions made some of the toughest quit, though Harry bore it stoically. One day, however, when the Champ was in a particularly foul temper, things got out of hand. The Champ slung the most vicious punches, badly hurting the sailorman, and kept inviting him to 'make a fight of it'. Throwing caution to the winds, Harry decided to take him at his word.

To the horror and consternation of those present, Harry knocked his famous opponent out cold and it was only with great difficulty that they were able to revive him. The incident was never made public but the Champ was finished for good as a boxer. Needless to say, Harry was 'fired'. Behind the blow that put the Champ to sleep were years of toil on schooner's windlasses and dollies.

In schooners equipped with motor winches, the power was used for heaving up anchors. A messenger with a 'dog' stopper at its end was clapped on the cable just abaft the windlass and its fall taken to the motor winch. I never cared for this method of heaving up: fiddling with an engine, rigging a messenger and overhauling it time after time, but worst of all, mud half the length of the deck. I doubt if much time was saved, either! I may be prejudiced as I was only in two vessels using power winches for this purpose, thank God!

Making sail, hoisting the heavy gaff fore-an'-afters, required plenty of muscle, especially for the big mainsails of the two-masters. I can imagine the tough job it must have been when hand-reefing these sails before the introduction of our most efficient roller reefing gear. This consisted of a heavy iron ratchet and pawl and drum with a chain wound round it, at the inboard end of the boom.

To reef, the pawl was shipped on the ratchet, the end of the chain hooked on a burton and the weight of the boom taken on its lift. The halyards were settled as we hove on the burton, unwinding the chain from the drum and revolving the boom, the slack of the sail rolling around it.

To shake out the reef, the pawl was disengaged, the halyards manned and as the sail was rehoisted the chain rewound on the drum.

Again, the inventor of this simple method of reefing is nameless.

Schooners were the People's ships. They were built, owned, manned and managed by maritime folk of very modest means and they were a classic reminder of the independence, enterprise and skills of our island people who had made our country great in the past.

Most of the vessels were lavishly fitted with beautiful teak and mahogany skylights and companions, an abundance of brass-work and bow and stern ornamentation, clearly indicating their owners' pride.

To sailormen, the ultimate adornment was a figurehead or, failing that, a well carved billethead with trailboards. In my time, the finest figurehead on the coast was that of my first schooner the *Via* of Brixham. It was a lovely carving of a young girl with a nosegay of flowers in her hand, a real work of art. Some of the schooner figureheads were rather crude examples of woodcarving but were highly regarded, nevertheless, for they were often likenesses of a wife or daughter of a first owner. Many happy hours were spent by sailormen painting and beautifying these adornments. When figureheads and other ornamentation went out of fashion, I believe the pride of sailors for their ships began to decline.

A real schoonerman was dedicated to his ship. I recall as a boy, sprucing up for a brief spell ashore. Dressed in my one good suit I was about to leave the schooner when I was halted by the mate. 'When you get on the quayside, boy, just take a look at your ship to see that nothing's adrift,' he said. 'If there is, come back and put it to rights.'

This 'looking back' at the vessel in which I served became a habit and I was soon as keen as any mate that my schooner should be the smartest wherever sailing vessels were gathered together.

Of course, there were a few slovenly schooner captains with dirty, unkempt vessels but they were the exception. The rule was that 'the ship came first', and even during the hardest times, the majority of owners and captains made great personal sacrifices to keep their vessels smart and seaworthy.

As late as the Second World War, the schooner *Katie*, commanded by the redoubtable W. F. Cort, was still trading under sail alone in the Irish Sea. On passage, she was bombed and machine-gunned by an enemy plane with the result that Clunes of Par, her owners, received orders from the Admiralty to lay her up for the duration. With the *Katie* laid up in the Tregaskis dry-dock at Par, Captain Cort found himself without a ship for the first time in his long, eventful career.

Living with his married daughter in Par, he spent all his time tending the *Katie*. Every morning, after breakfast, the old captain stumped off down to the laid-up schooner and worked aboard her until dusk, whatever the weather.

His daughter was very concerned about her father's health and worried about the long hours he spent alone working in the schooner. She tried to persuade him to take it easy, reminding him of his age, but he wouldn't listen and continued with the same daily routine.

One evening, when he returned from the *Katie*, she said: 'I can't imagine what you find to do all day, every day, in that rotten old ship, Dad!'

'She ain't a rotten old ship!' he retorted, angrily, and stamped upstairs to bed in a huff.

His work aboard the *Katie* continued for a few more days. Then, one morning, his daughter went to his bedroom to give him the usual call. Getting no reply, she shook him but found he'd passed away peacefully in his sleep.

Captain W. F. Cort thus ended his long and remarkable life in schooners on 24 February, 1944, lovingly caring for one of the little vessels to which he'd devoted his whole life. He was highly respected by shipowners, sailormen and all who knew him.

To men such as he, backbreaking work, hardships and danger were commonplace, with little remuneration in return.

One old schoonerman humorously summed up his life to me by remarking: 'It's been all Armstrong's Patent—main strength and stupidity!'

9

Shore Gang

In 1930, the British Sailing Ship Owner's Association listed the number of pure sailing vessels in the Home Trade as: 612 vessels totalling 44,051 tons net, belonging to 300 owners and comprising 3 barquentines, 40 schooners, 40 ketches, the remainder 'spritty' barges. Statistics can be very misleading, for I'm sure that there were at least double that number of vessels trading at the time. Perhaps the large schooner fleets of Eire and Ulster were omitted from the list, also vessels whose owners weren't Association members? And, of course, the many vessels with small auxiliaries were left out, though some of the motors were so unsuccessful they had but short lives. One fine ketch I remember had a single-cylinder semi-diesel installed and within the first few months the large, heavy flywheel had detached itself from its shaft no less than three times, nearly killing the captain on one occasion. Numberless mechanics and even the engine makers failed to cure this dangerous fault, so, after the third accident when the flywheel almost went through the deckhead, the ketch reverted to a sailing vessel although still listed in the register as an auxiliary.

The schooner *Katie* of Padstow, Captain Cort's last command, had an even shorter life as an auxiliary. When her owners decided to fit her with a motor, her master strongly disapproved but George, his son and mate, rather enjoyed the prospect of being in charge of an engine-room. He told his father that they had to move with the times.

The auxiliary was duly installed and soon afterwards the schooner was leaving port under sail and power, making a good seven knots. The old captain became infected with his son's enthusiasm at their speed. Grudgingly he allowed 'there might be something in these engines, after all'.

'I told you that you'd soon get used to an engine, Dad!' exclaimed George, excitedly. 'I reckon I'll get another knot or two out of her yet, with a bit of tuning up!'

A terrific bang from the engine-room interrupted his remarks and sent him diving below to investigate. A moment or two later, he reappeared on deck with a woe-begone countenance.

'The cylinder head's gone,' he reported. 'The engine's done for, Dad!'

'Well. That's that!' said the captain, a satisfied gleam in his eyes. 'I told you I never did hold with these new-fangled contraptions. Better get the gaff taups'l on her, George.'

To Captain Cort's delight, the engine was scrapped and for the remainder of her life the *Katie* traded under sail alone.

In fact, few auxiliary schooners deserved their prefix M.V., for they were primarily sailing vessels with their canvas their true means of propulsion.

Up to the thirties, sailing vessels and auxiliaries trading on the British coast together made a most impressive total.

This fleet of small ships supported a large workforce afloat and ashore, with trades and skills peculiar to them. In the ports most frequented by schooners, there were independent people with their own small businesses, anxious and pleased to attend to the wants of the small sailing ships and quite content with a modest return. With all who were connected with our schooners, we had a close, personal relationship. We knew the grocers, chandlers, sailmakers, riggers, shipwrights, stevedores, pilots, harbourmasters, customs officers and surveyors in most of the ports within Home Trade limits.

Our captains were greeted by their brokers and merchants as old and valued friends. In the few ports where pilotage was compulsory for a schooner, the pilots seemed to get nostalgic pleasure from being aboard a 'sailorman'. The traditional foe of seafarers, the Waterguard, often looked the other way when there were small transgressions in schooners. Even the dignified Board of Trade surveyors came under the spell of our little wooden ships.

Runcorn Lay-by, on the Manchester Ship Canal, the terminal for the sailing vessels bringing china clay from Cornwall, was a very busy schooner port. On the dockside there was a little grocer's shop where the schooners were provisioned. It was kept by a widow, affectionately known as 'Ma'. She was an untidy, wispy-haired woman of indeterminate age with a heart of gold. Every ship's boy who collected an order received a small gift of a few biscuits, a handful of sweets or a bar of chocolate. But, I best remember her for the time she helped me overcome a bedding problem.

Schoonermen, like all sailing ship crews, had to provide their own mattresses and blankets. The comfortable pipe cots in the *Via* allowed me to dispense with a mattress but when I left her I found the worn wooden bunks in other schooners hard resting places. To buy the usual straw palliasse was beyond my means. When discharging at Runcorn, a shipmate advised me see 'Ma'.

Entering her dusty little shop, I hesitated before blurting out my difficulties, but 'Ma' soon put me at ease. She ushered me into her parlour at the rear of the shop, sat me in a comfortable chair and like magic, produced bread and butter, fruit cake and a pot of tea.

'Help yourself, boy,' she said. 'I know all you lads from the ships are always hungry!'

As I waded into this unexpected treat, she brought out her sewing machine and stitched together two clean hessian sugar bags; chattering away as she worked in her shrill, high pitched voice, telling me about her only son who'd shipped in a schooner and sailed away, never to return.

'He was a big, strong boy, just like you,' she said. 'He would have been a fine sailor by now . . . perhaps even a ship's captain, but he was washed overboard and drowned on his first voyage. Pour yourself another cup of tea and have some more cake. That's my boy's photo over the mantlepiece. . . . There! I've finished now. Get some clean straw from that packing case in the shop and then you'll have a nice soft bed to sleep on.'

I returned to my schooner, carrying a first rate 'donkey's breakfast' on my back and it had cost me nothing. I learnt afterwards that Ma frequently helped hard-up sailormen in this way.

A ship chandler's best customers were the owners and masters of sailing vessels. The schooner fleets helped support many small chandlery businesses dotted around the coast. Following a long spell of bad weather, most of the schooners arriving in port would have some kind of storm damage and the chandlers would be busy supplying replacements for lost or broken gear. A good chandler prided himself on being able to supply from stock anything from a sail needle to an anchor.

Up to the thirties, there were three ship chandlers within hailing distance of each other in the Dock Road, Garston. I often went on errands to a chandlers and loved the atmosphere and smells of the old-type chandler's store. At Garston, the one most patronised by schooner captains was in an unimposing, one-storey building. Within the ramshackle premises was the essence of a whole fleet of ships. The shop floor was stacked with acrid smelling bolts of canvas, coils of golden manila rope, kegs of tallow, drums of Stockholm tar, paint, black varnish and bottom compositions, so that there was scarcely enough room for a customer to walk around. Shelving and counters were crammed with a jumble of gleaming copper navigation lamps, brass compasses, patent logs, foghorns; a fascinating miscellany without any apparent order.

Overhead, the ceiling and rafters were nearly hidden by hanging lifejackets, lifebuoys, strings of blocks, deadeyes, bullseyes, parrel beads and mast hoops; festoons of steel thimbles, shackles, clew spectacles—all the complex needs of sailing ships. Yet, whatever a customer required, however large or small, the little, white-haired bespectacled chandler always produced it instantly, without a moment's thought or hesitation, from this confusing mix-up.

Chandlers such as he had an intimate knowledge of the ships they served and their requirements. They also knew the schooner captains personally and understood their problems and difficulties. It wasn't unusual for a chandler to say to a customer: 'Settle up with me, Cap'n, next time you're here!' when times were hard on the coast.

Many of the chandlers were Scandinavians, former sailormen who'd 'swallowed the anchor'. With the passing years I've forgotten most of their names, though I still recall three excellent ship chandlers; James Tedford of Donegall Quay, Belfast, Monsen of Plymouth and Falmouth, and Christiensen, West Hartlepool.

Tedfords, like several of the larger chandlers, had a sail loft above their premises where new work or repairs were done quickly, efficiently and at prices that suited schoonermen.

These lofts bore no resemblance to the factory-like premises of modern yacht sailmakers. They were generally on top floors, partly in the roofs. A spacious, wax polished floor was a desirable requisite, but for some sailmakers space was very restricted and I've seen some enormous sails made in very small lofts.

Experienced sailmakers acknowledged that machine sewing was greatly inferior to good hand sewing and it was only when the cost of hand-sewn sails became prohibitive that machining was accepted in the trade. Seams, tablings and linings were then stitched with heavy-duty, treadle Singer machines. Apart from the addition of these manually operated sewing machines, the lofts hadn't changed their appearance in a hundred years. The traditional low sailmaker's benches, equipped and flanked by the craftsmen's hand tools, were still their main features.

Each bench had a shallow tray holding knives, serving boards, rubber, palms, beeswax and twines. Close to the tray were a row of fids, spikes and prickers stuck through holes in the bench. Fixed by a lanyard to whichever end of the bench best suited the worker—for some were right-handed and others left—was a steel sailhook for holding the canvas when hand sewing. In a pot of grease or tallow was a selection of sail needles. Near at hand were setting punches and dies, hammers, mallets and the largest of the hand tools, lignum-vitae setting fids, some as much as three feet high, with bases of five or six inches. These simple tools were all the equipment necessary for turning out a suit of sails for the finest windjammer afloat.

From the bolts of cloth and coils of tarred boltrope stacked around the polished floors came the pungent though pleasant odours of new flax, cotton, hemp and Stockholm tar.

Sails for a schooner were made from Scotch or Ulster grown and woven flax canvas supplied to the sailmaker in bolts of approximately 40 yards, 24-inch width. Nos 1, 2 and 3, weighing 46, 43 and 40 lb per bolt, respectively, were most used for working sails.

Bolt ropes were of soft-layed, best quality Riga or Italian hemp in sizes from about $4\frac{1}{2}$ inches downwards, tarred with best Stockholm tar. An average mainsail for a two-masted schooner would be about 1200 sq. feet, weighing in the region of 3 cwt. Making sails for merchantmen was a job for strong, highly skilled men and most of the old sailmakers were ex-sailormen who'd settled ashore after plying their trade at sea. These were the best craftsmen who knew the importance of strong, well cut sails and could never skimp their work.

Sailmaking was a very exacting and highly skilled ancient craft with only a poor monetary return. The true reward was the pleasure of working with the hands, creating strength, efficiency and beauty from natural materials possessing an almost sensuous quality of scent and texture. I remember an old sailmaker delivering a new sail to a schooner, saying: 'I'll be sorry for you, Cap'n, if you blow that sail away!' There was a wealth of pride and satisfaction in his few words.

Due to the strains of their work and the long hours spent in cold, draughty lofts, all the elderly sailmakers I knew suffered from arthritis in their shoulders, arms and hands. This painful complaint obliged many to retire and their young successors had neither the patience nor the need to learn the old skills. Instead of making sails, they turned over to the easy and more lucrative jobs of producing lifeboat covers, hatch cloths, dodgers etc., for steamers. By the mid-thirties, there were few lofts on the coast making good commercial sails. At one nor'-east coast sail loft, which had been famed for the fine-quality sails made for the many brigs and schooners employed in the coal trade, the young sailmaker was very put out when he received an order for a sail. 'I'll see if my old Dad'll come in to do the roping, grommets and cringles, if his arthritis isn't too bad. Never had the patience to learn all that old-fashioned stuff,' he said. It was a sure sign that the arts of the sailmaker were dying along with the commercial sailing ship.

Yet, in 1945, Tedford of Belfast made me a fine suit of schooner sails from Ulster flax. I believe they were the last sails for a working schooner to be sewn in his loft and perhaps, the last full suit to be made in Britain.

Another old craft which was closely linked to the fortunes of wooden schooners and ketches was that of the shipwrights skilled in timber construction. By the twenties, there were few shipyards remaining where schooners could be repaired by men practised in the age-old arts of keeping wooden merchant ships tight and seaworthy.

Even the commonplace jobs of maintenance, recaulking and renewing trunnel fastenings required long experience if they were to be done properly.

Naturally, the surviving yards were in areas where schooners and ketches were still owned. The workforce in some of these small shipyards often looked like a bunch of countrymen straight off a farm. But their deftness and assurance with their tools was something to marvel at. To watch an experienced old shipwright with an adze, fashioning an intricate ship's timber out of a massive oak log, was an unforgettable experience. Fiercely proud of their skills which had been handed down in their families for generations, they were accustomed to working for a mere pittance, yet retained a sturdy independence of spirit and strong individualism.

Some of the shipyards, with their dilapidated buildings surrounded by rotting deckhouses, stove-in boats, broken skylights, the accumulation of years of repair work, looked like the premises of marine junk dealers. Even the tidiest yards had an appearance of disorder, due to the large stocks of timber held for seasoning. Every available space was cluttered with logs and crooks in various states of maturity. English oak was particularly in evidence, being so slow to season that it was still too 'green' for high-quality work when ten years old. Without well seasoned timber a yard couldn't operate, and this caused the closure of many fine shipyards after the First World War, when stocks were used up and couldn't be replaced.

By the thirties, few of the old shipyards remained. Of these, the most notable belonged to Tregaskis of Par, P. K. Harris of Appledore and Tyrell of Arklow, Eire. In the past, these yards had built many fine schooners and they continued repairing them long after the work had ceased to be profitable. Wooden shipbuilding was in the blood of their people.

All the schooners of my time were very old but most of them were so well maintained their age wasn't obvious. About the oldest I can remember was the *Baltic* of 87 tons gross, built by R. Jones at Rhyl in 1857. When I knew her she was owned and commanded by Jack Ward of Wicklow. I remember her by her truly remarkable stem which was pieced together like a jigsaw puzzle after being severely damaged in a collision. The way it had been repaired always fascinated me. But, perhaps another reason for recalling her was that Captain Ward frequently had his teenage daughters in the schooner.

As the ravages of time could not be denied, the periodic Board of Trade surveys of these elderly vessels were always a strain on

the slender resources of their owners. If a surveyor ordered extensive work to be done, there was seldom enough money to pay for
it, which meant the end of another schooner.

This rarely happened, as most of the ship surveyors were very
knowledgeable men who took into account the massive construction of the ships, which allowed a generous margin for deteriora-
tion, and they knew that the high quality of the original building
materials could no longer be matched. Also I suspect that they had
a great interest in these historic wooden vessels and a genuine
liking and respect for the men who sailed them.

Whenever possible, the B.O.T. officials would co-operate in
keeping expenses to a minimum by surveying a schooner when
dried out between tides in small harbours, thus saving the owner
the high costs of dry-docking. On one occasion, a surveyor
arrived aboard our schooner looking every inch a Civil Servant in
his smart city clothes and with the very correct and stand-offish
manner expected of officialdom. Shortly afterwards, he was
splodging about under the schooner with our old captain, in a
boiler suit and rubbers, as much concerned as his companion that
practical solutions to any defects should be found so that the little
ship could continue trading.

A ship surveyor with a particular interest and affection for
wooden schooners was Laurie Hislop. For some time he'd been
responsible for surveying the County Down schooners of Kilkeel
and Annalong. He once told me that this was the most interesting
and happy period of his professional life. Many years later, I was
delighted to learn that this most gentlemanly and human official
reached the peak of his profession as Chief Ship Surveyor for the
Ministry of Transport. I can vouch for it, that if Laurie Hislop
hadn't been a ship surveyor he'd have been a sailor, for he loved
ships.

In the tight little world of schooners, we had few opportunities
of making worthwhile relationships ashore. Sailormen, like all
nomads, have always been regarded ashore as a shiftless lot, with
no interests but drink and women. This false prejudice together
with the shortness of our shore leaves left us little scope for
meeting people and making friends. Although shipboard life
suited me admirably, there were times when the constant hard

work, the same faces and the same surroundings got me down. If I had this stale feeling when we were lying in some small harbour, I'd go for long walks alone, exploring and enjoying the country-side and this never failed to raise my drooping spirits. But in large ports like those of Merseyside, a walk ashore generally depressed me for the streets of towns such as Garston couldn't be described as 'up-lifting'.

At first I wouldn't accept that the answer to my needs was right under my nose. At weekends, if we were anchored in the Sloyne, inward or outward the Mersey, we were visited by the padre from the Liverpool Mission to Seamen. He came off to us in a sturdy, black-painted motor launch flying a flag with a white 'Flying Angel' on a blue ground. We looked forward to seeing him as he always brought us a pile of old magazines, mostly *Spheres*, *Illustrated London News* and *Graphics*, which were greatly appreciated for they were the only reading matter we ever saw. He never mentioned religion, but chatted with us about seafaring. Before going off to another ship, he'd invite us to call at his mission, whenever we were at a loose end ashore. The religious aspect of the Mission put me off—I imagined it as a bun and a cup of tea in exchange for a church service and hymn singing. Even-tually, however, my curiosity got the better of me and I ventured into the Liverpool Mission, very much on my guard. My fears were groundless for there I found a place to relax, a good library and friendly company. Ever after, wherever I happened to be, I took full advantage of the excellent facilities provided by this fine organisation for seafarers.

For the tough, understanding men of the 'Flying Angel' I've the greatest admiration. So anonymous that I can't remember even one by name and I doubt if any of them ever knew mine, yet I'll never forget their hospitality and the many kindnesses I received from them during my sea life. My happiest memories are of the Seamen's Missions at Liverpool, Belfast and Dublin.

When in port, we seldom saw much of our captains, as they spent most of their time ashore, presumably at their agents', attending to the ship's business.

None of my shipmates had the slightest inkling of what went on at the agents', nor did they care. The general impression was that our captains enjoyed the hell of a good time ashore while we worked harder than we did at sea.

Determined to learn all I could about schooners, I was dying with curiosity whenever I passed an agent's office, many of which were situated in roads to the docks. It seemed highly improbable that I should ever know more than my shipmates of what went on inside a shipbrokers. Then unexpectedly, the mate of Westcott's homely old barquentine *Francis & Jane* entrusted me with a message for the master, Captain Cort. He was at his agents' in the Dock Road, which allowed me my first glimpse inside a brokers' office.

The outside of the building, which was very old, was of mellowed brick. It had a bow window and a Georgian doorway. Above the brightly polished brass plate inscribed with the name of a family business which had transacted the affairs of sailing ships for many generations were a number of plaques of national emblems with a notice stating that the firms's principal was Vice-Consul for those countries.

My timid knock on the door halted the hum of voices within. A gruff voice bade me: 'Come in!'

The 'Captains' Room' was filled to overflowing, for there was a big fleet of sailing vessels in the port. Through a thick haze of tobacco smoke I saw a dozen or more of the masters from schooners I knew, most of them middle-aged or elderly men with ruddy, weather-beaten faces, their hair and whiskers greying or already white. Among them I recognised gaunt old Charlie Deacon of *Waterwitch*, Beynon of *Lydia Cardell*, Williams of *Mary Sinclair* and Dudderidge of *Englishman*. Under the unwinking, critical scrutiny of this formidable company, I self-consciously delivered my message to Captain Cort, then hastily withdrew.

The scene in that broker's office is one of my most treasured memories. It would have been hard to find anywhere a more notable gathering of famous schoonermen.

The senior captains, Deacon, Beynon and Cort, had spent their lives in schooners, commencing as small boys only twelve years of age, in the vessels of the hard but lucrative Newfoundland saltfish trade. Schooners in this exacting trade rarely exceeded 200 tons and some were as small as 70 tons, with crews of three or four men and a boy.

107

They voyaged across the Atlantic Ocean in winter and summer to St Johns or Harbour Grace with fishery salt, then tramped along the Newfoundland coast picking up small parcels of salt cod here and there at the tiny fishing settlements. Cargoes complete, they returned across the Western Ocean to Italy, Greece, Portugal or Spain and generally finished the voyage by loading fruit homeward to the U.K. To survive and work up from boy to master in this trade was a great achievement. During their lives, these three great captains saw the schooners reach their peak of prosperity and development, then sadly decline.

Their careers ran on parallel courses, even to the extent of losing their commands by U-Boat attacks in World War I. Telling of his wartime sinking, Captain Cort's only complaint was about the German submarine crew stripping the schoonermen of their guernseys before casting them adrift in their punt. Hardships and dangers had been the normal patterns of their lives from their earliest seagoings, when they'd often suffered harsh treatment. In spite of this, they were all kindly, humane men, exemplary in the way they treated their crews and almost puritanical in their behaviour and language. Although making no outward show, all shared a most trusting faith in God.

The business relationships of schooner captains with their agents were on a very personal basis. It was unthinkable for a clerk to deal with them. A personal greeting from the broker, a comfortable chair and a good cigar was their invariable welcome by custom.

Long after typewriters became the normal way of corresponding for businesses, both large and small, letters between schooner captains and their agents were handwritten and some of them were beautiful examples of copper-plate penmanship. Shipbroking must have been the last business in Britain to use this means of communication as it was also the last to transact important deals by word of mouth. To this day, the motto of the Institute of Chartered Shipbrokers is, 'Our Word, our Bond'.

Some of the best known agents for schooners were Marwood and Clarke & Grounds, both of Runcorn; Brown & Kinch of Liverpool; Fisher of Barrow; Betson of Dublin; Fox of Falmouth and Tamlyn of Plymouth. These firms were closely connected with the schooner trades and many of them had owned their own vessels. Fisher's had formerly owned one of the finest schooner fleets in Britain until they sold their sailing tonnage in the twenties. Clarke & Grounds had a small fleet of schooners trading well into the thirties.

As a young man, I was unaware that I was seeing the gradual ending of many ancient crafts, trades and businesses dependent on wooden sailing vessels. In the short period of ten years, the few which remained had completely changed their characters. In particular, a shipbrokers' business became the same as any other in the modern business world and shipmasters found themselves treated with the impersonal efficiency of a new age. Gone were the centuries old traditions, customs and courtesies, and I believe the status of a master mariner suffered as a consequence.

10

Sea Lore

When I began seafaring in the twenties, the First World War had brought about revolutionary changes to sea transport, in ships, methods of navigating and conditions of service for seamen. Life in Home Trade schooners, however, remained practically unaltered from the way it had been for a hundred years.

The wooden vessels and the more mature schoonermen were products of the last half of the previous century, when schooner building was most prolific. At that time, it was difficult for boys of humble circumstances to obtain a rudimentary schooling in the three 'R's' before commencing work at twelve. In schooners, training consisted of hard experience, with a little useful information occasionally being passed on by word of mouth by well disposed mates or masters. To gain advancement, a boy with a natural aptitude for the life needed keen powers of observation and a retentive memory. Promotion was slow and it was only after years of service as boy, seaman and mate that there were any hopes of a command. Few achieved this before middle age and by then they knew their trade and the coastlines of Britain and the Continent like the palms of their hands. Seamarks, anchorages, harbours, tidal streams and hazards above and below the sea were well known to them after sailing Home-Trade waters for forty years or more. Courses and distances between their principal trading ports were memorised so that references to charts were necessary only in unusual circumstances. I've never ceased to marvel at the vast amount of knowledge the experienced old mariners carried around in their heads.

In my first schooners I rarely saw a chart. Occasionally, I glimpsed one of the 'blue backs', published by Imray, Laurie, Norie & Wilson, which were the most popular, being easy to read and covering a large area of the coast.

When I was 'boy' in the *Via*, her old captain once proudly showed me his one and only chart. It was of the Irish Sea and was the oldest chart I've ever set eyes on, outside of museums. Tattered, yellow with age and so stained and mildewed it was almost unreadable, it reminded me of the one in the story of the old shipmaster and his mate poring over their chart and the captain, with his spectacles perched on the end of his nose, stubbing his thumb at a mark on the chart, saying: 'Is this 'ere a buoy, Bill, or is it just another bit of fly muck?'

Light lists were not much in evidence, either. I can only remember once seeing an out-dated Reed's Home Trade, opened at the light list, during my early schoonering.

The essential items for navigating a schooner were a good steering compass and a leadline. The few vessels streaming a log used the obsolete harpoon type. Even barometers and cabin clocks were considered luxuries.

I gradually picked up the arts of a schoonerman in the time-honoured way: by keeping my eyes and ears open. I soon realised our greatest danger was the land and the prime factor in navigating a sailing vessel was to give her a safe offing under every condition of weather. Our captains had the most intimate knowledge of the sailing qualities of their commands and, making due allowances for tidal set and leeway, they were able to make the most astonishingly accurate estimates of our progress. Headlands and seamarks always materialised as predicted. I doubt if a mechanical log could have measured our erratic progress with such accuracy. It certainly couldn't have compensated for tide and leeway.

Very early on, I learnt to box the compass. In my watch below, I was expected to master the thirty-two points and did so at the expense of my sleep. To my great satisfaction, from then onwards, the captain allowed me to spell him for short periods at the helm.

I was always under his critical eyes, for a schooner's 'boy' traditionally stood watch with the master. Having a natural 'feeling' for sailing vessels, I was soon doing my regular two hour 'trick' and was able to claim that I could 'hand, reef and steer'.

My wheels became the most enjoyable part of the daily sea routine. I found that schooners varied as much as we do; some were wild and intractable, needing a strong pair of hands to control them; others sailed steady and true, obedient to the lightest touch on the wheel-spokes. Except for the shelters at our backs, we were completely exposed to the weather when at the helm. We had some tough times in the winter when the cold could make a two-hour trick seem an eternity. On occasions an hour was all the strongest could endure. Snow was a great hazard. It blinded a helmsman so that he was unable to see the compass or anything else. Braced against the backboards of the half-round, trying to ignore the searing cold which penetrated to the marrow, he was obliged to steer by instinct during winter blizzards. In these situations we all swore that we'd never again ship in a schooner, but when it was over we instantly forgot our good resolutions. In fact, such incidents only bound us closer to our little ships.

Fast steam and motor vessels were an increasing danger to schooners. It wasn't enough to know the simple steering rules for sailing ships; the whole of the Regulations for Preventing Collisions at Sea had to be thoroughly understood. There seemed no end to the Articles as we called them, until I met up with the aids to memory in verse regarding the movements of power-driven ships. I don't know if modern seafarers still use the verses I found so helpful, but here are two of them:

> Green to green,
> Red to red;
> Perfect safety.
> Go ahead.
> When all lights are seen ahead,
> Port your helm and show your red.

In addition to verses covering the Rule of the Road, there were many other handy rhymes. On the subject of weather, this very true couplet is a good example:

> When the rain's before the wind,
> then your tops'l halyards mind;
> When the wind's before the rain,
> you may soon make sail again.

A rigger's procedure for covering a rope with small stuff was remembered by:

> Worm and parcel with the lay,
> Turn and serve the other way.

A real gem was a pilotage rhyme of the East coast, used by mariners in the coal trade between the Tyne and London River. The hoary old sailorman who passed it to me had learnt it during his hard service in North-Country collier brigs and schooners. Quoting the lines, I can still hear him recite in his broad 'Geordie' accent:

When it's high water at London Bridge,
It's half-ebb at Swin.
When it's low-water in Yarmouth Roads,
It's half-flood at Lynn.
First the Dudgeon, then the Spurn,
Flamboro' Head comes next in turn.
Filey Brigg is drawing nigh,
Scarboro' Castle stands on high.
Whitby Rock lies out to sea,
So steer two points more northerly.
Huntscliffe Foot is very high land,
Twenty-five miles from Sunderland.
Hartlepool lies in the bight,
Seaham Harbour is now in sight.
Our 'Old Man' says: 'If the weather's right,
We'll be in the Tyne this very night,
But if the wind's at East and the tide is least;
It'll be, ratch off, ratch on!'

These rhymes were very old, dating back to an age when few seamen were able to read and write and everything was passed on by word of mouth.

Courses taken by schooner captains in established trades were also traditional. From the Mersey, bound around the Land, we steered from Liverpool Bar to get a good offing from the Skerries. From the Skerries we sailed across the Irish Sea for Wicklow Head then changed course for the Smalls and then the Wolf Rock, before rounding the Longships. If caught by strong sou'-westerlies, we were thus assured of being well away from Cardigan Bay with its powerful insets and dangerous coastline and had plenty of sea room at all times.

I well remember a time in the barquentine *Francis & Jane*, bound from the Mersey with coal for Falmouth Gasworks. Down to the Smalls we had good weather but then it began to pipe up from the sou'-west. In severe and continuous gale-force winds our little vessel clawed away to wind'ard, the deck flooded and the pumps manned day and night. There was a mountainous sea rolling in from the Atlantic and somewhere under our lee, towered the high, inhospitable shores of North Cornwall—'a sailor's grave by day or night'—as the Cornish verse describes it.

We made five attempts to round the Land, but were driven back to Lundy each time.

Although bundled up in oilies with 'soul and body lashings', we were soaked to the skin and perished with cold. After a week of fierce gales we were all showing signs of exhaustion. The captain's little terrier dog Toby was in no better shape. Time after time we put him below but whenever the cabin slide was opened, he leaped out and was in great danger of being swept overboard. Alternately swimming in the boarding seas then standing shivering with cold and fear as the deck cleared, he seemed too scared to stay below.

Captain Cort was apparently immune to cold, salt water and weariness. A sturdy figure in well darned slacks and woollen guernsey, a battered old cheesecutter firmly jammed on his grey head, his only concession to the bad weather was a red and white spotted handkerchief knotted about his throat. In attempting to weather the Longships, he drove the *Francis & Jane* hard but without losing sails or gear. At all times we had sufficient sea-room to work a not particularly handy vessel.

At the height of the gales, a number of racing pigeons exhausted by the storm took refuge in our rigging. A lesser man would have ignored them, but our captain had food and water put on the galley roof for the weary birds.

When the wind finally blew itself out, it was no coincidence that we were in a perfect position for slipping around the Land and Lizard into Falmouth Bay.

Captain Cort's assessment of the weather, his seamanship and navigation were so naturally intermingled there was only one way to describe it; sea lore. To serve under this great schoonerman was a privilege and a most rewarding experience.

In the North Sea and English Channel we always 'worked the tides', using the extra thrust of strong tidal streams to good advantage. When the tide turned and the wind was light, it was customary to anchor under a headland or in a bay or roadstead until the sting had gone out of it. Many hard-won miles were saved this way. Constant watchfulness was necessary in these temporary anchorages, for a sudden change of weather could make them dangerous. Anchor watches had to be alert but in spite of this I've assisted in many speedy, unpremeditated departures when a wind has unexpectedly flown round and freshened.

Schoonermen have sometimes been scornfully called 'dog barking navigators'. Meant as a slight, it was partially true. In thick fog, when sounds carry a great distance over the sea, a schooner's change of motion, the scent of the shore, the sounds of a crowing cock or a barking dog were all useful aids when closing the land. At such times we were kept busy with the leadline and, given the soundings and samples of the sea-bed brought up in the tallow 'arming', a good captain could unerringly find his way. In fact, our greatest danger in fog was the possibility of being run down by a steamer. With visibility down to a few yards and a wind so light we scarcely had steerage way, it was nerve-wracking to hear the tell-tale throb of a steamer closing us. All we could do in these circumstances was frantically crank our Norwegian-type box foghorn, giving the signal for a sailing vessel under way and hope the steamboatmen in their enclosed wheelhouse could hear us and alter course. Fortunately, I was never involved in a collision, though I had my quota of narrow escapes. Two vessels I knew well were sunk by steamers during fog. The barquentine *Lydia Cardell* was lost by collision with S.S. *Broadgarth* off Flamborough Head in 1929, and the *Hilda*, of the same rig, foundered after being struck by the steam trawler *Kudos* off Hartlepool in 1930. I'd tried unsuccessfully for a berth in the *Lydia Cardell* just before she was lost, so was third time lucky.

Our captains' weather forecasts were commonsense deductions from observations of the sea, sky, temperature and humidity. The natural changes going on around them were sufficient for them to make remarkably true forecasts of local weather. A big swell in a moderate wind and they knew there was heavy weather to wind'ard. A change in wind direction was often indicated by a sea running contrary to the wind. A low dawn, with heavy clouds massed on the horizon, was a sure sign of bad weather. The types, formations and height of clouds spoke volumes to an experienced mariner. Sudden drops in temperature following sunshine generally meant rain or fog, especially on the East coast.

Long after wireless receivers were available at a modest cost, few schooners had them. Most of the old captains preferred their own judgement to the wireless Shipping Forecasts.

The adroitness of veteran schoonermen in dealing with the ever-changing facets of the sea was taken for granted. Yet, around us instruments and machinery were replacing traditional skills. Steel ships of awe-inspiring size were the order of the day. For our small wooden schooners to survive was nothing short of a miracle. It never occurred to me that masters such as Cort, Deacon and Beynon were the last of a line of sailormen dating back to Drake. Stubbornly, all in schooners refused to accept that our way of life was an anachronism. We lived in a world where time stood still.

Having acquitted myself well as boy and seaman, I set my sights on a mate's berth. This was no sinecure in a schooner. For about a pound a month more than an A.B., plus a small cabin of his own at the foot of the companionway, a mate was required to be a thoroughly practical seaman, strong as a horse to lead in all the back-breaking tasks and untiring and patiently loyal to his captain's slightest whim. At sea it was a most satisfying position, sharing the responsibility of the schooner, watch and watch with the captain, except in bad weather. In port it was more difficult. With the captain ashore most of the time, discharging was under the mate's surveillance. In small ports where the crew dollied out the cargo, it was he who set the pace for the hands on the winch handles and, at the same time, endeavoured to maintain the schooner to his commander's high standards. His reputation depended on the smart appearance of his charge. I noticed that the best mates also did tasks which were not so obvious but much more important than spit and polish. One of these was the ventilating of a schooner's timbers when her hold was empty. This was done by opening the air ports and lifting the limber boards in her ceiling, allowing the air from an open hatchway to circulate around her framing. It helped prevent rot in a wooden ship and was as necessary as the never-ending 'airings' to preserve her sails.

Some captains were noted for being over critical and too demanding and rows often occurred between testy masters and overtired mates when we were in port. They were usually of a short duration and in most instances it was the captain who 'climbed down' and made the peace, for efficient schooner mates were indispensable, being difficult to replace. Many of the most sought-after mates were competent enough to have had their own commands but for an inability to cope with ship's business and in some cases, a dread of decision-making. Perfectly content in the role of second-in-command, these stalwarts were the backbone of the schooner trades, serving both ships and masters faithfully to the end. Jim Weddock of the Down schooners, George Cort, the dependable West Countryman, and the veteran Phil Allen were typical mates.

Cargo loading and stowage, strictly speaking, were a mate's responsibility, but I can't ever recollect a master being absent during these operations. Apparently leaving everything to the mate and keeping well in the background, nothing escaped the 'Old Man's' eagle eyes. The sailing qualities of his vessel and even her safety could be jeopardised by careless stevedores. The peculiarities of different cargoes greatly influenced the behaviour of a sailing vessel and a correct seagoing trim was essential.

Coal, that mainstay of schooners, was speedily teamed through a schooner's small hatchways and when properly trimmed, it filled the hold to the tops of the hatch coamings, distributing the weight of the cargo throughout the vessel. It was a sea-kindly cargo, allowing the timbers of a wooden schooner to work freely, which contributed to her speed and handiness. I was unaware that different kinds of coal varied considerably in the amount of hold space required for a ton weight—the stowage factor, we call it—until it was brought to my notice by a very practical experience.

I joined a handsome three-master as seaman, attracted to her by her spick and span appearance. I was soon to regret it, for her young master-owner was so exacting that however hard we worked, we were unable to satisfy him. One of his main obsessions was the cleanliness of the deck and we were for ever sanding and scrubbing, trying to reach an impossible standard for a working vessel. The long-suffering mate was driven frantic, but by dint of hard labour we achieved the nearest thing to perfection—and then learnt we were about to load a coal cargo. Before warping under the tips, we took great pains to protect our precious deck but as soon as loading commenced, it disappeared under layers of coal.

Eventually, the trimmers crawled out of the tiny hole in the

117

filled mainhatch, signifying that loading had finished. Their foreman was donning his jacket, ready to leave, when he was accosted
by our captain.

'Here! You haven't finished yet,' he snapped aggressively. 'I
loaded twenty tons more than this, last time I was here. Before you
knock off I want at least another ten tons in the ship.'

'But she's full up, now, Cap'n!' answered the foreman quite
civilly. 'These are different coals to your last cargo. There's no
room for any more!'

'You can't fool me,' came the scornful retort. 'You haven't
stowed it properly. Call your men back. I insist on having another
truck.'

The trimmer gave our captain a dirty look. 'There's not room
for a bloody rat in your hold, Cap'n!' he protested. 'But if you
want another truck, you can have it. Bill, give us another truck for
the Cap'n!'

From somewhere up in the gloom of the tip, there came a string
of oaths. Waggon wheels rumbled; the tip guides squealed and a
further ten tons of coal roared down, piling up into a big heap
over our already over-filled mainhatch.

'There's your extra truck, Cap'n,' said the foreman with relish.
'Fucking well stow it yourself!'

After that parting shot he clambered ashore, leaving our 'Old
Man' choking with rage.

Overnight, the mountain of coal remained undisturbed but by
morning the captain had things all worked out. After breakfast,
dressed for the shore, he called over the mate and issued instructions. 'Stow the small coals down in the forepeak and build the big
lumps into a breakwater around the wheel,' he said. 'I want the
hatches cleared and battened down by the time I come back this
evening.' The mate opened his mouth to protest but before he
could utter the captain was ashore and gone.

'My poor bleedin' deck!' moaned the mate. 'After all that work
and putting up with the bastard's grizzles at the slightest stain on
it ... now we're going to have sodden' great lumps of coal
everywhere. Aw, hell! Let's get crackin'.'

Shifting the big mound of coal off the hatchway was tough
work for two men and a boy. Stripped to the waists, we toiled
throughout a broiling hot day, filling coal baskets, manhandling

them for'ard and lowering them through the small fo'c'sle scuttle to the peak beneath our living quarters. We built a massive waist high wall around the wheel with the big lumps of coal as instructed, and when it was finished the sweating, black-faced mate swore profusely.

'If that lot take's charge at sea, someone's going to get bloody well killed,' he grimly prophesied. 'Whatever made me come in this schooner? I must be off me flamin' rocker!' His words echoed my own gloomy thoughts.

Never had a schooner's company so anxiously studied the weather as we did from the Mersey to Cornwall. But we had the finest passage I've ever known all the way around the Land to Falmouth and the only injuries we suffered from our dangerous deck cargo were a few bruises and skinned shins from colliding with it in the darkness.

As we made fast to a quay punt which was about to tow us up the Fal to Truro, I expressed my thankfulness at getting off so lightly. The mate glowered aft to where the upper half of our captain was visible above the coal surrounding the wheel. He spat disgustedly over the bows and growled sourly: 'The devil always looks after his own!'

Coal to the West Country was generally followed by a cargo of china clay to Runcorn.

Fowey, Charlestown and Par were all 'clay' ports but Par was the one most used by Home-Trade schooners. I disliked loading the kaolin even more than coal. It was teamed into our hold down wooden shutes, covering everything with a coating of white dust which penetrated into every nook and cranny of our living quarters; even into our food. Loading coal, we'd been as black as Christy minstrels; taking in clay we looked like a troupe of circus clowns. If it rained, the clay dust turned to a slurry as slippery as grease, making it difficult to keep a footing on the deck. When loaded and battened down, it needed a lot of effort with our deck scrubs to get rid of the tenacious white coating. However hard we scrubbed, there was sure to be a little clay we'd missed, somewhere. We usually found it by slipping and falling flat on our backs when swigging up gear in the dark.

The stowage factor of china clay is about half that of coal so our hold would be barely three parts full when a schooner was down to her marks. If the clay was in a vessel's hold for any length of time, it settled down into a solid mass which impaired her sailing qualities. But fortunately the prevailing sou'westerly winds usually enabled a northerly bound schooner to make a quick passage; a week to ten days was a fair average time from Par to the Mersey.

Occasionally I saw cargoes which required a lot of digging out at Runcorn, where the clay was discharged in big iron tubs, craned ashore into a warehouse.

I was very curious about what happened to the clay after it disappeared into the cavernous building, for I'd heard its ultimate destination was the Staffordshire Potteries. I found the answer at the rear of the warehouse. A large canal lay-by was filled with narrowboats, taking in the clay we'd brought from Cornwall. The inland craft were a picturesque sight, the sides of their tiny cabins emblazoned with the owner's name surrounded by elaborate scrollwork and the traditional castles and roses painted in bright colours. Smoke wreathed from chimneys banded with burnished brass or copper. Each boat had gaily decorated water-carriers and a most intriguing feature to me, a rope Turk's head, pipe-clayed white, nailed to the rudder head. It was plain that the narrowboat families were very proud of their horse-drawn craft.

My interest in cargoes gave me my first insight into some of the problems of a schooner captain.

Loading during heavy rain or snow, cargoes which absorbed moisture weighed considerably more than the tonnage on the Bills of Lading. The increase in a vessel's draught was clear proof of this. Building bricks, which we frequently carried, noticeably gained weight after exposure to the weather in open railway trucks. Sometimes the discrepancies between the tonnage indicated by the draught marks and that of the Bills of Lading were so big, it was obvious that a merchant was adding a few extra tons without paying freight for them. This unfair practice was grudgingly accepted by captains when it was kept within reasonable bounds. This wasn't always done, and I remember how one disgruntled captain took his own drastic remedy after losing a considerable sum over a long period. Without further protest he continued to load the overweight brick cargoes but, on passage, managed to get off course during the hours of darkness so that he was conveniently near some of his friends' trawlers working off his home port. When his schooner arrived at the discharging port, the weight of cargo landed barely exceeded the documented tonnage.

Agents and merchant frantically telephoned one another without being able to solve the mystery and for several months they refused to accept that the biter had been bitten. In the hopes of catching the captain out they continued to charter the schooner but excess tonnage nearly always vanished. In the end, they took the captain to court on a charge of alleged barratry.

The captain calmly asserted that all his cargoes when discharged tallied with the tonnage on the Bills of Lading and the case against him was thrown out. The news was received with delight by his fellow schooner captains who'd been similarly imposed upon from time to time.

With freight rates at rock bottom, the subsidised Dutchmen multiplying at an alarming rate, and too many ships chasing too few cargoes, things were so bad that no schooner captain could afford to let anyone take an unfair advantage of him. I recall how shocked I was during a night watch with a harassed captain when he said, bitterly: 'If somebody ashore would offer me a dustman's job I'd take it, for I'd be a sight better off on a dustcart than sailing this schooner!'

These were sad words indeed, from a man who'd spent his entire life in such an exacting trade, yet he continued to ply it until a few years later, when he was swept off the deck of his schooner and drowned.

It was rare for the master of a schooner to hold a 'ticket'. The march of progress had made the B.O.T. examinations too up-to-date for our obsolete mode of seafaring so that their contents were almost totally irrelevant to us.

A story worth telling about this subject of certificates was related to me by an indignant old mariner with over sixty years of schoonering to his credit. He spun the yarn to me in the fine, spacious cabin of the veteran three-master that had been owned and commanded by members of his family for several generations. The schooner had been built in 1859 and her conservative owners maintained her in her original state, refusing to add even a motor winch, although the year was 1947.

121

My old friend had been practically reared in the vessel, accompanying his father on all his voyaging from a mere toddler. He'd seen his gallant old ship through two wars and the lean times between, but eventually his advancing years and the difficulty of finding employment for his vessel became too much for him. Some young men made him an attractive offer for the schooner, so reluctantly he agreed to sell but with a proviso that he remained in command until he had taught them enough to sail the schooner.

The new owners proposed using the little windjammer for carrying paying guests on yachting cruises. Then the Ministry of Transport appeared on the scene, informing the old seadog that he needed a certificate if passengers were to be carried. He was summoned to appear at an appointed place and time for examination and duly presented himself, badly shaken by all this official tomfoolery.

The subsequent happenings, difficult to piece together from his garbled version, must surely rank as one of the most extraordinary examinations ever conducted.

It began with an oral on the Rule of the Road. Although very nervous, he acquitted himself well, for steamers had been a source of danger to him all his life. The next questions were on seamanship and ship handling and, as the old captain put it: 'Them young fellers didn't know the first thing about a schooner!'

From then onwards the proceedings were a riot. Instead of answering questions he took over completely, giving his former inquisitors a long and detailed lecture on the way a schooner should be handled in every kind of weather and emergency, using the most colourful and forceful language to drive home the important points.

In an effort to shut him up, one of the examiners produced a sextant. The captain fixed him with a steely glare: 'Take that there sexteroon away, young feller. Never had no truck with them things!' he said severely. 'An' as I was just saying . . . we backed her taups'ls, hove in on our cable until it was nearly up and down, then with a nice bit o' sternway, she drugged through a little gut atween the banks into deep water.'

Thoroughly warmed to his subject there was no stopping him with his endless reminiscences of a truly remarkable life in schooners.

I never heard how the officials finally got rid of him and it was only after repeatedly asking if he got his 'ticket' that he answered: 'Oh, aye! But what bloody use it'll be I dunno!'

Weighed against a lifetime's stringent testing by a pitiless sea, the pasteboard and paper document seemed totally insignificant and superfluous.

11

Depression and War

In schooners, without radio or newspapers, we were quite out of touch with events ashore.

The state of merchant shipping has always been a reflection of the country's economy. Although we were constantly having our own minor recessions owing to the Dutchmen and steamers, we were soon aware of something serious happening as the Fal, Medway, Jarrow Slake and other laying-up berths around the coast became filled with idle tramp tonnage.

The great depression of the thirties gradually brought British shipping to a virtual halt. Previously in bad times we'd blamed the 'bloody Dutchmen' or Coast Lines, but now our hated rivals were in trouble, too.

Naturally it was the out-dated sailing vessels that were worst hit by the chill draught of recession. The London River barge trots filled to overflowing with out-of-work 'spritties' and the moorings were so crowded off Woolwich that they were nicknamed the 'Starvation Buoys'.

In spite of an impossible situation, most schooner-owners fought desperately to keep their vessels in commission. The most obvious signs of hard times in the schooner fleet were the many vessels with extensive patching on their sails, for such vital necessities as sails, rope and paints had to last until trade improved. Vessels became very run-down and many were put up for sale at ridiculously low prices, but there were few buyers. Some were sold to foreigners; many lay on the mud in remote rivers and creeks, neglected and forlorn.

I heard of two old schoonermen pooling their meagre savings to invest in one of these 'bargains'. A schooner's mate, when yarning, told us the sequel. On passage, he sighted a schooner under full sail just ahead of them and saw it was the new owners proudly sailing their purchase to their home port. A sudden squall struck both vessels, not enough to inconvenience a well-found schooner but for the new owners it was a disaster. Every threadbare sail blew away, leaving just the boltropes.

'One minute they was under full canvas, the next there weren't

13. Traditional sailmaker's bench and hand tools; the simple, inexpensive equipment used for making flax and cotton handsewn commercial sails. (*Richard Hayward, Litlington*)

14. The little 'Dutch Clog', *Schollevaer*. (*The late Captain Joe Sabiston*)

15. *Nellie Bywater's builders at Millom Shipyard, 1873. Hugh Jones, centre back row, wearing a bowler.* (*Family of the late Hugh Jones, Millom*)

a bleedin' rag left,' the eye-witness informed us. 'Quickest snug-down I ever did see!'

One day, shrewd old Captain Cort said to me: 'Now's your chance, Dick. You can have your schooner for a hundred or so!'

How he'd guessed my secret ambition I'll never know, as I'd never confided it to a soul.

The *Francis & Jane* was soon a victim of the depression. She was due for her quadrennial survey, and her Plymouth owners withdrew her from trade rather than face the heavy expenses involved. She was put on the mud of the Pont Pill, Fowey Harbour, where she looked a pathetic sight, listing over, her yards awry and Irish pennants fluttering everywhere. She was soon out of Lloyd's register. Her master was immediately given command of another fine sailing vessel and was never without a schooner throughout the depression. As the Fowey pilot said to me: 'Cap'n Cort will never be without a command while there's a sailing vessel in trade!'

For me the depression seemed the end of my schoonering. A period as mate of a very run-down schooner settled things. The promotion I'd so looked forward to proved a most disheartening experience. I had my own small cabin below the after companion-way but no extra pay. My captain was an unhappy, dispirited man with no further interest in his command. The schooner was crying out for attention but I could do nothing as we were without oils, paints or Stockholm tar. Even paraffin was in such short supply that our side lights were only lit when other vessels lights were near. We were for ever turning running gear end-for-end and patching our worn-out canvas. Our food was insufficient and of the poorest quality. Fortunately I'd enough sense to know that if I didn't make haste about changing my occupation I'd end up in one of the ever lengthening dole queues ashore.

With the supreme optimism of youth, I decided to leave the sea temporarily, find a lucrative shore job and earn sufficient for a share in a schooner by the time shipping got back to normal.

I returned home, a gaunt, tough young man with a weather-beaten countenance and calloused hands, full of confidence but without any other qualifications for employment ashore. My family accepted my return without comment, as if I'd never been away, but if I spoke of seafaring there was a tight-lipped silence and the air was charged with antagonism and disapproval. Both my parents fondly imagined I'd worked the sea out of my system and gave me invaluable help in my efforts to equip myself for a new career in civil engineering. By studying myself sick, I succeeded so well that I was even gaining some advantage from the sad plight of others at the peak of the depression. Based in a Midland town, far from the sea, I was working on engineering projects for the relief of the unemployed under the Government's Unemployment Grants Scheme. I had the unenviable task of supervising the works, aided by a very tough Irish foreman.

Our labour was obtained through the Employment Exchanges on a rota system which allowed each man only six weeks' work. It was heart-breaking to see a batch of men arrive on a site to begin the first job they'd had for months. Whatever their age, size or shape, all had the same pinched faces and lack-lustred eyes. Their working clothes hung loosely on undernourished bodies. Accustomed as I'd been to the tanned, weathered features of sailormen, the pallor of these men horrified me.

After a couple of weeks at work, the changes in the men's appearance were amazing. Their faces were regaining their colour, the purpose as they worked gave the illusion that their shrunken bodies had filled out and their eyes had brightened with hope: hope which was soon to be destroyed. It was about their third week in work when this happened. As I went my rounds, one of the men would stop me to inquire if his efforts were satisfactory and, if so, could I retain him for the duration of the scheme. I had to explain as gently as I could, that I hadn't the authority to keep anyone beyond the stipulated six weeks. Some of these men were old enough to be my father!

Once the gang had received the message, their work slackened to a snail's pace despite the hazing of a very truculent foreman.

I came to dread these interviews, comparing my own comfortable status with theirs. Although working hundreds of hours of unpaid overtime, my pay allowed me to be well dressed and fed, with a few simple luxuries, and yet to save a pound or so each week. I'd every reason to be thankful.

The Grants Schemes had a short life. They weren't of sufficient magnitude, were uneconomical to operate and were brought in too late to alleviate distress. Also, they were measures without compassion.

With the depression at its worst, I met a small, quiet, soft spoken girl and married. This wholly illogical step was taken with the 'Jeremiahs' prophesying disaster for the pair of us. I've never ceased to marvel at the way fate directed me to that Midland town, so far from the sea, where I stayed just long enough to find my staunch, lifelong partner. Fortune indeed smiled on me.

Britain's economy gradually moved out of the doldrums, the dole queues shortened and the hard times were quickly forgotten.

I prospered with work for which I'd inherited talent but no stomach. My initial temporary appointment became permanent and pensionable. Rapid promotion brought with it a salary far in excess of that earned by a schooner's master. Working hard, I refused to join the 'rat race' for advancement and well remember a lecture about this that I received from a very old, self-made businessman of the area.

'Young man,' said he. 'Tha's too perfect t'live. If tha lives as long as me, aa'll be reet sorry f'r thee!'

It was a kindly, well intentioned homily but it was wasted on me. Further promotion was near but it meant nothing to me as I was missing the sea and my beloved schooners. I was impatient to get back to the coast where I could obtain information regarding the state of the schooner fleet, though the scanty news I'd received from various sources was far from reassuring. With my young wife's enthusiastic support, I resigned my post and took a lower paid one at a Medway port. It meant leaving behind a lovely bungalow home, surrounded by a well kept flower garden, also my wife's parents and friends. This was the first of the many surprises my apparently quiet and timid partner had for me in our lifetime together. Although we had a tiny daughter, just old enough to travel, her unseemly haste to leave her native town has caused us amusement ever since.

We set off for Rochester in an ancient Morgan three-wheeler and she never gave a backward glance at the bungalow which had been the envy of her friends. With the baby and a road map on her knees, she piloted me to our destination without error although it was her first experience of map reading and mine of driving a car.

When she saw the Medway, busy with tramp shipping and red-sailed barges, her eyes shone and even a dreary temporary home failed to dampen her elation.

A few weeks later, at her instigation, we began exploring the numerous alleys and concealed wharfs at the rear of the Rochester High Street. It was our lucky evening. Near the bridge, we turned down a side road to the river and espied the mast and rigging of a small sailing vessel rising above the buildings at the Medway Steam Packet Company's shipyard. The unusual masthead with the remnants of a very long wift fluttering above a gilded truck immediately aroused our curiosity. The vessel proved to be a sturdy Dutch galliot and from the yard watchman we learned that her owner had recently died and she was for sale. Keys were produced and in the failing light we made a quick inspection below. The appeal of the galliot was so strong, we both knew at once that we'd found our home.

Within a few days we were the proud owners of *Schollevaer*, a forty-eight foot steel lemster of about twenty tons. Alow and aloft she had the generous proportions and ample curves of the traditional 'Hollander', even to the bowed gaff at the head of her mainsail.

She was very run down when we found her but we gutted her to her ballast and in six months transformed her into a fine seagoing home. I'm sure her former owner, who'd lived and died aboard the little galliot after a colourful career as a rum-runner captain during America's Prohibition, would have approved of our handiwork. After the refit, his Pisces medallion with its inscribed name of his command, S.S. *Newton Bay*, Rum Runner, Rum Row, still remained undisturbed on the cabin bulkhead.

My wife and our small daughter Jo took to life afloat as if born to it. *Schollevaer* was berthed in a small dock off Limehouse Reach. Abreast of her were the mooring buoys for deep-sea shipping, and below them the sailing barge trots. From our deck we had a panoramic view of the commercial Medway from Rochester Bridge to Chatham Ness. On days of fresh winds, the sailing barges winded close to our stern. It was a lovely sight to see a deep-laden 'spritty', lee deck awash, bear down on us with her bluff bows shearing through the water with a sound like ripping silk. Slatting sails thundering, she'd round to so close that her ochred canvas towered high above us. A moment's hesitation as her bows swung to the backed fores'l, then we'd hear its traveller slam over the horse and she'd fill away on the new tack leaving behind her a broad, white frothing wake.

My wife confessed that she was so entranced by the maritime activities going on around her that she was often unable to attend to her housewifely duties below.

There was a close camaraderie on the river and we were accepted into it. My wife was soon known by all on the Medway as 'Bill', a nickname she bears to this very day, and our toddler daughter became a favourite with everyone. On fine days the river police made a habit of nosing their patrol launch under our stern and hailing: 'Where's our little "Shirley Temple?"'. Immediately she heard the call, Jo would scramble on deck to welcome her blue-uniformed admirers and accept their small gifts of sweets or chocolate.

In my free time, we'd sail *Schollevaer* down river, exploring the Thames Estuary and the Kentish coast. An old barge skipper who'd taken a very professional interest in my re-rigging of the galliot, surprised me on our return from one of these short voyages by remarking: 'Dang me! When it come on to blow after you left, I couldn't help worrying about you two and the babby. But I'll not bother no more. You'll do.'

On another occasion, we were dropping down river on the tide, with Bill at the wheel as I made sail. An Admiral's barge, proceeding upriver, changed course to close *Schollevaer*'s stern. A naval officer I immediately recognised as 'Evans of the *Broke*', then in command of the Nore, jumped to attention in the barge's stern-sheets and gave Bill a salute fit for royalty. It was a gesture typical of that great, democratic sailor.

In retrospect, this was the most idyllic period of our lives. I had a job which wasn't too exacting yet brought in sufficient for our needs; we had a happy family life, a stout, seaworthy little ship with every comfort below and, best of all we'd the youth, good health and strength to enjoy everything. But even in those halcyon days it was unwise to plan too far ahead. Being close to the Naval bases of Chatham and Sheerness it was impossible to ignore the danger signs that trouble was brewing in Europe.

Since the Depression, the sailing barge trades had recovered.

Every tide saw scores of these fine craft entering or leaving the Medway, but schooners were completely absent from the scene. From all sources the news was the same; the schooner fleet had been dealt a mortal blow when trade had been at a standstill. I learned that the laid-up *Jane Banks* and *Snowflake* had been sold abroad. *Ocean Gem, Dispatch* and *C & F Nurse* were either scrapped or cut down to towing barges. *Pet, Ethel May, Julia, Nellie Fleming* and *Flying Foam* had all been lost at sea. The former fine Down fleet was reduced to three schooners, *Nellie Bywater, Volant* and *Ellie Park*. The evidence pointed to an end to sailing vessels on the British coast, yet I stubbornly refused to accept it. I had a tempting opportunity to buy *Katie* but instinct warned me not to commit myself with war a likely possibility. Instead, I took a better paid shore job on the Nor'-east coast and sailed *Schollevaer* to Hartlepool.

It was the end of December when we left the Medway and the North Sea was in its most inhospitable mood with bitterly cold, gale-force nor'-easterlies. Anticipating bad weather, I'd prudently sent my wife and child ashore and was crewed by two volunteers, a retired steamer captain and a tough young yachtsman. It was a hard beat up to Tees Bay but *Schollevaer* was as buoyant as a cork and took the steep seas in her stride. We were very exhausted by the violent buffeting and it was a great relief to us all when we rounded the Hartlepool breakwater.

To my consternation, our arrival in the bad weather had front page coverage from the local press. This sparked off an absurd controversy in the newspapers about the risks Bill and our child would take by living afloat in the docks. The busybodies were finally silenced by a satirical verse entitled 'You can do that there anywhere else, but you can't do that there 'ere!' which appeared in one of the papers. We were then made thoroughly welcome by the hospitable townsfolk and the residents of Middleton, a rather dilapidated village in dockland which was surrounded by water: the sea on one side and dock basins on the others. This community depended on the sea and ships for its livelihood. The older people remembered the many Dutch galliots, crewed by families, formerly trading to their port and saw nothing strange in our mode of living. They called *Schollevaer* 'the little Dutch clog' and took a proprietory interest in us. The harbour master ensured we had a snug berth and the minimum trouble when locking in and out of the docks. Nowhere have we met kindlier folk.

Our second daughter was born in Hartlepool and christened in the sailor's church of the Mission to Seamen. She was a most contented baby, lying in a small netted hammock which swung to the movements of her floating home. She went to sea when she was six weeks old.

Our happiness was short-lived. In Spain and Ethiopia the Fascist leaders of Germany and Italy were testing their armaments on defenceless civilians. A Ropner tramp steamer arrived in port damaged by a German plane. She'd been running the blockade with food for the starving Spaniards and, when discharging, was bombed and her bridge wing and topside were stove in by a very near miss. Seafarers knew what was coming.

I attempted to join the Naval Reserve but I was discouraged by the apathy. Then I was seconded from my civilian occupation to Air Raid Precautions by the Home Office to form and operate a rescue service for West Hartlepool. War was officially declared a few days later. It wasn't the wartime role I desired, though it helped when I found myself working under a Regional Commissioner who, as a very young man, had been second-in-command to the legendary Lawrence of Arabia.

The Nor'-east coast was an early target for the Luftwaffe. When the first bombs dropped on the port, we had an efficient and well equipped force to deal with rescue operations. It wasn't a job for the squeamish and I was soon sickened by the sight of old people, women and children being horribly maimed or killed by the raiders. I scarcely saw my wife and children during the frequent bombings and could only pray they were unharmed.

Throughout the raids, Bill remained with the two children aboard *Schollevaer* in a very vulnerable area of the docks. It must have been nerve-racking for her alone with her small daughters without anyone even calling to see if they were alright. She told me that when the sirens sounded, she took the children from their beds, wrapped them in blankets and carried them to the safest corner of the cabin within easy reach of the companionway. To take their attention away from the noise of the gunfire and bombs she read them stories. Sometimes, when the explosions were unpleasantly close, she'd stop in the middle of a sentence, trembling with fear, only to be urged on by Jo saying: 'Go on, Mummy. What happens next? Why are you shivering? Are you cold?'

She listened to low-level raiders machine-gunning freighters at the lockpits less than a cable's length away; saw Gray's Shipyard on the other side of the basin, blazing from an incendiary attack; experienced near misses which blew the roofs, windows and doors from dockworkers' cottages only hailing distance away, and in daylight, from the deck, witnessed a mustering convoy in the bay nearly destroyed by German planes flying only masthead high. When one of the few survivors was towed into the docks, a smouldering mass of twisted steel which no longer resembled a ship, she joined the people of Middleton gathered on the quayside, bareheaded and silent; a tribute to the dead crew. Never at any time did she utter a single complaint.

The suffering inflicted on civilians by the enemy raiders, seen during rescue operations, made me determined to take a more active part in the War. I trained one of my best men to take over my duties, then continuously requested a transfer to the Royal Navy but without success. However, Fate took a hand, for almost the last bombs to fall on the town caused a difficult incident which landed me in hospital very close to death's door. In lucid moments between long periods of unconsciousness, I swore that I'd have a crack at those who'd caused such bloodshed, destruction and human misery, if I should recover.

I was so emaciated when I left hospital I was unable to stand and was written off as being of no further use to the War effort.

A few weeks later, with the invaluable assistance of Captain Shelley, R. N., a bag of bones was piloted through the medicos and an application to join the Royal Navy, when blocked by higher authority, switched to the Royal Marines. In less than four months I was serving in the 40th Royal Marine Commando, a small unit of adventurous young men, all carefully selected volunteers. There had been difficulties, as my thirty-four years were regarded as advanced old age, but a small incident during a night exercise on Exmoor eased the impasse.

The Brigadier in command of the manoeuvres attempted to

disarm me in the darkness and found himself spreadeagled in the mud with my bayonet pricking his throat. There were no further objections to my transfer to a commando unit.

Before leaving Bill and the children, I sailed *Schollevaer* to a good laying-up berth in the River Tees, provided free by a patriotic businessman. My wife sent me off with her heartfelt blessing and I promised to return. It proved a difficult promise to keep, as the Commando was kept fully occupied for over two years, a long time to stay alive.

This is not the place to describe my experiences in the Mediterranean theatre of operations. It is enough to say that, of the original 40th Royal Marine Commando which spearheaded the invasion of Sicily, there were but few survivors who returned home. I was extremely lucky to keep my promise to my wife. Badly wounded by an enemy landmine, I was flown back to Britain to do the rounds of naval hospitals and was a shadow of my former self. Bill cried at her first glimpse of me. At my most urgent request, I was invalided out of the Service with an almost useless right leg and arm, the beginnings of a breakdown and a war-weariness that is indescribable. A humiliating 'disabled serviceman's' job didn't help. The utter disillusionment fighting men have always experienced on their return to 'civvy street' was far more difficult to bear than all the fighting.

Bill roused me from a severe depression with a sharp lecture, then reminded me of our pre-War ambitions.

During service abroad, I'd been in close contact with the small sailing vessels of the Mediterranean and Adriatic, also the shipyards where wooden *barcas, trabaccolos* and *golettas* were built and repaired. The Jugoslav partisans shipped their stores and munitions in schooners at Italian ports, consigned to the Dalmatian island of Vis, and it was there that I'd met up with an old favourite of mine, the *Snowflake* of Runcorn, still giving excellent service, though masquerading under the name *Hvrat*. These vessels had kept alive my former hopes until my physical condition made an end of them.

Bill's words brought back all my old longings. With her encouragement I packed in my miserable job and began a drastic course of therapy for my injured limbs by working as a labourer on a building site for several months. My employer, who'd known me before the War, thought I'd gone crazy but the experiment paid off. Heartened by a slight improvement to my leg, I began a determined search for a schooner—if such a vessel existed in a seaworthy state after the long and gruelling War.

PART TWO

FULFILMENT

The sea gives but hard days and harder end.
We do not heed the end, we only care
To take the ship and wander anywhere;
To mind her, day and night, while underneath
The mouth of ocean opens, showing teeth,
To give her beauty, though ourselves have none,
And let the others have the wealth that's won.

Masefield

12

Full Circle, 1945

My first port of call was Par, Cornwall, where the schooner *Katie* of Padstow had been laid up for the latter part of the War. She was still in the Tregaskis drydock and had been well cared for by her last master, Captain Cort, until his death, but had received little attention thereafter. To bring her up to Certificate standards would have cost a great deal so I ruled her out although she was still a fine vessel.

I combed the Devon and Cornish coasts from the Exe to the Fal without finding a single seaworthy schooner. Falmouth was particularly depressing, with several hulked schooners rotting in the mud off Penryn and Flushing. I'd known them all before the War, the pride of their masters and owners until they'd been requisitioned in the War for harbour barrage balloon service. By the end of hostilities their working days were over. I still have the Ferguson and Baird brass nameplate of one of these schooners, the *Earl Cairns* for which I'd a particular regard and happy memories.

A 'For Sale' notice in *Lloyd's List* sent me to Bideford, Appledore and Avonmouth with no better success. I inspected the ugly *Haldon* and several ketches but none of them were in a serviceable condition. The only exception was the wellfound, trim little *Irene*, still under her original ownership and busily trading between Bristol Channel ports.

Undeterred, I switched my search to Chester River where I'd heard that a number of Marstal schooners had found sanctuary during the War years. The Danes were preparing to leave when I arrived at Connah's Quay. The schooners were fine vessels but too big for my purpose. Before returning to Teesside, I called at the home of Captain John Wynne the last of the very tough, frugal, Welsh Chester River schoonermen. His wife informed me he was still trading with the family-owned *Useful* and was currently on passage to Belfast. The Captain's lady proved to be as formidable as her husband and when I told her the purpose of my visit to the Quay, her eyes gleamed and she became reminiscent.

'The Cap'n nearly sold our *Useful*,' she said. 'A man came up from the West Country and talked him into it. I didn't like it a bit but the deposit had been paid at the broker's office, so I couldn't do a thing. This feller moved his gear into our schooner but after a few days I heard he'd been saying things about our ship at the pub. So I went down to the *Useful* to have it out with him. He wasn't to be seen on deck, so I knocked with my umbrella on the companionway. He heard me alright and poked his head up to see who it was.

"Good morning, Ma'am," says he. "Come below". "You come up here, my man," I says. "What's this you've been saying about the *Useful*? Let me tell you, she's far too good for the likes of you. Just you step along with me to the brokers and you can have your deposit back. And, get your things off our schooner before I lose my temper!" I soon got rid of him, I can tell you!'

I could well imagine the discomforture and rout of the West Countryman when faced by the very angry lady armed with a gamp. A disparaging remark about one of these family-owned schooners was a personal insult to the owner's kith and kin. It reminded me that to negotiate the sale of a schooner could be a very delicate matter indeed.

I returned to *Schollevaer*, lying at the Tees Graythorpe Shipyard, heartened by the knowledge that at least one schooner and several ketches were still finding employment on the coast. I was as sure of finding my schooner as I'd been about surviving the War, although in both instances, I couldn't give the reasons.

Then, one day, in conversation with a Ministry of Transport ship surveyor who'd been stationed in Belfast prior to the War, our talk naturally turned to the Down schooners, many of which he'd surveyed. He said that one of these vessels, the *Nellie Bywater*, was just coming off Ministry of Sea Transport charter and her master-owner, Captain William McKibbin, spoke of retiring and selling his vessel. Within hours of hearing this news I was on my way to Belfast.

Landing from the mailboat on the Donegall Quay in the early morning it was only a short walk around the Clarendon Dock to the shipyard where the *Nellie Bywater* lay in a graving dock, her hull fully exposed, and my heart leapt at my first glimpse of the schooner I'd not seen for nearly twenty years. From the kerb of the dock, I ran my eyes over the beautiful underwater lines. Her moderately raked stem with its slightly rounded forefoot swelled into full, buoyant bows. Amidships the bilges were firm, with little deadrise to her floors and this section rapidly developed into a very long clean run finished off by a Lancashire stern and an 'out-of-doors' rudder. I'd never seen sweeter or more sea-kindly lines and I knew my search was over.

With her fiddle cut off, bowsprit removed and all her spars but the fore lowermast gone, she bore no resemblance to the tops'l schooner I'd known as a boy. This didn't bother me, as her Wartime charterers were responsible for restoring her to the rig she'd had when requisitioned.

I spent several hours down in the drydock, thoroughly examining the bottom of the schooner, which was bone dry and scraped to the bare wood. Keel, garboards and skin planking were in excellent condition and all she needed was the renewal of a few trunnels and a bit of recaulking and hardening up of seams. I was amazed at the skill of her builders in constructing such a fine run to the schooner with scarcely any 'stealers' and it was obvious she was the work of superb craftsmen.

Willy McKibbin, the owner's son, was on board the schooner. I could see he was very fond of the *Nellie Bywater* and it must have hurt him to know she was about to be sold out of the family. But he was most friendly and helpful. The extreme delicacy of the negotiations was apparent when sturdy, white-haired Captain McKibbin arrived from Annalong.

He was a man of few words, and after exchanging a pleasantry, neither of us broached the reason for our meeting. In silence, he pottered around the ship, taking in the progress of the shipwrights. After a bit, he announced that he'd a bus to catch back to Annalong and he'd like me to accompany him as far as the 'stop'.

Neither of us uttered as I limped along beside him until we'd nearly reached the bus stop. Then he asked, suddenly: 'Would you be telling me what church you attend?'

Hiding my surprise, I answered: 'The Church of England, which is the same as your Church of Ireland.' Satisfied, the staunch old Orangeman named his price for the *Nellie Bywater* and I accepted. The simplicity of our verbal transaction left me unprepared for the complications that followed.

The deposit was paid, but because the schooner was still on charter to the Ministry of Transport, their approval to the change of ownership was required before the sale could be completed. A period of great frustration and expense began, for I couldn't get officialdom to move. During this time, I'd no say in what the shipyard was doing to the *Nellie Bywater*. In desperation I travelled to Blackpool, where the offices of the M.O.T. Finance Department were located, occupying several hotels in various parts of the town.

I shall never forget that day, hobbling from one hotel to another, meeting the most charming officials and discussing every subject except the one I'd come about. It was a complete waste of time and money, for in turn, each civil servant disclaimed responsibility for the schooner's charter and passed me on to yet another official in another hotel. It was a complete stalemate for several weeks until I remembered a friend with great influence in 'high places' and with his assistance, the sale difficulties were ironed out with lightning speed. With the change of ownership legalised, we sailed in *Schollevaer* to Belfast, taking with us two young men who were keen to become schoonermen. This proved to be a sad and very expensive mistake, for neither of them would accept my description of the tough life they wished to embark on when I sketched out the unglamorous truth. One was a young engineer, just out of his time at Gray's Shipyard, whom I'd sent to Widdop's of Keighley for a course on our auxiliary motor. His first sight of the *Bywater*'s tall masts totally un-nerved him and he was gone by the first available mailboat. The other, an ex-R.N.V.R. officer, a friend for a number of years, persuaded me to take him as a working partner, although I'd doubts about it from the beginning, for the contrast between the life of a Royal Navy 'Jimmy-the-one' in big ships and the mate of a schooner was too great to work out successfully. From our arrival in Belfast, the erstwhile cheery friend became morose and uncommunicative, but I put this down to his difficulties in mastering a completely different kind of seamanship. I've blamed myself ever since for not sending him home immediately, for the consequences later on were disastrous to all concerned.

With delays and unforeseen expenses, our capital was rapidly diminishing, so it was essential to speed up the refit of the *Nellie Bywater* which was proceeding at a most leisurely pace. I'd been out of schooners so long that I was unknown, and the shipyard took me for yet another adventurous ex-serviceman about to embark on a yachting cruise. It took a sharp encounter with the foreman shipwright to clear the air and put things on a proper footing.

In my absence, a new mainmast of Norwegian spruce had been made and stepped in place of the former beautiful Oregon pine 'stick' which had gone 'missing' from a shipyard during the War. I wasn't too pleased about that, but when I saw some other work vital to the safety of the schooner being scamped, I refused to accept it. This caused an unholy row with the tall, saturnine foreman with the peculiar gait. We slanged one another, and I said angrily: 'You should be bloody ashamed of yourself, you, an old sailorman, allowing work to be done that could lose the schooner and all aboard her!' The shaft got home. He shut up, eyed me warily as if to get my measure and, apparently satisfied, the anger on his face vanished. To my bewilderment, he stooped and rolled up one of his trouser legs to a point above his kneecap. Instead of a normal leg, I saw the old foreman had an artificial one, which explained his odd manner of walking. But it was no ordinary artificial limb. It was a creation of his own, beautifully made in polished hardwood, with the most ingenious brass jointing and a feature quite unusual in such aids . . . a small compartment, just above the knee joint, concealed by a sliding door. The foreman opened the door by pressing a button, revealing a half bottle of rum, which he extracted from it's snug hiding place.

Deftly removing the cork, he handed me the bottle, saying: 'Here, Cap'n! Have a swig and let's forget our differences. You're right about the work, it's a bloody disgrace and it'll come out. Those young fellers don't know nothing . . . they make me sick. But, on the Bible, I'll swear to it you'll never again have reason to complain about anything in my department. Here, have another snort!' He was true to his word and the shipwright's work was excellent from then onwards. Big Jim, as he was known in the shipyard, became a good friend of ours and we enjoyed many a yarn together.

We moved into the *Nellie Bywater* as soon as the accommodation had been painted out. It was a tight squeeze for my family in the Master's quarters aft, but Bill and the children adapted themselves perfectly to their new surroundings. Our ex-Navy friend slept in the fo'c'sle, as the Mate's berth had been lost when an auxiliary was installed, but he messed with us in the cabin. I'd a feeling he was dissatisfied with this arrangement, no doubt comparing his quarters with the luxurious cabins he'd occupied during the War. But he was much better off than we were aft, for the fo'c'sle had been fitted out by the Admiralty and was the roomiest and best furnished crew's accommodation I'd ever seen in a schooner, with four spacious bunks with comfortable mattresses, varnished hardwood surrounds and bunkboards, cushioned locker seats, ample locker and cupboard space, solid-fuel heating and table. The bulkheads and deckhead were enamelled white and the sole covered in heavy, dark brown cork lino. In fact, the fo'c'sle was far superior to the after accommodation.

During the remainder of the re-fit, Bill quietly and efficiently dealt with food rationing, victualling, cooking in her tiny deckhouse galley, washing clothes and keeping the two children and our living quarters spotlessly clean. In addition, when there were problems she was a tower of strength to me with her plain commonsense judgements.

The shipyard responded well to my appeals to expedite their work, but post-war shortages of suitable materials were a serious difficulty. James Tedford's of Donegall Quay were responsible for the rigging and sailmaking. Manila rope was still issued on licence solely for lifeboat falls, and I had a hard fight to get it for the most essential running rigging. The riggers were told to use manila lanyards for setting up the standing rigging but I refused point blank to accept them. I was informed that Italian hemp was unobtainable, but after a practical demonstration for the Ship Surveyor aboard the *Nellie Bywater*, the hemp arrived. Even the Stockholm tar was a wartime substitute which was scarcely safe to use.

The least of my worries were the new sails, for Tedfords turned out a fine strong suit of working sails in Irish flax which gave splendid service in the years that followed.

Much of the schooner's gear was missing and the shipyard seemed to have forgotten the details of such vessels, so I was kept busy drawing the parts that were needed, and they made a capital job of everything I'd sketched. But it was sad to see that the equipment peculiar to schooners was already unknown in a shipyard which formerly repaired and maintained hundreds of these vessels.

The Widdop auxiliary engine and the Crossley motorwinch caused the most serious delays. The shipyard ordered spares for both engines and the makers replied that deliveries couldn't be made for at least a year. I journeyed to Keighley and Manchester to make personal appeals and both firms responded magnificently, getting the vital parts to Belfast in record time. I'd never been in schooners with power but I realised it was now a necessity. Gone were the days of a thirty-bob tow from Liverpool Bar to Garston, and I couldn't imagine my crew 'dollying' out cargoes as we did in the past.

As the shipyard work neared completion, a hefty moon-faced local lad was engaged as 'boy', but I guessed he wasn't too bright when I caught him chopping kindling for the galley range on a hatch that had just been covered with new tarpaulins. He seemed strong and willing so I overlooked this stupidity and hoped he'd soon learn, for there was plenty to be done to get the schooner ready for sea. By the time the shipyard engineers had finished assembling the winch and auxiliary we'd thoroughly overhauled the ground tackle, catted and fished both anchors, oiled and greased the windlass and steering gear, restowed the forepeak, lamplocker and halfdeck, bent the sails and finally, after clearing away all the refuse of the refit, scrubbed her down.

Resplendent with new paintwork, rigging and sails, the *Nellie Bywater*, now a fully rigged fore-and-aft schooner, only needed hard work from her crew to make her shipshape.

We did a day of dock trials, with the motor running against doubled up moorings, followed by the sea trials.

The weather was ideal for our purpose, with a light westerly wind and good visibility when we left the fitting-out berth in the Clarendon Dock with a large company aboard, including several shipyard men, M.O.T. surveyors, the compass adjuster and a Belfast pilot. I was merely an observer, as the schooner was still the responsibility of the Ministry, but it was a great moment for me as I felt the little ship come to life after her long docking. We motored down the Lough to just outside the Copeland Islands, where we swung ship for the compass adjuster.

Bill was having a busy day, supplying endless mugs of tea and coffee to all and sundry. She cooked and served everyone with a roast beef lunch, seating them in relays at the cabin table. Her only helper was little Jo, who washed up stacks of dirty dishes and fetched and carried for her mother between the cabin and the galley. Not only was this a culinary feat, it was also a masterly job of victualling under post-war rationing.

With everything in her favour: light, a clean bottom and a following wind and tide, the *Nellie Bywater* had handled very well under her small engine until it was time to return to Belfast. Motoring back up the Lough against the ebb and an ever freshening head wind, she slowed down to a mere crawl. The Pilot Lightvessel abeam, the real test of the engine's capabilities began. Coming up the Lough as the daylight faded I'd heard the steady beat of the motor take on a more urgent note for the yard men in the engine-room were getting impatient to be home with the coming of darkness and were boosting the motor to its limit. In the River Lagan the schooner just stemmed the tide and when the pilot asked for more power, he was assured the engine had reached its limit. Seeing from the shore lights that we weren't gaining an inch, he turned to me saying: 'She won't make it, Cap'n. She won't make it!'

'Let me try her, Pilot,' I answered, and he obligingly moved over so that I could take the wheel. Gently nursing her as if she were under sail in light airs, I started inching her up against the wind and tide. Gradually we snaked up river, using every inshore eddy and lull in the wind until the entrance to the Clarendon Dock was under the bow. I then turned her over to the pilot for docking.

A check line on the dock entrance knuckle unfortunately parted as the schooner swung on it and the tide took charge, slewing her stern so that she was in great danger of losing her headgear by collision with the dock wall.

'I'll take her,' I exclaimed urgently to the pilot, who unhesitantly turned the wheel over to me. Like a lamb, the *Nellie Bywater* answered my hands, passing safely through the entrance without even the need of a fender and berthing with the utmost docility. I can't explain it but I had an instant rapport with the schooner which lasted all the time I had her.

I apologised to the pilot for taking over in the heat of the moment but, good man that he was, he brushed aside my regrets and congratulated me on the handling of the schooner. It was the beginning of a most pleasant relationship with that fine body of seamen, the Belfast Pilotage Service. Subsequently, on the many occasions when they took the *Nellie Bywater* up and down the Lagan, it was always a pleasure to have these friendly pilots aboard and I believe they enjoyed being with us.

It took another two days to complete the ritual of the change of ownership, one spent signing the Off-Survey acceptance documents in the Belfast M.O.T. Ship Department. During the refit, I'd found their officials to be practical, friendly men and our relationships had been most cordial. They had been tireless in their efforts to obtain suitable materials for the schooner at a time of shortages and were most generous with her equipment. In one instance they were too thorough, for in the place of the traditional 'punt', I was supplied with a tanked lifeboat with full equipment. I believe the *Nellie Bywater* was the only Home-Trade schooner ever to carry such a boat and gear. But I'd gladly have changed it for the usual workboat as it was really too heavy and cluttered with gear to be practical as a schooner's punt.

Had it not been for the annual surveys, I'd have stripped her down to essentials.

The most valued item they supplied was the fine, fully corrected steering compass in a teak and brass binnacle with electric lighting. Their interest greatly contributed towards giving the *Nellie Bywater* a new lease of life.

On the second day, the sixty-four shares of the schooner were duly registered at Newry, with twenty-four under my name as Managing Owner, twenty under my wife's name and twenty to our gloomy friend. Six months later, the latter shares were nearly to be our undoing.

In common with most ex-servicemen who'd been abroad for most of the war years, I'd little knowledge of the way in which conditions had changed whilst we'd been absent. I fondly hoped that the business side of schooners would be the same as in pre-war days but when I began seeking employment for the *Nellie Bywater* I was quickly disillusioned.

In a dingy shipbroker's office in the city, I had my first taste of the difficulties ahead. After the usual preliminaries, I asked the broker if he could fix my schooner, preferably to the Mersey.

'I expect you have your Coastwìse Licence, Cap'n?' he enquired blandly, looking at me over his glasses. Of course he knew very well that I was ignorant of a measure brought in during hostilities.

Trying, but not very successfully, to hide my alarm—for I'd suffered more than my bellyful of forms and permits during the past few months—I asked him to fully explain this additional obstruction.

His mournful face creased into what I assumed to be a smile.

'Oh! It's nothing to worry about,' he said, reassuringly. 'Just a mere formality. We can obtain the licence for you, if you wish. Your schooner will come under the Belfast Coasting Committee and it will be granted as soon as we apply to them. It costs nothing but we, as your agents, have to keep them informed of the full details of your schooner's activities. It's a formality, that's all. Shall I make the application?'

I nodded an affirmative, too full for words. His smooth talk couldn't hide the implications of the licence terms. A wartime regulation was being used to place the 'one ship' owner at the mercy of the big operators. But there was worse to follow!

With the *Nellie Bywater*'s pre-War trades in mind, I next brought up the subject of possible coal cargoes from Garston to Ulster.

'Coal comes under the Ministry of Fuel,' replied the broker. 'You'll need a permit from the Ministry before you can carry coal.' 'Well! How about potatoes the other way?' I suggested hopefully. 'Oh! that's the Ministry of Food. You can't carry potatoes without a permit, either.'

So this was the 'freedom' we'd been fighting for, I thought, bitterly.

Aloud, I asked: 'What about a stone cargo, Annalong to Liverpool. Surely there's no permit required for granite kerbs?' My sarcasm was wasted, but for the first time the broker showed mild interest. 'Ah, now! Perhaps we could do something there, Cap'n. Hang on while I use the phone.'

I waited anxiously as he spoke to somebody over the telephone. He broke off his conversation to say to me: 'Our friends at Annalong can rustle up about a hundred tons of kerbs for you,

Cap'n. The rate to Liverpool is ten shillings a ton, F.I.O. Shall I tell them you'll accept?'

The quoted figure was the pre-War rate. Hiding my dismay, I suggested that twelve and six would be nearer the mark.

There were a few more words exchanged between the broker and his 'friend' over the wires, then he put down the receiver.

'My friends can't increase their offer, Cap'n. They say, take it or leave it but they must know one thing or the other within the hour. What do you say? You'll take it? Right! When shall I tell them to expect you in Annalong? Day after tomorrow.' He jotted the date on a scribbling pad, then consulted a tide table lying on his desk.

'Let's see . . . High Water's 9.30 a.m. You say you'll be off the port at nine? Anything else I can do for you before I confirm with our friends?'

'Yes!' I answered. 'Order me a hoveller to pilot us in, and make sure he's ready to board us at nine, sharp. It's a difficult entry for a stranger!'

He assured me the order would be passed on, we shook hands and I left the office.

On my way back to the docks, my feelings were mixed. I was disappointed that our first charter for the *Nellie Bywater* should be at a rate so poor that it would scarcely cover our expenses to Liverpool. But it was a start and perhaps we could do better in the Mersey. On the other hand, I was struck by the extraordinary way my life had turned full circle.

I should have been filled with triumph at the thought of returning to Annalong with a vow made there as a ship's boy an accomplished fact. Instead, I experienced a deep thankfulness that I'd been spared in the War to see this day. I only hoped I'd prove worthy of the little schooner, in spite of my disabilities and make her a happy ship for all who sailed in her.

Our future fortunes now depended on the *Nellie Bywater* and the key to the future is often to be found in the past. My knowledge of the schooner's past was confined to particulars in her documents, the brief entries in Lloyd's Register of Shipping and the occasions when I'd met up with her during my early days in the *Via*. But, over the ensuing years I gradually pieced together the vessel's complete history, from the time she was built until I became her third owner.

13

Nellie Bywater, 1873–1945

In the year 1800, Millom, Cumberland, was a tiny, straggling village of sandstone and slate cottages, with the massive bulk of Black Combe rising steeply to the north and the broad, shallow estuary of the Duddon River to the south.

About 1850, rich deposits of purple-coloured iron ore were discovered near the shores of Hodbarrow Point and with the opening of the Hodbarrow Mine, a small, thriving town sprang up which soon eclipsed the old village. Mining was closely followed by the building of blast furnaces for the Millom Ironworks so that by 1870, Millom had become a booming industrial town served by the railway.

To protect the mines from flooding at high tides, a sea wall was built from Hodbarrow Point to Haverigg, with a pier to accommodate the many ships arriving in the Duddon with cargoes of pit props, coal and other necessities of industrial development.

To add to the town's prosperity, in 1873 a famous Welsh shipbuilder, Captain William Thomas of Amlwch, Anglesey, opened a new shipyard on the shores of the Duddon at Borwick Rails. He entrusted the yard with its workforce of twelve men to a talented, twenty-five-year-old foreman shipwright, Hugh Jones. The first vessel to be laid down was a schooner of 99 registered tons to the order of the Hodbarrow Mining Company.

Hugh Jones carved the laminated, yellow pine half-model from which the lines of the schooner were to be taken, and his handiwork delighted the prospective owners and his employer, for the design incorporated seaworthiness, stiffness and speed.

Early in the spring, keel blocks were laid near the water's edge and the sawyers commenced cutting the schooner's timbers from selected logs. They toiled in pairs, using seven foot taper-bladed pitsaws with T shaped wooden handles at the broad ends for the top sawyers who stood on the logs being cut. The narrow ends of the saw blades had adjustable wooden handles which were held by assistants working in 15 ft × 3 ft × 7 ft deep pits, under a constant stream of sawdust. The yard supplied ale at intervals for the men engaged on this arduous and thirsty job.

The schooner was built under special survey with the finest materials and workmanship. Her scantlings were exceptionally heavy. The oak keel measured 15 in × 12 in and the floors shaped from 15 in × 10 in. Futtocks sawn from oak bends tapered from the floors to the frame heads which finished 7 in × 6 in. The sawn timbers were turned over to the shipwrights for finishing with broad axe and adze.

With the keel laid on the keel blocks and stem and sternpost erected, the finished frames were positioned only 6 in apart. Then a massive 24 in × 12 in keelson, topped with a 12 in × 6 in sister keelson, was bolted above the frame floors with wrought Swedish iron keelbolts forged by the yard's blacksmith. This nearly indestructible material was used for all metal fastenings. To complete the enormously strong framework of the schooner, 15 in × 4½ in shelves were bolted on the inside of the frame heads for supporting the 9 in × 9 in deck beams.

At this stage an onlooker could visualise the form of the unfinished ship.

There were plenty of critics, for the shipyard drew nearly everyone in Millom on Sunday evenings after chapel. The tough miners and ironworkers all agreed that Hughie Jones and his men were building a 'girt' ship and even the strict Lloyd's surveyor found little to fault.

Deck beams were stiffened with wrought iron knees and the edges of frames adzed to true lands for the skin planking and ceiling.

These outside and inside skins were constructed simultaneously. Long, accurately shaped planks were rushed from the steam chests, clamped in position, then fastened to the frames with alternate wrought iron bolts and oak treenails. 5 in thick American elm was used for the bottom with oak, graduated from 5 in to 3 in, above it. The hold was lined with a 3 in durable oak ceiling with removable limber boards and airports.

Bulwark stanchions had been inserted at intervals between pairs of frames and when the sheerstrakes were in position, the laying of coverboards, waterways and deck began. King planks and the deck beneath the windlass were 5 in thick pitchpine and the remaining decking 3 in.

Up to this stage of the building, the air had been sweet with the scent of newly worked timber and the yard sounds mainly a soporific rasp of pitsaws, a muted 'chunk' of razor-edged cutting tools biting into timber and a measured beat of mauls driving home fastenings. When caulking began, dense black smoke and choking fumes wreathed about the shored-up hull from the fires and heating pitch kettles. The insistant, rhythmical ring of caulking mallets echoed far across the Duddon estuary as the tarred oakum was driven into the vessel's seams. Each caulked seam was payed up with boiling pitch, its acrid odour penetrating into the whole of the schooner's structure and remaining there to the end of her life.

The hull completed, fitting-out commenced. Windlass, dolly winch, galley, rudder and steering gear were added and joiners constructed the accommodation below for officers and crew. On the slipway alongside the schooner, adzemen were fashioning huge Oregon pine logs into lowermasts and bowsprit. The spars were given four, then eight and finally sixteen sides before rounding with drawknives and planes. The masts, fully banded and furnished were lifted with sheerlegs and stepped, and the bowsprit shipped between the knightheads above the stem.

Captain Richard Morgan, who had been engaged by the owners to command the new vessel, took charge of the rigging and final equipping of the schooner, for she was to be launched fully rigged and ready for sea.

She was masted, rigged, painted and ready for launching ten months from the laying of her keel.

On a cold December day, 1873, the first of the many schooners to be built by the Millom Shipyard was named and launched. She was christened *Nellie Bywater* after one of the owner's family, and, bright with bunting, slid down the tallowed ways into the Duddon without a hitch. The event was witnessed by all of Millom who could attend and the opinion of those present was that 'ur schooner'll stan' abeun aw udders!' Hugh Jones affirmed in later years that she was the finest schooner he ever built.

Her Lloyd's Survey Certificate dated 1 May, 1874, stated:

The Schooner NELLIE BYWATER of WHITEHAVEN, Richard Morgan, Master. 99 Tons, has been surveyed at MILLOM by the Surveyors to this Society and reported to be, on 11th. April, 1874, in a good and efficient state and fit to carry dry and perishable

Cargoes to and from all parts of the World, and that she has been CLASSED and entered in the REGISTER BOOK of this Society with the Character A1 for TWELVE Years from DECEMBER, ONE THOUSAND EIGHT HUNDRED AND SEVENTY-THREE subject to periodical survey.

LAUNCHED, DECEMBER, 1873.

Built under Special Survey,

Witness my hand,

THO. J. WALKER

Chairman

The *Nellie Bywater*'s principal dimensions were: Length from knightheads to half-round, 98 ft. Between perpendiculars, 89.7 ft. Beam, 22.2 ft. Depth of hold, 10.1 ft. Draught loaded, 11.5 ft.

She was rigged as a double tops'l schooner. Her number in Lloyd's Register was 69715 and her signal letters MSFV. Other details are given in the appendix.

Loading a cargo of ore at the Hodbarrow Pier, the *Nellie Bywater* began her maiden voyage, sailing down the Swash and over the Duddon Bar, her new canvas hard with wind and her spars and paintwork glinting in the pale, wintry sunlight. She quickly established herself in the West Coast trades, her principal cargoes being ore from the Duddon to the Clyde, Mersey and Bristol Channel, with coal, coke and pitprops homeward. In addition, she carried bricks and tiles from Connah's Quay to Ireland and fishery salt from Runcorn to the Western Isles.

Her masters spoke highly of the schooner's sailing qualities, her seaworthiness and tightness and she became very popular with charterers and agents. In 1890, Captain Soloman Ellis in command, the *Nellie Bywater* carried a cargo of salt from Runcorn to Stornoway and the captain received the following letter from the Stornoway agent:

Stornoway. 2 July, 1890.

Dear Sir,

        I have much pleasure in certifying that you delivered a cargo of first and second fishery salt from Runcorn to me this week in first class order and condition, and I consider the vessel

151

Nellie Bywater commanded by you most suitable for carrying salt.

Yours faithfully,

J. N. ANDERSON

A ship's economics are rarely mentioned outside professional circles, yet her life span depends on her earning capacity. When she ceases to give dividends, she's either sold or scrapped.

The Hodbarrow Mining Co. were fortunate to have masters for the *Nellie Bywater* who were keen businessmen as well as excellent mariners. Following Captain Ellis, in 1891 Captain James Fairclough of Ulverston took command. His son of the same name succeeded him in the *Nellie Bywater* until 1902. During the eleven years of Fairclough command, the schooner loaded, delivered and discharged an average of twenty-eight cargoes a year, many of them 'dollied' out.

A Charter Party for the schooner at this period indicates typical freight rates. The cargo was 170 tons of fireclay goods, Queensferry to Belfast, at 4s.6d. per ton, F.I.O., with a guinea gratuity to the Master. Brokerage at 2½ per cent. It can be assumed that the *Nellie Bywater* grossed over £500 in a half-year, out of which came wages, victualling, insurance, port charges, repairs, sails, rope, paints and other stores. A Statement of Accounts for the half-year ending 30 June, 1899, has a dividend for the owners of £1.18s.10d. per share. Only the master's disbursements are itemised: Sails £21.17s.0d.; Rope £10.11s.0d.; Paint £1.18s.0d.; Stores £5.3s.2d.; Management £5.0s.0d.

Wages at the time were approximately £6 per month, Master; £5 per month, Mate and £3 per month for seamen. Victualling allowance was about a shilling a head per day.

The owner's dividends were hard-won by the *Nellie Bywater*'s captains and crews. A terse entry in the schooner's log for November, 1898 records: 'Ernest Ray, Seaman, of Ramsey, I.O.M., lost overboard off Milford, when on passage from Swansea to Duddon with 172 tons of coal.'

It was a tough life in schooners but there was never a shortage of men and boys to man them. The trade bred the finest type of sailormen who were proud of their ships and their calling. Captain Fairclough spent the whole of his working life in these vessels

152

and when retired, he delighted to yarn about the schooners he'd known and served. This fine old mariner died in 1944, at the ripe old age of 88 years.

The *Nellie Bywater* retained her Whitehaven registry and was owned by the Hodbarrow Mining Company for forty-eight years. In 1921, she was sold to Irish buyers for the sum of £1,825 and was re-registered at Annalong, Port of Newry. The local school-master, doctor and publican had shares in the vessel, with Captain William McKibbin, former master of the *Hunter*, the new manag-ing owner and commander.

The new owners suffered the most outrageous bad luck at the start of their venture. Captain McKibbin sailed the *Nellie Bywater* to Whitehaven to load a coal cargo and here he was caught in a long-drawn-out strike of Cumberland coal miners. For weeks the schooner lay idle under the deserted coal tips until her share-holders were nearly ruined. Before they'd fully recovered from this disastrous beginning, ill fortune struck again. During a violent gale in the Firth of Clyde, the *Nellie Bywater* was trapped on a lee shore of Holy Island. It was a wild, dark night and Captain McKibbin tried to wear the schooner round, but with insufficient sea room she struck, broadside on. Pounding on the sharp rocks, the schooner drove further inshore and Captain McKibbin and his crew took to the rigging to avoid being swept away by the heavy seas. For three hours they clung there until, eventually, the *Nellie Bywater* brought up close to the shore. At 3 a.m. it was low water and, assisting each other, the exhausted men were able to scramble over the slippery rocks to the safety of the land. They staggered to the lighthouse, shocked and suffering from exposure, where the keepers cared for them. It was a very close call for the McKibbin family, for the captain had his son Willie with him as mate and a nephew James as A.B.

Next day, at low water, the schooner was high and dry, listing far over to starboard and surrounded by enormous boulders, some of them crushed by the schooner's pounding during the gale. Her position seemed hopeless. The underwriters thought other-wise, however, for they engaged a salvage firm to clear a channel through the rocks, refloat the *Nellie Bywater* and tow her to Irvine.

Her keel and bottom planking were badly damaged and it says

much for her builders that she survived a battering which would have broken up most vessels. The insurance barely covered the cost of the salvage operations, so the captain and his shareholders had to pay for the extensive repairs.

Undaunted by his narrow escape, and recognising the outstanding qualities of his command, Captain McKibbin worked hard to recover his losses. He installed a 50 h.p. auxiliary motor in the *Nellie Bywater* and modified her to fore-and-aft rig. In December, 1928, the schooner had another test of her strength and seaworthiness when she was one of four Annalong schooners to be caught by fierce gales in the Irish Sea, resulting in the loss of one of them, the *Bengullion*, which foundered with all hands.

Comparing the schooner's work as an auxiliary with her records when under sail alone, her cargo book in 1931 showed that she loaded twenty-six cargoes of coal, granite and potatoes, carrying between Northern Ireland and the Mersey. To do this, she was obliged to make twelve light passages. Between 1932 and 1940, she averaged twenty-two cargoes a year plus twenty-two light trips. No unprofitable light passages had to be made when Captain Fairclough averaged twenty-eight cargoes per year under sail alone.

In March, 1934, the *Nellie Bywater* stranded on a sandbank in the treacherous Chester River near Mostyn, where groundings were often fatal because of the bore. With Captain Tom Coppack of Connah's Quay supervising and Captain John Wynne and the *Useful*'s crew assisting, the schooner was hauled off into deep water without serious damage, although again it was her stout construction which undoubtedly saved her.

With the outbreak of the Second World War, the *Nellie Bywater* continued normal trading until 1 July, 1940, when Captain McKibbin received Admiralty orders to proceed to Belfast. Here the vessel was requisitioned for war service.

Her bowsprit and mainmast were lifted ashore and the fiddle bow cut off, completely altering her appearance. For the next four years she played a valuable role in the war effort. She began by carrying stores and equipment from Belfast to the many ships brought up in the Lough. When the enemy commenced using the deadly magnetic mine, the *Nellie Bywater* was converted into a mobile degaussing workshop, taking the heavy cables to the anchored merchantmen in the Lough for fitting on the spot, without the delay of the ships' docking. Two cracked deck beams, caused by loading degaussing cable on her deck, were the evidence of this service she bore to the end of her days.

Finally, she became a fueller for the M.T.B's and M.G.B's of the Navy's Light Coastal Forces.

Captain McKibbin was seventy-three years of age when the War ended, and he retired after twenty-four years in command of the *Nellie Bywater*. When I became the third owner of the schooner, she was seventy-two years old.

14

Return to Annalong

The reactions of my partners to the stone 'fix' at Annalong were characteristic; Bill asked, 'Can I have the boy this afternoon to help me bring the provisions from McArdles?' The mate was silent and increasingly glum.

We decided to leave the children with a friend in Belfast until the end of the school term. They were happily attending school in the city and had made many friends. In the dock area they were known as the *Bywater* kids.

The following day our crew was made up by a young marine engineer who joined us as a rather reluctant motorman. Shortly after dark, we dropped down river with a pilot aboard. He left us at the lightvessel and we made sail. Rounding the Copelands, we jogged comfortably along the Ulster coast at about five knots to a cold, light s'uth-easterly breeze. It was a lovely night for December with just enough sea to give the deck a buoyant lift.

At the *Nellie Bywater*'s wheel, with my pipe drawing nicely, I felt happier and more relaxed than I'd been for months. Every mile we sailed put the cares and worries of the long refit further behind us. I was looking forward to revisiting the scenes of my early days in schooners and wondered if I'd meet John Doyle and others I'd known as a boy. The return of the *Nellie Bywater* to her former home port would be quite an occasion for the people of Annalong. I thought of the arrival of a local schooner when I was a ship's boy, every able-bodied man and boy assisting with the berthing of the vessel; we should be assured of a hearty welcome when we sailed into Annalong in the morning. My nostalgic reverie was interrupted by Bill's voice: 'The boy's seasick! Shall I tell him to turn in? I'll stand his watch.'

As it was a fine night, I agreed and she vanished in the darkness to ease the lot of a lad making his first acquaintance with the sea.

When dawn broke, we were close to our destination. The sun's crimson orb rose above the rim of a calm sea, tinting the snow-capped peaks of the Mourne Mountains a delicate pink. Slieve Donard seemed unnaturally near.

We took in sail and under power nosed cautiously shorewards,

16. Dockers discharging the *Nellie Bywater*. (*Author*)

17. Everything set and drawing. View aloft of *Nellie Bywater*'s foremast. (*Author*)

18. Master and mate. The author with trusty second-in-command, Colin Potter. (*Western Morning News, Plymouth*)

as I searched with my binoculars and found the small granite pier marking the entrance to Annalong.

The mate hollered for the boy, who appeared from below, his round, rubicund face shining from a recent wash and his hair plastered down with a highly scented dressing. He'd changed into a clean khaki shirt and trousers and his first words were: 'Good morning, Mrs England, what's for breakfast?' The look my tired, grimy-faced wife gave him should have killed him. An angry bellow from the mate sent him scurrying away.

The schooner approached the harbour entrance at 'Slow' speed. The brief early morning sun had gone, its glowing disc completely hidden by a bank of dense fog which was rolling down on us from the horizon.

I sounded the horn for the local pilot and we all strained our eyes for some sign of life in the little port, but there was none. Already fog was wreathing around the *Nellie Bywater*, then it closed down on us, as thick as pea soup. I stopped the motor and blew the horn, again and again, listening intently between the blasts, but our signals were unanswered. All we heard from the invisible shore were the sounds of a cock crowing, followed by the mournful barking of a dog.

The mate took a cast of the lead. 'Seven fathoms and a hard bottom,' he reported. A hard, foul bottom, too risky for anchoring.

Cursing the missing hoveller under my breath, I concentrated on keeping our position with the lead on the bottom, correcting the drift with an occasional engine burst. For about twenty minutes we jockeyed about in complete frustration, then as swiftly as it had closed down, the fog lifted. Without further delay, I swung the schooner's head towards the harbour and motored in. I was relying on a twenty-year-old memory but as we closed near enough to see the details, everything came flooding back. 'Steer parallel to the pier, keeping just clear of its projecting toe. As the basin opens up, poke the headgear and bows obliquely through the entrance and get a checkrope on a pawl at the knuckle!' For the first time, I noticed a helper on the pier who took our check and made it fast. 'Now! Slow ahead, gradually checking until more than half the schooner is in the dock, before making the full turn, otherwise our stern will foul the big boulders in the narrow river. There! She's through.' A few moments later we were safely alongside the dock wall.

A poker-faced crowd of men and boys appeared like magic on the quay, some of them assisting in mooring up and the rest swarming over the *Nellie Bywater*'s rails, milling about and examining everything aboard with silent curiosity. From my early experiences in Down schooners I was prepared for this, but to Bill it came as a shock.

'They're in the fo'c'sle, the engine-room and even in the cabin, opening all my lockers,' she protested indignantly.

As I explained what had always been customary in these small Down ports, she suddenly pointed to the wheelhouse, which was filled with jostling, jersey-clad visitors. 'Is that customary, too?' she demanded.

To my amazement and horror, I was just in time to see my parallel rulers being tucked inside a man's jersey. A few quick steps took me to the wheelhouse door and I angrily requested the return of the instrument. The offender calmly replaced the rulers on the chart-table without changing his expression or uttering a word.

Thoroughly upset, I abruptly cleared the schooner of sightseers. Within minutes the quayside was completely deserted and the harbour became as silent as a grave.

It was worrying: first the non-appearance of the hoveller, then the incident in the wheelhouse, which was obvious provocation. In spite of the great interest in the *Nellie Bywater*, so far we hadn't received a single friendly word in a port previously noted for its hospitality.

Bill, who is particularly sensitive to atmosphere, voiced her feelings: 'After all you've told us about Annalong, I don't think much of our welcome. The sooner we're loaded and away, the better, I say!'

Tommy, our boy, provided us with some much needed humour. Throwing his head back, with his nostrils quivering like a hound's, he took loud sniffs of the air and growled: 'Be Jasus! There's a straang smell of fish here. Glory be t'God! Whatever can it be, Sorr?'

The Annalong fleet was at sea, but there was plenty of evidence that we were in a fishing port, with a couple of ring netters moored astern, piles of empty fish boxes on the quay and screaming gulls circling overhead. The absurdity of the boy's remark reduced us to tears and removed some of our tension.

With such a poor freight rate, I was naturally anxious to load and get away as quickly as possible, but our luck was out. It was next morning before the local granite merchant arrived to talk business. He was friendly enough and our business was soon completed. The weather looked very threatening, with the glass falling and a very fresh easterly wind blowing, dead onshore, so I took the opportunity of asking our visitor the whereabouts of the harbourmaster, in case of the need to close the basin with the timber baulks provided for that purpose. He told me the harbourmaster lived some distance from the village, somewhere on the mountainside but 'Ach! He'd be down!'

Seeing the merchant ashore, a strong gust of wind nearly whipped my cap away. The *Nellie Bywater* was beginning to surge about, her moorings and fenders creaking and groaning. She was listing to the wind which bowed her running gear and the windsock at the maintruck was ashiver. It was high time to find the harbourmaster, for the baulks could only be put in when the harbour was dried-out and the tide was already falling fast.

Leaving the lads to treble the doubled moorings, I climbed the hill from the harbour to the main road, following the haphazard directions I'd been given, but without success. For a couple of hours I trudged over the wild countryside without meeting anyone or seeing a single habitation, and then gave up the search. Back on the main road, I was alarmed by the deteriorated weather. A low unbroken ceiling of sombre, oily-black clouds covered the sky, blotting out the high mountains at the rear of the village. From the horizon, the slate-grey sea was ploughed into white-rimmed ridges which swelled perceptibly as they neared the shore, and the sound of the rollers had risen from a murmur to a dull boom. Below me I could see the little basin and as I looked, a giant wave topped the breakwater, leaped high in the air and dissolved into a curtain of spray which blew over the harbour, hiding everything from sight.

Hurrying down the hill, I had to lean forward against a wind which had reached gale force.

The *Nellie Bywater* was on the mud with the tide making and in a few hours she would be afloat. In my absence my anxious-faced crew had laid out four brand-new lines across the basin in addition to trebling all others. The 'nips' had all been parcelled with canvas. Every available tyre and log fender was in position. Everything had been done for the safety of the schooner.

I asked if anyone from the village had been down and they said they'd not seen a soul whilst I was away.

I told them to snatch all the rest they could before the *Nellie Bywater* floated, and then followed suit. It had been an exhausting hike over the rough country with my 'gammy' leg but, with the urgency of the situation, it was only when I relaxed in the cabin that I realised my weariness. Bill's hot meal revived me, then I dozed uneasily on the settee for a spell.

Thump . . . the concussion of the schooner striking the ground instantly roused me. The wind was shrieking overhead and the sound of the sea on the breakwater was like gunfire. Thump . . . another heavy blow sent a shudder through our little vessel's fabric. I grabbed my oilskins and hastily pulled them on as an even heavier bump shook the *Bywater*.

Bill's scared face peered round the door of the sleeping berth. 'Shall we be alright?' she enquired anxiously. 'What can I do to help? Oh! I hate this place and the people here!' Another violent shock sent us both staggering. No wooden vessel could take much of this treatment, I thought grimly. To Bill I said: 'Stay below, but be ready to come on deck when called!'

Within a few minutes of reaching the deck, I was soaked to the skin in spite of my oilies. The air was a lashing turmoil of wind and water, salt spray and torrential rain blew with stinging force across the schooner in the pitch darkness, making it difficult to see, even with a powerful torch.

Fortunately, the heavy bumping on the ground stopped soon after we floated but in a welter of spume and spray, the schooner was plunging and rearing as if possessed, threatening every moment to part her moorings. The strain on her rails was terrific. Every now and again the seas swilled right over the breakwater, filling the basin to overflowing. As high water approached, the *Bywater*'s movements became wilder.

The four of us had our hands full, taking in the slack as the warps stretched under the strain, replacing parcelling as it chafed through and tending the grinding fenders. I'd never before seen a schooner take such punishment. As she tried to tear herself free of the restraining moorings, she snubbed so viciously that it was difficult to keep our feet on the streaming deck, and the rails creaked and groaned their agony. I wondered how long it would be before she pulled herself apart.

As the schooner's rails plunged below the quay, someone boarded us with a flying leap. In the light of my torch I saw it was Willie McKibbin. In my ear he yelled: 'Mind if I help, Cap'n? Make your best lines fast to the masts before the rails go!'

This we did with his powerful aid, for he was as strong as a bull. 'Now get some strops on 'em and take up the slack with the burtons.' This eased the strain on the rails considerably.

'Tis all we can do for her now, Cap'n,' he panted breathlessly. 'Don't let on about me giving a hand, will you? Ach! I'll away home.'

Brushing aside my thanks, he waited in the lee of the galley until the schooner rose above the quay, and then with a catlike leap he jumped ashore and disappeared in the darkness.

For another couple of hours we pulled our hearts out tending the network of moorings as the tide fell. A short period of heavy bumping before we took the ground was followed by blissful stillness. Completely exhausted, we all staggered to our bunks and passed out.

'Wake up! Wake up! We'll soon be afloat again.' Bill's voice roused me after what seemed to be a very brief rest. There was barely enough time to snatch a few mouthfuls of food and gulp a mug of strong coffee before our struggles of the previous tide were repeated all over again.

If anything, the gale was more severe and the scene in broad daylight enough to scare anybody. Great snarling whitecaps rolling shorewards, piled up in the narrow bottleneck of the harbour entrance where they collided with the torrent of fresh water pouring down from the Mournes. The battling waters turned the little basin into a boiling cauldron seething with foam, swelling above the quays one moment and subsiding the next. The highest seas swilled right over the breakwater into the dock, aggravating the situation.

Trapped in this maelstrom, our little schooner's movements

were so violent it seemed that no moorings could possibly hold her and her masts would be torn bodily out of her tortured hull. The squat stone buildings on the quayside strongly emphasized her wild motions. But, miraculously, everything held through the second tide.

Several times during our daylight struggle to save the schooner, I'd glimpsed local men watching us from sheltered vantage points. It seemed incredible that they offered no assistance although they could see my wife, on the point of collapse, hauling and pulling with us. Apart from Willie McKibbin, who'd acted like a true sailorman, I despised the lot of them. My boyhood image of Annalong was completely shattered.

The last tide had so completely sapped the strength of my small, inexperienced crew that they were in no fit shape to withstand another gruelling night. Before the next tide, the baulks had to go in, with or without official permission. With only the briefest rest, I again searched the mountainside, in the furious wind and rain, for the elusive harbourmaster but I never found him then or afterwards and very much doubt if such a person existed. I'd done my best to avoid antagonising anyone but, in my crippled state, it had been a big effort. I returned to the *Nellie Bywater* dead tired but even more determined to get those baulks in position.

It was already pitch dark and my lads' morale was at breaking point. With difficulty I got them on their feet and hopes of a night's security encouraged them to buckle to on the wet, slippery piers. The hand crane for lifting the baulks was rusty from disuse and many of the massive timbers ill-fitting. Buffeted by the wind and lashed by rain and spray, we were lucky to accomplish our task without accident, for it was difficult to see what we were doing, with our torches but feeble glimmers.

Thankfully, we came to the last baulk, successfully dropped it in place and passed the securing chains. The *Nellie Bywater* was safe for the time being.

Our relief was short-lived. On my way back to the schooner, the mate, who'd remained behind to collect some gear, came dashing up to me in great distress.

'There's a crowd of men on the piers taking the baulks out again!' he yelled above the wind.

As my tired brain grappled with this new development, a gang of tough looking men appeared in the beam of my torch. Their attitude was so menacing, my mate and crew scurried back to the *Nellie Bywater*, leaving me to face them alone. A tall, rawboned fellow, obviously the ringleader, yelled: 'Aye! We're takin' out the baulks so our boats can get in.'

No fishing boat could close the land, let alone attempt to make Annalong in such terrible weather and well they knew it. With an effort, I controlled my anger and tried to reason with them. I told them we'd remove the baulks at the first break in the weather, but it was a waste of breath. The baulks were now nearly all out and their answer was: 'T' Hell wid y'r ould ship. The baulks come out and who's t' stop us?' It was a deliberate taunt to rouse my temper and it did. I was about to attack the speaker when a small figure showed up in the darkness and clutched hold of me. 'Don't do it!' I heard Bill scream. 'It's just what the cowards want . . . a cripple to beat up. Come back to the ship, please.'

I begged her to let go of me and move out of the way so I could tackle the ruffians but she gripped me even tighter and then my madness passed. She was right. I was one against half-a-dozen or more.

Keeping a tight hold on my good arm, she led me back to the *Nellie Bywater*.

I was physically and mentally drained but Bill was now thoroughly aroused. 'We won't let them beat us,' she said. 'There's two hours before the ship floats again. We'll find a magistrate and get him to take our statement of what's happening, then have him sign it. If anything happens to the ship, we'll make those ruffians answer for it in court. Come on, there's no time to waste.'

Buffeted by wind and rain, we set off, first to the merchant's home to obtain the whereabouts of the local J.P. and then up the mountainside to the magistrate's house.

All we succeeded in doing, however, was to get two irritable old men from their beds. The magistrate was the most difficult of the two. We hammered away at his door for some time before he stuck his head out of his bedroom window, yelling: 'Stop that noise! Whatever you want, come back in the morning!' The window slammed down.

We redoubled our knocking until it had the desired effect. A ribbon of light showed beneath the door and we heard the sound of several bolts being withdrawn. The door flew open and a testy voice growled: 'Come in, come in and hurry! You'll give me my death of cold. What do you want at this time of night when all decent folk are in bed?' We stepped over the threshold and the speaker slammed the door to. By the light of the candle he was holding, we saw an irate old man in nightgown and nightcap, glaring at our dripping forms with anger and suspicion. Our brief interview was a failure. The magistrate refused point blank to take our deposition or sign it.

'No, no. I can't do what you ask,' he said plaintively. 'I wouldn't be allowed to live here if I did.'

Sick with disgust, we left the old man to his night's sleep and set off back to the harbour. As we clattered down a narrow street of the silent, sleeping village, Bill stopped suddenly, pointing to a lighted sign reading R.U.C.

'Why didn't we think of it before?' she gasped. 'The police station, they'll have to do something for us here!'

Opening the door, she hauled me into a warm, brightly lit office, where a stout, jovial faced sergeant of the Royal Ulster Constabulary sat toasting himself in front of a blazing fire. He wasn't the least bit surprised to see us, even at that late hour.

'Good evening, Cap'n! Good evening, Ma'am!' he greeted us. 'An what can I do for you?'

For the third time that night we told our story.

'Sure, sure! I know how it is,' he sympathised.

'You mean to say you knew what those ruffians have been doing down at the harbour, tonight, Sergeant?' I asked, unable to believe my ears. 'And you've done nothing to stop it?'

'Tis little I can do, without a proper complaint,' he replied, quite unperturbed. 'Now, it's a different story. I'm a foreigner meself . . . from Liverpool, an' I'll be pleased to take down your statement, Sorr!'

With obvious enjoyment but tantalising slowness, he wrote down our deposition which was duly signed and witnessed. The hands of the station clock showed it was time we were back aboard the schooner, so we hurriedly thanked the officer and left.

Almost running down the hill, we noticed a slight easing of the wind and hoped fervently it wasn't just a temporary lull. True enough, the gale was decreasing at last, but for the remainder of the night there were no noticeable improvements in the harbour conditions. Tommy and the motorman had given up and lay in their bunks, too done in to care what happened. It was the mate, Bill and I who had to save the schooner from damage. The *Nellie Bywater* was unscathed until the last of the tide, when one of the lines to the mainmast parted and with practically the final big surge, the massive half-round timber on the schooner's port quarter drew out of its scarfs and disappeared overboard. I could have wept. Nothing further could be done until daylight so we turned in and slept like logs.

When I awoke refreshed by a few hours' sleep, the wind was reduced to a pleasant breeze and even the sun was shining. We made a leisurely breakfast and then began clearing the raffle from the deck.

A group of local men were on the quayside and the damage to our stern seemed to amuse them. One of them, with a silly grin, called out to me: 'Nasty bit of damage to yer stern, Cap'n. That'll cost a bit to put right. I'll away an' fetch me brother, the shipwright.'

'Mind your own damn business!' I answered, which brought a burst of derisive laughter from his cronies.

At low water we recovered the half-round from the harbour mud and hove it back in place with tackles. A short bus trip to neighbouring Kilkeel in quest of ironwork and coachscrews for completing the repairs turned out to be a pleasure. The blacksmith immediately remembered me as the *Via*'s boy. To attend to my modest requirements, he took staff from their jobs in the fine modern engineering shop which had replaced the old forge. During the wait, my old friend entertained me in his home with a lovely meal and a yarn about the past. The ironwork was finished in record time at a cost which couldn't have paid for the materials. After the recent events, the blacksmith's kindness was greatly appreciated and I returned to the *Nellie Bywater* in a much happier frame of mind. Before nightfall the repairs were completed and the schooner looked no worse for her ordeal.

After being storm-bound down the coast, the Annalong fishing fleet returned to port on the next tide. Captain Chambers and the other skipper-owners of these fine, modern motor fishing vessels were from schooner families, dating back for generations.

They were furious at the way we'd been treated. During the two days we were loading, they showered us with kindness to make up for the inhospitality we'd suffered. Loading was speedy and efficient. When we were battened down and ready for sea, the fishermen invited us to be their guests at the little pub on the quay. It was a happy ending to a most unpleasant experience. During the evening, my wife and crew saw for the first time the real Annalong of my youth and Bill was toasted, time and time again, by its tough seaman, who recognised her courage and spirit.

At breakfast, the following morning, we had a most unexpected caller.

'May I speak with you, Cap'n?' a voice sounded from the companionway.

'Aye, come below. We're eating!' I called back.

Down the narrow stairway scrambled a tall man who I recognised as the leader of the gang who'd removed the baulks.

Looking thoroughly uncomfortable and twiddling with his cap, he said in a bashful voice: 'Tis me, Cap'n. Sure! I'm ashamed of meself about the other night!' An embarrassed pause, then he asked, anxiously: 'Could ye forget ut, now, Cap'n?'

'It's over and done with,' I replied, and we shook hands. The relief showed on his face. I guessed it had taken a big effort to apologise.

When the tide served, we warped the *Nellie Bywater* out of the little dock with the motor winch. A rush of compressed air, ignition, and the Widdop burst into life. Gliding parallel with the pier, the schooner motored slowly out of the harbour. The breakwater was thronged with well-wishers. 'Happy Xmas and the best of luck!' someone shouted. A chorus of farewells and good wishes followed us.

Clear of the pierhead, I brought the vessel on course for the Chickens and faintly over the sea I heard: 'God bless ye, Cap'n. Come back to us!'

15

'Just Around the Corner'

I shall always be grateful to the Chambers, the McBurneys and others for their kindness which helped restore my shattered image of Annalong, but the unpleasant incidents there were to have serious chain reactions later on.

The nerves of the mate and crew had been badly shaken, and this became manifest on our arrival in the Mersey, after a quiet and uneventful passage across the Irish Sea. We ran into dense fog near the Crosby Lightvessel and soon there were sirens and bells sounding all around us. The mate was in such a nervous condition that Bill had to con me through the river traffic up to the dimly lit entrance of the Canning Half-Tide Dock. We were guided to our berth by the voice of a dockmaster we couldn't see for the fog.

Bill's reward for her efforts was a cursing from the dockmaster for missing a thrown heaving line.

'Pipe down, Dockmaster!' I yelled. 'Don't use such filthy language to my wife!'

Next morning, a shocked official came aboard the *Nellie Bywater* to apologise; 'Sorry, Cap'n. Thought it was your ship's boy, it was so thick last night.' We had a good laugh about it, for Bill's small body had been so muffled up against the cold, with a woollen balaclava covering her head and most of her face that the mistake would have been allowable even in good visibility.

Our cargo of granite kerbs was craned out of the schooner at the Liverpool Corporation quay in two days, but I was unable to draw my freight owing to the intervention of the Christmas holiday.

The children were coming over in the *Ulster Prince* in the care of Captain 'Joe' Wilson, her genial master, and we were looking forward to a day or two's peace, re-united as a family, when our troubles began afresh. On the morning of Christmas Eve, the mate packed his bag and left, without explanation or a business discussion. His face was like a thunder cloud.

After breakfast, the motorman and boy requested their discharges so I paid them off, gave them their fares back to Belfast and, at Bill's insistence, added the extra for Christmas dinners for both of them. None of our crew had given any notice of their intentions to leave beforehand, but they were no loss. Unfortunately, they cleaned us out of ready cash until after the holiday.

Our recent experiences had proved it was difficult to operate the schooner without a sailorman as mate. Where to find a suitable sailing ship mate was a real problem and all I could do before Christmas was send a wire to a seafaring friend, asking for his help.

We spent a spartan Christmas without seasonal fare or gifts for the children, who'd arrived safely.

'Don't worry, Daddy,' said Jo, our eldest daughter, when I tried to explain the absence of Christmas dinner and presents. 'We don't mind, really!'

The big, tough padre of the Liverpool Seamen's Mission found me a new motorman on Boxing Day; a cheerful little Indian who was staying at the Mission, awaiting repatriation after paying off a ship in the Mersey. Before leaving the Mission, the padre invited us to dine with him that evening and the four of us enjoyed a superb Christmas dinner with all the trimmings, in the company of a most charming host. Next morning, he sent a bundle of woollens down to the *Nellie Bywater*, 'to keep the Indian motorman warm' as he tactfully put it. There were guernseys, seaboot stockings, mittens and balaclavas, enough for the full crew, and they proved a great comfort to all in the schooner, for the winter turned out to be the severest in living memory.

The padre was typical of the anonymous men of the 'Flying Angel', who perform the difficult and often thankless task of spreading the Gospel to merchant seamen by deeds, not words, in seaports throughout the world.

Boxing Day had been a good day for us; in addition to a motorman, we engaged a strong, clean lad of seventeen, recommended by the dockmaster, and in the afternoon a new mate arrived.

'I'm Potter,' he said in a quiet, cultured voice. 'Your wire was passed on to me.' At this first meeting with the tall, lean, hawk-faced sailorman, I never guessed how important he was to become to us, not only as mate but as a true friend. I'd just fixed the *Nellie Bywater* to load a cargo of bricks and tiles from Connah's Quay to Belfast and it seemed a miracle to be fully manned just in time to sail light to Chester River.

We also had two unexpected visitors; John Henry, the former Rhyl smacksman and his brother Bob, the lighterman, both now well into their seventies. They wanted to inspect the *Nellie Bywater* from stem to stern, and at the beginning it was amusing to watch their reactions. Age hadn't improved them; they were now a pair of gaunt, stooping, lugubrious old men. All I could get out of them as I took them round the schooner was a mournful repetition: 'Well, well, well!' but they couldn't entirely hide their admiration for the vessel. Their misgivings were for her master, and although they didn't say anything, it was quite obvious.

My pleasure at meeting my old friends after so many years was soon evaporated by their gloom, but I consoled myself with the thought that they would soon be gone. Bill made them tea in the cabin and during the meal I incautiously disclosed that we were bound for Connah's Quay in the morning. The result was disastrous. 'Oh dear me!' exclaimed John Henry. 'Oh dearie me!' Alarm and deep concern puckered his lined face. 'Chester River's a very dangerous place. Us knows, as me an' Bob was brung-up there. Oh dearie me! Me an' Bob'll have to come an' show you the way, won't we, Bob?' Dolefully, Bob agreed it was the least they could do for their young friend.

I tried every excuse to dissuade them from coming with us but failed. When they left the *Nellie Bywater*, Bill looked at me with consternation written all over her face. 'We can't have those two miserable old men with us tomorrow,' she complained. 'We've enough to worry about without having them with us!'

'Oh, they won't be with us for long,' I assured her, more hopeful than I felt. 'They only want a busman's holiday and it's just around the corner to Chester River. John Henry's still a tugmaster and Bob's a lighterman, so they shouldn't be any trouble. They were very good to me when I was a little boy.'

'Yes!' she replied. 'And that's the problem. They still see you like that. A few minutes ago they were speaking to you as if you were about ten years of age.'

Of course she was right, and it would have been better for all if I'd heeded her warning, but it seemed churlish to me to refuse the

169

old men the short trip around the Wirral, after the pleasure they'd given me as a youngster.

At dawn the following morning, the moorings were singled-up and the motor warming, ready for leaving the Canning Half-Tide Dock. It was bitterly cold, with a very fresh nor'-easter and a leaden sky. To the very last moment I hoped the old timers would decide against their trip but I was disappointed. Just as we were letting go, they scrambled aboard the schooner and John Henry immediately elbowed me away from the wheel. Resigned to the odd situation, I allowed the old man to undock the *Nellie Bywater*, but our erratic course through the dock entrance nearly gave me heart failure. The two old men in the wheelhouse were in rollicking high spirits as we made sail and clipped down river in fine style. We took the Rock Channel out of the Mersey then our course was through the Hilbre Swash and North Channel into Chester River. We'd timed our departure so as to have ample time for reaching Wild Roads anchorage before the daylight failed, as the Swash was like a dog's hind leg, marked only with unlighted buoys, and the river was even worse, for here the buoys were quite unreliable.

The wind had been steadily backing, with a build-up of low angry-looking cloud on the horizon. It was about two o'clock in the afternoon as we entered the Swash and I was worried by the deteriorating weather. The sky to wind'ard was black as jet and the narrow, tortuous channel was a bad place to be caught out.

Colin, our new mate, came out of the wheelhouse which the two old mariners had tenaciously occupied since boarding us. John Henry was steering with Bob at his side and they were guffawing loudly at some private joke.

I pointed to the muck to wind'ard and advised the mate to stand by the halyards as it was travelling towards us fast.

'Aye, Aye!' he acknowledged, a troubled frown on his face. 'Do you know those two in the wheelhouse have been drinking rum ever since we left Liverpool? They're laughing because I caught them at it and said "There's a strong smell of rum in here" and they answered: "Aye! An' that's all you'll get!"'

So that explained the unusual hilarity of the pair and also the near collision that occurred as we left the Liverpool dock . . . it horrified me to think I'd trusted a couple of 'drunks'. Very angry, I jumped into the wheelhouse and unceremoniously barged John Henry away from the wheel. I was only just in time, for as I grasped the spokes, a shrieking blast of wind struck the schooner, laying her on her beam ends. Although the mate had let all halyards go with a run, the wind struck with such speed and ferocity that the sails wouldn't come down the nearly horizontal masts and stays. With one foot on the wheelhouse side to keep upright on the steeply inclined deck, I'd only a glimpse of the situation before everything was blotted out by blinding snow and pitch darkness. It was a regular blizzard and daylight had gone for good. I knew the mate had done his job with the canvas by the way the schooner righted herself. As I took a quick look at the chart with the aid of a torch, Colin poked his head round the door to advise me that the main was fast and he'd reefed the boom fores'l. 'There's only a close reefed boom fores'l and stays'l on her, now,' he said. 'I've sent the Indian below to stand by the motor.'

I telegraphed for the motor which coughed into life and under power, groped my way by guess and by God through the narrow, twisting gutway towards the invisible Welshman buoy, with the sea picking up fast. The chart had shown an emergency anchorage near the buoy, where the sandbanks provided a little shelter. Colin checked the depths of water with the lead—a difficult task in the rough sea—and when they agreed with the chart soundings we let-go in about six fathoms. After veering out four shackles of cable and readying the other anchor we'd done all we could for the time being apart from praying we wouldn't drag in the very exposed anchorage.

I'd been too occupied to bother about the old men until then. They'd gone to pieces from the first blast of wind. In the torchlight they were a pitiful sight; soaked to the skin and their teeth chattering with cold and fright.

'She'll never hold. There's no anchorage out here! Us're all done for!' they gabbled, despairingly.

'Get below where it's warm and dry, and turn in, the pair of you,' I snapped. 'Colin. Get these two off the deck if you have to carry 'em.'

The mate's size and grim expression had the desired effect. Moaning 'they wouldn't be able to rest when they were in such danger', they were escorted to the fo'c'sle scuttle by Colin, who slammed the slide to after shoving them below.

With the premature darkness so early in the afternoon, the night seemed overlong. The wind had backed right around to the sou'west and settled there, blowing at gale strength. The overfalls over the shoals of the Dee estuary caused a steep and very confused sea. It was bitterly cold and the snow continued until well after midnight. Colin and I kept the long vigil together in the wheelhouse, after sending the motorman and boy below on 'standby'. For the worst of the night, we alternately steered the *Nellie Bywater*, to prevent her breaking sheer and this helped a lot, for she never shifted her position and buoyantly rode out the blizzard.

At intervals throughout the night, Bill struggled from the cabin to the galley to dish up mugs of scalding hot tea and coffee, which were a great comfort. Early in the morning, as the wind eased a trifle I'd a twinge of conscience about our two ancient mariners and decided to take them a mug of tea apiece and see how they were faring.

After the arctic conditions on deck, the fo'c'sle was a haven of warmth and comfort; the bogey well stoked up and the Tilley lamp shedding its bright light on the occupants of the four bunks. John Henry and his brother were buried under the blankets, snoring their heads off, so I didn't bother to wake them. The little Indian and the boy were awake but resting, so I left them the tea.

About 4 a.m. I saw the first star appear in the sky as the heavens cleared. Gradually wind and sea moderated until, by dawn, the weather was fine enough for entering the river.

The sudden blizzard of the previous day had proved one thing; Colin was a cool, fearless and highly skilled mate, who could be relied on in any situation. The motorman and boy had also done very well under such difficult conditions.

I was anxious to learn how Bill and the children had coped in the cabin when the schooner had been knocked down by the first furious squall. 'Oh!' said Bill when tackled. 'The wind came down the stovepipe and blew the fire right out of the grate. The kids and I stood on the bulkhead picking up the red-hot coals and throwing them back into the fireplace and the coal scuttle before they set the cabin alight. It wasn't any good calling for help as I knew you'd all

have your hands full on deck. Then I put the children to bed and
dozed on the settee between making you hot drinks. The children
slept through it all!' This, in a matter of fact voice, as she began
preparing breakfast for nine persons in the little hutch of a deckhouse galley.

As we hove up, the sounds of the windlass pawls roused John
Henry and his brother and they staggered on deck, looking as if
they'd suffered the most terrible hardships.

'Us never slept a wink all night,' groaned John Henry. 'An'
never so much as a mug o' tea, though us was perished an' wet
through!' his brother complained in funereal tones.

'Bloody old liars!' *sotto voce* from the mate.

Under power we entered the river and off Mostyn found a local
motorvessel at anchor awaiting her pilot. Her captain invited us
to lie alongside his vessel until the pilot arrived. He gave us a pluck
up to Connah's Quay when the tide served to save the pilot two
journeys.

Immediately we were tied up, Bill served us a magnificent
breakfast of porridge, bacon and eggs, toast and marmalade, tea
or coffee, all piping hot and prepared and cooked in a way that
would have done credit to any housewife ashore. She served the
old men first.

'Us never eats porridge or bacon an' eggs,' grumbled Bob,
sourly, pushing his plate aside. 'Ain't you got a bit o' saut fish,
Missus?'

'No, I haven't!' replied Bill, curtly. 'That's your breakfast. Eat it
or leave it!' They both left it.

Bill dried out the old men's clothing but their boots were
beyond her. None of our shoes would fit them. To the last moment they moaned and groaned about their pleasure trip which
had turned sour on them. It was with immense relief that we
watched them walking down the quayside, on their way to the
railway station. They looked the picture of misery and I heard
John Henry say to his brother: 'Mark my words, Bob. Us'll both
get pneumonia!'

Their many friends and relations in Connah's Quay were certainly in for a tale of woe about their little jaunt in the *Nellie
Bywater*.

I blamed myself for having them with us but I'd never realised how age had changed them. Perhaps I'd be even more cantankerous if I lived to be their age?

Bill and the children never let me forget my blunder, however. Ever after, when we were leaving port with threatening weather conditions and I minimised the discomforts ahead, I had to listen to three female voices chanting in unison: 'Go on, say it! We're only going "just around the corner".'

About two years later, we had a last brief encounter with John Henry. The *Nellie Bywater* was brought up in the Sloyne anchorage in the Mersey, waiting for the tide to lock-in at Eastham, when a tug towing a string of lighters rounded to under our stern. The gaunt, stooping figure of John Henry emerged from the tug's wheelhouse. To my shouted greeting and enquiry regarding his and his brother's health and wellbeing, he replied in melancholy tones: 'Bob's dead. Never got over that trip with you, he didn't!'

With that parting shot, John Henry vanished into his wheelhouse and the tug with its tow steamed away up-river.

16

Arctic Winter

January, February and March 1947, were the coldest three months I can ever remember on the British coast. Blizzard followed blizzard without a break and temperatures were so low the sea froze solid in little-used estuaries. Throughout this trying spell of bad weather we were trading across the Irish Sea; Connah's Quay to Belfast with bricks and tiles, and scrap metal back to Summer's Steelworks, Shotton. Freight rates for both commodities were so poor that to be weatherbound inevitably meant a loss, yet the weather became increasingly severe each passage, and life was hard in the *Nellie Bywater*. The icing-up of rigging and sails was a constant worry and we were forever freeing frozen running gear blocks and shovelling snow overboard.

The arctic weather had obviously come to stay, so we sent the children ashore to some relatives for the duration of the freeze. We were very thankful for the fine, safe port of Belfast at one end of our Irish Sea crossings as Chester River was truly a desolate spot in such bad weather.

The river was fringed by extensive sandbanks through which there were two approaches; Hilbre Swash to the north and Welsh Channel to the south. Over ten miles long and four miles broad, the estuary was bounded by the low, featureless Wirral peninsula on one hand and the narrow Welsh coastal plain on the other, but navigation was confined to the Welsh side, where the deepest channel lay. Owing to the strong tides and the narrowing of this expanse of water into a bottleneck, the river had a tidal wave; a bore which at times assumed alarming proportions. The inner channel buoys were unlighted and as the bore frequently altered the navigational channel the buoyage was unreliable. The Chester River pilots responsible for the safe navigation of vessels above Mostyn marked the edges of the ever-moving banks with 'withies'. As these temporary markings were swept away by the bore, they were patiently replaced by the pilots, who certainly earned their modest fees.

At Low Water Spring tides, the whole estuary dried out, except for the navigational channel of Wild Roads and the mosaic of

175

rivulets intersecting the glistening, grey mudbanks. Sometimes, channel buoys dried out on the highest part of the shoals which must have prompted a humorist in the past to name one of the buoys the Seldom Seen.

Connah's Quay had been a very prosperous sailing ship port. At the turn of the century, Ferguson & Baird built fine schooners in a yard at the seaward end of the long, piled quay, and there were four schooner owners in the town, Reney, Foulkes, Royle and Coppack.

The waterfront had been a hive of activity with a forest of masts bordering the quay. Gradually the schooner trades declined and although the little port was the cheapest outlet for the products of the North Wales brickworks, the quay was allowed to fall into disrepair. By 1947, all that remained of the former busy waterfront was a tumbled down quay with just a single loading berth served by an antiquated steam crane but, worst of all, the river had been left to silt-up until the channel between Mostyn and Connah's Quay was only deep enough for a loaded schooner near the tops of the Spring tides.

The *Useful*, owner-master Captain John Wynne, was the sole survivor of the former large, local schooner fleet, and her master the last of the hardcase Chester Rivermen. Short, broad, with a face like wrinkled leather, Johnny Wynne was in a very truculent and critical mood when he came to inspect the rival *Nellie Bywater* during our second visit to the Quay.

In colourful language, with frequent pauses to hawk and spit on our clean deck, he informed the mate of his poor opinion of our schooner. Nothing about the *Nellie Bywater* met with his approval.

He began with a derisive comment about the clean deck and burnished brasswork; 'a waste of time, the sea'll wash 'er down!' His opinion of the working gear was that it was too substantial; 'break yer 'earts luggin' yer guts out!' His remarks about the lifeboat were unprintable. Then, with an expression of the utmost contempt he pronounced his final judgement on our vessel; 'an she's as narrer as a weasel!' When he'd stumped away, we were helpless with laughter at his picturesque invective.

The *Useful*, loaded with bricks and tiles for Belfast, was anchored off Mostyn, and a few hours after visiting us Captain

Wynne was outward bound. During the night there was another blizzard in the Irish Sea and the *Useful* was driven ashore at the base of the lofty cliffs near Douglas, Isle of Man. Distress signals from the stricken schooner were unseen.

The heavy seas began to break up the little vessel but her crew managed to jump to a narrow ledge near the bottom of the cliff. In pitch darkness, and blinded by driving snow and spindrift, the exhausted men, nearly paralyzed with cold, struggled inch by inch up the ice-coated cliff face. The mate, Captain Wynne's son, carried the ship's dog which his father had refused to leave to drown. With unbelievable endurance they all succeeded in reaching the cliff top, but fifty yards or so beyond the edge of the precipice they collapsed in the deep snow and would have died there from exposure had it not been for the little dog they'd saved.

A sheep farmer in search of stock trapped in snow drifts heard its whining. He found the unconscious men nearly buried under the snow and summoned help from his farm. The frozen schoonermen were carried to the farm where, with care and attention, they recovered and even made light of their ordeal.

Twenty-four hours later, they were back in Connah's Quay. Captain Wynne's son called to see me as we were loading, and gave me a first-hand account of the wreck and their remarkable escape. When I sympathised with him about the loss of the family schooner, he brushed aside my commiserations and said: 'Oh, Dad'll miss the *Useful*, but I won't. I'll be far better off with a job in the steelworks with a hell of a sight more money for half the work I did in the schooner. And I'll get a proper sleep at night!'

The loss of the *Useful* ended the long and stirring history of Welsh schooners, for Captain Wynne had commanded and owned not only the last Chester Riverman but also the last schooner belonging to the Principality.

The *Useful*'s fate was a grim reminder to us not to take risks in the arctic weather which was becoming even worse. But to remain solvent we were obliged to take chances.

The brick and tile cargoes were F.O.B., so when loading at the Quay, we had to do the stowage. We bottomed out with facing bricks, then stowed roofing tiles on edge above them. The tiles were topped off with glazed earthenware pipes, 4 to 18 in bore, the smaller nesting inside the larger. Working at top speed, it took us two and a half days to load about 140 tons and get battened down, ready for sea. This strenuous work was immediately followed by a sea passage. With the arctic conditions, there were certainly easier ways of earning a living.

At Belfast, we were discharged by dockers. They formed a human chain and, using stages, threw our cargo out entirely by hand. It took them a week to clear our hold and effectively neutralised our own frantic labours to make the cargoes pay. When I suggested quicker ways of discharging, I was bluntly told that this was the traditional method of discharging bricks and tiles in Belfast docks and it couldn't be changed by anybody.

I mentally resolved that I'd find a way to speed things up by some means or another, otherwise bricks and tiles were a dead loss.

Scrap metal, our return cargoes, only took a day to load and under two days to discharge. Before loading began we protected the deck with hatch boards. Then the hold was lined with a generous cushion of baled light scrap. The heavy stuff followed and it could be anything from massive steel girders to heavy engine flywheels, dropped in by a grab. It made a horrible clatter as it fell into the hold and the poor little schooner reeled to the shock. When working scrap, the mate had to be very alert to prevent damage to the *Nellie Bywater*'s wooden hatch coamings.

At Shotton, the scrap was lifted out with a large, circular electro-magnet on the end of a crane wire. It was dropped through a hatchway from a considerable height, picking up a tangle of rusty, jagged metal. The magnet with its dangerous looking attachment was hoisted and swung ashore. A snag when lifting could inflict severe damage to a schooner. I hated scrap cargoes and was always relieved when the last lift had swung shorewards.

My new crew were doing well in spite of the trying weather. The little Indian motorman proved to be a skilful engineer; far too good for a small schooner where, most of the time, he was doing sailor's work. He certainly did his share of handling frozen canvas and iced-up running gear and never complained although the intense cold was a great trial for him. He was so bundled up with clothing, only the top of his face was visible when he was on deck but, whatever the situation, his eyes were always smiling. He was perfectly happy with us for two months and then the authorities arranged his repatriation. He begged me to let him stay but officialdom refused to allow it and they made me responsible for his departure. He sailed from Belfast on the *Ulster Prince* to join his ship at Liverpool and we all missed him when he'd gone.

As a replacement for the Indian, I engaged a Belfast foyboat-man. Jack, a sturdy Ulsterman in his mid forties, had been discharged by his former employers without a reference. I took him on trust, and during the very worst of the winter's weather he proved to be the best motorman we ever had.

Ready for sea, with another cargo of scrap under hatches, we were unable to sail owing to a severe blizzard, the worst to date. For over a week we were held up at a berth near Queen's Bridge, our freight for the scrap being swallowed up by expenses. The master of the packet *Ulster Prince*, Captain Wilson, confirmed that conditions in the Irish Sea were the worst he'd ever experienced.

'Stay where you are, Cap'n, whatever it costs,' he advised. 'You wouldn't get round the Copelands in this nor'-easter. It's difficult even for the *Ulster Prince*.'

Joe Wilson spoke from experience, for he'd been in schooners in his early days. Several times during that winter he'd seen us from the *Ulster Prince* battling our way between Belfast and Chester River, and he greatly admired the hardihood of my wife and children.

During this worrying period of delay, it was most infuriating to read in a newspaper that potatoes were being rationed across the water as supplies were running short. Ulster was full of them, yet we'd failed to get a licence to carry them after repeated attempts, although friends in Kilkeel had offered us regular cargoes if we could get the Ministry permit. Carrying potatoes right up to the War, the *Nellie Bywater* had never damaged a single bag in twenty years of trading, but the bureaucrats were deaf to reason. As a gesture, we bought a ton of best-quality Irish potatoes and loaded them on top of the scrap in full view of passers-by on the Queen's Bridge.

A brief lull in the blizzard allowed us to sail, and we made a fast, very rough passage to Chester River. Off Mostyn, the river pilot hailed us from his boarding launch with the unwelcome news that the river was impassable above that point, being completely frozen to a depth of over two feet.

'Just our luck!' groaned Bill. 'And after all we've done to get here!'

I turned the *Nellie Bywater* down river and motored to the deeper water of Wild Roads as a glum-faced crew readied the anchor. A flurry of snow suddenly blotted out the shores and we just had a glimpse of the N.E. Mostyn buoy before the driving snow reduced visibility to nil. We let-go in seven fathoms, and as the schooner brought up to her two-shackle scope I joined Colin in the bows, advising him to give her another shackle and ready the other anchor.

It was hellishly cold! The biting nor'-easter penetrated right to the bones. I could feel the rheum from my eyes trickling down my cheeks as I helped the motorman furl the stiff, ice-coated sails. Colin and the boy tackled the equally cold job of surging the heavy cable over the windlass barrel. We were all very thankful when our tasks were done and the schooner, with a riding light hoisted on the forestay, was as secure as we could make her for the night.

'Tea's up. Come and get it!' At Bill's summons, we gathered round the galley door, muffling our arms and stamping to restore the circulation in our frozen limbs.

Bill handed out steaming plates of stew and mugs of tea.

'This'll warm you all up,' she said. 'Hurry below before it cools.'

A hot meal in the warmth of the cheerful, lamp-lit cabin thawed me out, but I was very depressed by the unexpected setback of the frozen river. There was the bleak prospect of ten days at anchor in the exposed Wild Roads unless we could get through the ice to Summer's Jetty on the present tides.

'Do you think we can get to the steelworks before the tides take off?' enquired Bill anxiously, reading my thoughts. 'I don't want to worry you but I think I'm starting with flu'; I feel terrible.'

We were all showing signs of strain but my wife looked very ill. It wasn't surprising, as she'd taxed herself to her limits. Throughout the severe weather, she'd helped to keep us all going with a continuous supply of hot, nourishing food and drinks, day and night. Alternately roasting in her tiny, reeling galley and freezing on the gale swept deck, she'd had a tough time. In addition, she was constantly in demand when there were seamarks to be picked up in the bad visibility, for she had the best eyes in the ship.

With great difficulty, I persuaded her to turn-in and mixed her an extra strong tot of rum and lemon. She complained that the toddy was too strong but when I insisted on her drinking it, she got it down with a great deal of coughing and choking.

From the lively movements of the cabin and the gyrating lamp, I could tell the sea was picking up fast on the rising tide. The moan of the wind had risen to a high pitched whistle and the out-of-doors rudder, although checked by a taut kicking strop, kept up a monotonous thumping. With the noises of the wind and sea and every timber of the schooner protesting, the racket in the cabin was enough to waken the dead. In spite of this, by the time I'd donned my heavy-weather clothing, Bill was fast asleep, knocked out by the rum, for when pouring the spirit I'd failed to take into account her exhausted condition. It upset me to see my stalwart partner lying helpless in her bunk, but I'd done the best I could for her under the circumstances. Before going on deck, I turned the lamp down to a glimmer. For the remainder of the night I was fully occupied, attending to the safety of the ship.

By midnight it was blowing a severe gale, accompanied by continuous blinding snow. The nor'-easterly wind against the strong tide of the Dee estuary piled up a vicious, short, steep sea. We veered out extra cable three times, until we were riding to a full scope. As we worked, swirling snowflakes covered our faces and clothing and we were drenched by the sheets of icy spray flying over the rails. The schooner rolled alarmingly, and shortly after one o'clock she broke sheer and lay athwart her cable which sawed up and down her keel and bottom planking. Every moment I expected her to break out her anchor.

We tried every ruse I could think of to sheer away from her cable; using the helm, the motor and a tarpaulin in the rigging but without success. There was nothing further we could do but watch for developments and hope—with our second anchor the last resource. If we dragged, we would drive-down on the dangerous shoals of the estuary where there was no possibility of surviving in such dreadful conditions.

With this dire eventuality in mind, I went below to rouse my wife, to tell her to dress and be ready for any emergency.

She was still unconscious with a blissful smile on her face; shaking, slapping her face and shouting had no effect on her; she was dead to the world and I was obliged to leave her in her bunk.

The lads joined me in the shelter of the wheelhouse, silent and grim-faced. As the *Nellie Bywater* gave a particularly violent snatch at her cable, Jack the motorman muttered, plaintively: 'Aisy now, aisy y' bitch! It's taxin' me strength y' are. Boys oh boys! I'd give me own right haund to be in me own bed in Belfast, right now. I'd be traipsin' after nobody.'

Though oddly expressed, his words just about summed up our feelings. Miraculously, the schooner held her position until high water had passed.

With the ebb tide, we were able to sheer the schooner away from her cable and she lay more comfortably, though rolling heavily. The wind took off a great deal and it stopped snowing. The emergency over, normal anchor watches were resumed.

Another grey, bitterly cold day dawned. The *Nellie Bywater* looked like a polar exploration ship after the night's blizzard. Deep snow covered the deck, drifted to the bulwark cappings on the lee side. Everything had assumed massive proportions with the thick coatings of ice and snow. The running rigging resembled enormous tinsel pendants. Long icicles adorned the eaves of the deckhouses.

From the galley came the sounds of activity and a delicious aroma of bacon and coffee. It was Bill, preparing breakfast as usual.

I overheard the mate asking her how she felt. 'Not bad, thanks to the rum,' she replied. 'Damn this rolling! All my eggs are breaking in the pan.'

All day long we were hard at it, shovelling snow overboard and hammering and banging to clear our iced-up gear. Since the cold spell began we must have shifted tons of snow off the schooner.

Another tide, then as the ebb set in, Colin drew my attention to huge pieces of ice sailing past us. The heavy weather had caused a break-up in the frozen river.

We spent an uneasy night and with the first light began preparing for the passage up-river. Using hatch boards, log fenders and planks, we constructed a stout shield at waterlevel around the schooner's bows to protect them from the ice-floes. We shortened in our full scope of cable to the two-shackle marks. At half-flood we hove up and it required the help of the motor to break the anchor from its stubborn hold on the ground. The river pilot boarded us off Mostyn.

'You'll be the first vessel up since you were last here, Cap'n.' he said. 'We must keep her clear of the big floes. Tell your mate to warn me when he sees one ahead.'

Motoring up the tortuous river, we avoided the heaviest ice, but when we butted the smaller floes, it was as if we'd run full tilt into a dock wall. The ice sliding along the schooner's sides made an ominous grinding sound, but we reached Summer's Jetty with nothing worse than a badly scored waterline.

Even when tied up, there was little peace for us. On the ebb tide, ice commenced piling up between the *Nellie Bywater* and the quay, and to deflect it away from us we had to moor spars at bow and stern at an acute angle to the jetty.

On the next flood it was an extraordinary sight to see the Chester River bore, steeper and more spectacular than usual, roaring up the river, foam-topped and bearing great slabs of ice from the lower reaches. We'd taken precautions with our moorings and stood by when it struck the *Nellie Bywater*. It was like an explosion and over just as quickly. The schooner leapt upward in a great bound, the ropes and wires holding her groaning and creaking with the strain, then the tidal wave had passed. I could well understand why many schooner captains in the past had moored up here with their chain cables.

Ironically, after the discomforts and dangers of life afloat, the first time Bill and the ship's boy set foot ashore, they suffered an equally unpleasant experience. Bill told me she was taking the boy to the shipping grocer at Connah's Quay to replenish her stores which were running low.

'We'll walk round and over the bridge,' she said. 'The grocer will bring us back in his van. We should be back before the men knock off.'

I forgot about them being ashore until discharging finished for the day. As we covered up for the night, it was snowing heavily again and pitch dark. All at once I realised they hadn't returned, and feeling a bit uneasy about them, I decided to walk a short distance up the road to see if the van was coming.

Although equipped with a powerful torch, a few hundred yards away from the jetty I lost the road in the deep snow and several times got into drifts up to my armpits. I was now really worried about the missing pair as it was blowing up another blizzard and it seemed unlikely that any vehicle could make it in such weather. I began to call out at intervals and nearly shouted myself hoarse before I heard a faint reply. I found them floundering in a drift, burdened with two heavy kit bags of provisions. They were completely exhausted, their sense of direction gone.

Relieving Bill of her load, I helped her along but it was a struggle to get them back to the schooner.

'Thank goodness you found us,' said Bill through chattering teeth, as she thawed out in front of the cabin fire. 'The security men at the works gatehouse wouldn't let the van through. When it began to snow we couldn't see and got lost.'

Of course I should never have allowed them to go in the first place. It made me wonder what other unexpected hazards the grim winter had in store for us.

The scrap was out of the schooner the following day and we shifted over the river to Connah's Quay on slack high water. The Quay was a depressing scene; the little crane poking its jib into a leaden sky and the railway trucks containing our next cargo buried under drifted snow.

'Holy Mother of God!' exclaimed Jack, who was visiting the port for the first time. 'If this is Connah's Quay, let's get back to Belfast!'

I'd no intention of lingering for we'd earned nothing with the previous cargo. Bill disposed of our potatoes by selling them at full retail price to her grocer, who was delighted to get them.

'I'll be the only tradesman in the area to have good potatoes for customers,' he told her. 'I wish you'd brought a full cargo. I'd have taken the lot. As it is, I'll be the most popular man in Connah's Quay!'

In short, the situation was absurd. Bill had earned more with the sale of a ton of potatoes than we had received for carrying 160 tons of scrap metal.

Our agent was very pessimistic about loading, when I called at his office. 'The weather's brought everything to a standstill,' he said. 'We can't get water for the crane, as the water supply to the quay is frozen. It'll be almost impossible to get labour for loading your schooner under these conditions.'

It was snowing heavily again as he spoke.

When I pointed out that there was plenty of water in the river and, although brackish, it wouldn't hurt the crane boiler for once, he agreed. I told him we'd load the *Nellie Bywater* ourselves, using our motor winch if needs be, but we weren't going to be held up. He promised to do his best to muster a shore gang and solve the crane problem.

Next morning, loading began with a full shore gang and the steam crane. It snowed continuously, with a biting nor'-easterly wind which made it very unpleasant for the men on the quayside. The bricks and tiles were frozen solid in the railway trucks and had to be broken out in great blocks.

In the shelter of the hold it was still perishing cold and we worked at top speed stowing the cargo which was lowered to us on trays. In two days, the bricks and tiles were aboard, leaving about thirty tons of earthenware pipes to be loaded to complete our cargo.

I was feeling in a more cheerful mood at having overcome the problems of loading, for it seemed as if we were to have a quick turn around after all.

We were hard at work in the hold, stowing the first of the pipes when the hatchman shouted down that somebody wanted to see me. Straightening my back, I climbed out of the after hatch to be confronted by a very ill-tempered man, the owner of a small, local motor vessel.

'My full-powered motorvessel is just coming up the river, light from Liverpool. She has to be loaded and away on these tides,' he said without preamble. 'You know the rules, sail takes second place to power, so move your old windjammer out of the loading berth as I can't afford to have you delay us.'

I could scarcely believe it; the rudeness and cheek of bringing up an outdated custom was bad enough, but the fact that his demand was an impossibility staggered me. At high water the *Nellie Bywater* floated in a bed she'd made in the river mud. Around her was a bank, preventing her from moving for at least another two tides. Irritated by his high-handed manner, I foolishly neglected to point this out and told him we'd move the schooner as soon as possible after we'd finished loading.

The ship-owner lost his temper, abusing me and the schooner.

It was a storm in a teacup, for after completing our loading, we still had to wait for an additional tide before there was sufficient water to lift the *Nellie Bywater* over the bank. The motor vessel had ample time for loading and we were both ready for sea on the same tide. Her owner apologised and we agreed it was the weather that was getting us down.

Bill's health was of deep concern to me. She was suffering from delayed 'flu' and complete exhaustion. When the two children rejoined us just before sailing, I knew she was in no fit state to care for them and cope with her shipboard duties. With great difficulty, I persuaded her to take a short break ashore with relatives who would help her with the children.

As I saw them off at the railway station, Bill's last words were: 'Don't take any risks now we're out of the way! And wire when you arrive in Belfast.' The train pulled out before I could answer.

The *Nellie Bywater*, with the pilot aboard and moorings singled-up, was ready to leave when I returned. Astern, the local ship had her engines running so I told the pilot to let them get away first.

Jack poked his head through the engine-room skylight: 'Can't we make a race of it, Cap'n?' he asked. 'We c'd surely beat tat rusty ould flattie. Man, man! Would ye listen now? They've already trouble with their ingines.'

Jack was right. The rhythmic beat of the motor vessel's engines had changed to an unhealthy coughing, slowed and finally ceased.

We waited no longer. Under our little auxiliary, the *Nellie Bywater* drew away from the snow-covered wharf, rounded the first bend and quickly put Connah's Quay out of sight. The distinctive thump of our exhaust, echoing across the estuary, quickened and increased in volume as the motorman boosted the motor to its limits. The noise was impressive but we gained very little extra speed. There was still no sign of the rival ship following us when we were half-way down the winding channel to the sea.

Jack's head again appeared through the skylight and he scanned the grey, tumbling waters astern.

'Hurroosh!' he yelled, excitedly. 'Where's that full powered motor vessel, now? Boys oh Boys! *Nellie*'ll show 'em a thing or two.'

We all enjoyed the fun but not for long. The local ship appeared around a bend with a bone in her teeth, rapidly overhauled us and passed as if we were anchored.

Jack's face was a study as she went by. We were soon left far behind and she became a mere speck to seaward off the Point of Air.

My concern was the weather. The strong nor'-easterly of the upper reaches was fairly piping through the rigging as we neared the sea. After a succession of gales from the same quarter, I knew the kind of sea that would be running a few miles offshore and I wasn't prepared to face it. If old Tom, the master of the rival ship wanted to try it, good luck to him, for he'd need it. His vessel of about 200 gross tons, didn't look much of a seaboat to me.

I spoke to the pilot, who used his own marks to find us a snug little hole off Mostyn, with just sufficient water to float the *Nellie Bywater* at low tide. Here we anchored.

The lads were bitterly disappointed but soon all was well again for we saw our rival returning through Wild Roads and she went right into Mostyn Harbour.

The pilot, a Bennett, of the well-known Chester River schooner family, had put us in the best anchorage in the river. Although it blew very hard for the remainder of the day and throughout the night, we were safe and not too uncomfortable. With the dawn, the wind took off a bit and the sky looked less threatening.

About midday, the mate drew my attention to the rival ship sheltering in Mostyn. 'Reckon they're being chased out,' he said, handing me the binoculars.

Through the glasses, I could see exhaust fumes puffing from the ship's funnel and her crew busy hauling in moorings. A saloon car was parked on the quayside. A few moments later, I saw the owner leave the vessel's wheelhouse and climb ashore. As Colin had forecast, our rival got under way and steamed out of Mostyn. Jack and the boy were beside themselves with excitement. 'Shall we heave up, Cap'n?' they chorused. 'No,' I replied. 'I'll let you know when I'm ready.'

There were sullen looks and mutterings at this and to make

things worse, Tom steered his vessel in an unnecessary turn around the *Nellie Bywater* and when close under our stern, he leaned out of his wheelhouse window, gesturing seawards with his thumb, a challenge if ever there was one.

'Divil take 'em!' moaned Jack. 'They'll be in Belfast tomorrow. A race, indeed!' He spat over the rail in disgust.

Colin gave him a bleak look. 'They'll find plenty of sea offshore,' he drily remarked. Finding no encouragement there, our crew retreated for'ard to chew me over.

I wouldn't have been human if I'd been unaffected by Tom's attitude or his owner's disparagement of the *Nellie Bywater*, but I wasn't going to let their behaviour cloud my judgement. It rankled, however.

Twenty-four hours later there was a break in the heavy clouds to wind'ard and the barometer had risen slightly. Although there was still plenty of wind the wireless forecast gave an improvement for the weather in the Irish Sea.

'Let's go, Colin!' I said to the mate.

The anchor was hove up in record time. When the sails were hoisted, great lumps of ice fell out of their folds; Jack roared with laughter as the boy dodged the barrage and all traces of their ill-humour had gone. Abeam of the Point of Air, we'd set everything but the tops'ls and were sailing at a real clip. Clear of the black and white striped West Constable buoy, I brought the schooner on course for the Isle of Man. For the first few hours we had a lee from the land and the sea was only moderate. Then, further offshore we began to feel the effects of a week of continuous nor'-easterly gales. On a broad reach, her sails hard and rounded with wind, the *Nellie Bywater* swooped dizzily over big, foam-laced rollers in a welter of spray. Under a lowering sky, the angry sea was an impressive sight, with the horizon a series of massive humps and hollows. The schooner was in her element and for the most part she took the steep combers in her stride, but when one caught her out of step, she staggered.

I was exhilarated by our headlong progress after the frustrations of the past weeks. Jack and the boy were very subdued by the rough sea and there were no further mentions of a race.

I'd never driven the *Nellie Bywater* so hard before, but with a bit of nursing in the squalls, she stood up to her big spread of

19. (*Left*) Bill in cabin companionway. (*Author*)

20. The children assisting with the
early morning deck scrubbing. (*Author*)

21. Bending *Nellie Bywater*'s foretopsail. (*Author*)

22. Crew making up headsail gaskets. (*Author*)

canvas magnificently without shipping heavy water. Studying the schooner's behaviour, my thoughts naturally turned to the rival ship, wondering what progress she could have made under such difficult conditions. I discussed it with the mate.

'She can't have got far,' he reasoned. 'The sea was even worse than this when they left Mostyn. And she doesn't look as if she could take much weather, to me. I expect she's in Douglas!'

The short day ended and through a wild, black night we drove the schooner as hard as she could go. We'd failed to sight a single ship since leaving Chester River as so often happens in bad weather.

The ten-second flash of Langness light, on the Isle of Man, showed up faintly at midnight and from the log reading, we were about ten miles off the point. I let the vessel's head fall off, as the lads eased the sheets, until the wind was on our starboard quarter. I wanted a good offing to round the Chicken Rock. The schooner was sailing very fast with the alteration of course and she was difficult to steer in the following sea.

Colin relieved me at the wheel. Before going below for a quick pipe of baccy and a warm, I told the boy to keep a sharp lookout for the Chicken's light and call me when it showed up.

After the freezing cold and driving spray, the cabin was cosy and warm. Flexing my stiff limbs, I thawed out in front of the fire and filled my pipe. As I lit up, I reflected that we were doing well, so far. It was the first time for weeks that we'd been without snow. I tried to relax but felt nervy and ill-at-ease. After only a few puffs at my pipe, some instinct drove me back on deck, where I sought out the boy to ask him if he'd seen anything of the Chickens. He answered: 'No!' As my eyes became accustomed to the darkness, I searched for the Langness light but failed to find it.

'Where's Langness?' I asked again. The lad replied 'It went out after you'd gone below.' So my senses had warned me correctly that something was wrong . . . it meant either snow or fog over the land, which accounted for the light being so weak when sighted. If the log was under-registering, as it could so easily do in a heavy sea, then we could be closer inshore than my reckoning. Sailing at our present speed, I couldn't afford to take risks.

In the wheelhouse, the mate was having a strenuous time steering, with the schooner yawing badly. I checked the course with him and told him of my suspicions. I said we'd get the mains'l off as quickly as possible. Our course was due West but, as a precaution, I had him fall off a couple of points. Bringing the wind further aft didn't help the steering and the schooner began a vicious rolling.

'Here comes your fog!' exclaimed Colin, as a thick blanket enveloped us, cutting visibility down to a few yards.

I mustered the two lads to tackle the mains'l but as I did so, the rhythm of the schooner's movements altered to a wild, disordered tumble and she began to take solid water over both rails.

Without sufficient experience, Jack and the boy were not much help in the frightening conditions, with the boarding seas sweeping them off their feet. The sail, when half lowered, was pinned against the backstays by the wind and stubbornly refused to come down. Gazing aloft, waiting for one of the violent rolls to ease the sail, I suffered a shock. Almost overhead in the thick haze there appeared a pale incandescence for a few seconds, then it vanished. I saw it again and automatically began counting. The thirty-seconds interval was enough . . . it was the Chicken Rock light.

I clawed my way to the wheelhouse to warn Colin of our close proximity to the Rock and told him to make as much southing as possible.

The next hour was a nightmare. Caught between the run of the steep seas and the backwash off the Chicken Rock, the *Nellie Bywater* was tossed about like a chip of wood. Great dollops of water leaped over the rails from every direction. The racket was indescribable, but above all the other sounds I could hear the ominous metallic clinking of the tiles in the hold. The partially lowered mainsail made the schooner almost unmanageable and it had to come down.

Groping blindly for the peak downhaul, I received a sharp blow in the face, then my neck was encircled in a vicelike grip and I soared aloft, caught in a bight of the downhaul whipped about by the flailing gaff. I knew no more until I hit the deck with a jarring shock and was in such pain I thought my right arm and shoulder had been badly broken. A boarding sea swept me against the wheelhouse and left me at the mate's feet. Before I could tell him what had happened another sea washed me for'ard and deposited me in the waterways.

I think I went temporarily crazy after that . . . picked myself up and muzzled the heavy mainsail practically unaided, for I remember securing the last gasket on a roughly furled sail, although in a state of shock.

Eased by the reduction of canvas, the *Nellie Bywater* gradually crept around the invisible Chicken Rock under the ghostly beam of the lighthouse. The fog-gun kept sounding, the reports coming from every point of the compass with varied volume and distinct echoes at times. I never trusted a fog-gun after that demonstration. Still in a daze, I wondered if the lightkeepers in their lofty eyrie could see us through the fog.

The bearing of the light altered with painful slowness but eventually we gained sufficient offing to scrape around the Chicken.

Later, when we'd gained a lee from the Isle of Man, we reset the mainsail and with much less sea clipped along for the Copelands with the fog left behind us.

Alone at the wheel when I'd relieved Colin, I took stock of the night's events. My 'cracking on' had endangered the ship and I blamed myself for allowing the competitive spirit to take over. The mate's steadiness under extreme stress had been the main factor in avoiding disaster. When I'd tangled with the downhaul my neck would have been broken but for the many thicknesses of the rucked hood of my duffle coat and although my throat was terribly swollen and my voice nearly gone, I'd got off lightly. The most fortunate part of the incident was the result of my heavy fall to the deck. Instead of suffering further injuries, my right arm and hand, which had been partially paralyzed since the War and had resisted hospital treatment, now seemed to be working normally. The drastic treatment of a severe blow had cured my painful handicap, but only time would tell if it was a permanent recovery. It was a miracle to me to be so unexpectedly relieved of one disability.

The *Nellie Bywater* arrived at her usual berth in the Clarendon Dock, Belfast on the evening's tide. There was no sign or news of the rival motor vessel but I'd lost interest in her whereabouts. My sole concern was the state of our cargo, for I fully expected a rubble of broken pipes and tiles after hearing the racket from the hold off the Chickens. To my surprise and relief, when we stripped the hatches the following morning, we found the cargo to be practically undamaged due to careful stowage and extra straw dunnage being used when loading. There was a lot to be thankful for.

There was a telegram from my wife at the agents'. It read: "Get us to Belfast immediately. Sailing tickets unavailable. Don't fail me. Bill."

It was almost as if she knew of our narrow escape.

Captain Wilson of the *Ulster Prince* kindly came to my rescue, so when the packet berthed opposite to us next morning, Bill and the children were with the first passengers down her gangway. Beforehand I'd briefed the lads to keep their mouths shut about the Chickens.

After the usual five days of discharging, we'd just finished cleaning ship when our Chester River rival steamed into the dock and berthed astern of us. As soon as she was alongside, Tom, her master, jumped ashore and made for the *Nellie Bywater*.

'How the hell did you get here?' he demanded as I welcomed him aboard.

'Where have you been hiding, Cap'n?' I countered. 'We've been here a week and thought you'd changed your mind about coming.'

Seeing the furious expression on the old man's face, I hastily added: 'No offence meant, Cap'n! Come below and have a drink.'

Still smouldering, Tom followed me down to the cabin where I introduced him to Bill. Over a drink and a pipe of baccy, I carefully explained there was nothing personal about our rivalry.

'But where have you been all this time, Tom?' I persisted. 'We're completely discharged.'

The old man seemed about to choke. 'Sheltering in the Menai Straits, of course,' he almost spat. 'You're young and foolish, that's what you are . . . young and foolish!' He returned to his ship, still muttering his poor opinion of me.

Bill had listened to our conversation without comment until we were alone, then she tackled me: 'Come on, out with it . . . what have you been up to while I've been away?'

I told her the full story, including our near miss of the Chicken Rock. When I'd finished, she said: 'Tom's right. You're crazy. You won't get me ashore again so easily. But, did you see Tom's

192

face? I'd like to see his owner's when he hears we were discharged before his vessel arrived. Full-powered motorship, indeed! I'm glad we beat 'em.'

The arctic weather was going but the gales persisted. Ships that normally carried deck cargoes had been unable to do so for months. Because of this, we were offered a most unusual charter for a schooner—baby prams to the Clyde. The prams were in open-work crates consigned to Glasgow, but I arranged with the manufacturers to deliver them to Bowling where I could discharge with my own winch and crew, thus cutting down their costs. The Belfast dockers seemed to think our cargo amusing and as they were finishing loading, they landed the last crate on deck by Bill's galley.

'This one's for you, Missus!' exclaimed the burly hatchman, which caused his mates to guffaw loudly.

There was a brief lull in the strong winds when we left Belfast, but it was soon over. Half-way across the North Channel we were hit by gale-force nor'-easterlies and torrential rain squalls.

With so little weight in our hold, the schooner had the high free-board of a light ship and was in poor trim for beating against a headwind. In the steep sea that rapidly got up we made slow progress under reefed main, boom fores'l and stays'l assisted by the motor.

Just before the weather broke, I'd noticed a steamer of about five hundred tons ahead of us, holding the same course. After it began to blow hard, I sighted her several times between squalls, rearing and plunging into the headsea, with dense black smoke pouring from her funnel as her stokers did their best to give her maximum speed. I saw my crew casting envious looks in her direction while she was still visible and I guessed their thoughts, for we seemed tied to the Killantrigan light on Black Head and were scarcely moving over the ground.

Wind and sea worsening, we had to battle every inch of the way to the red and white flashing light of Corsewall Point, where reluctantly, I decided to seek shelter in Loch Ryan. We were in bad trim for closing the lee shore of Arran.

Going about, we were hours making the loch and had to sail up to Stranraer to find a safe anchorage. Even at the head of Loch

Ryan the schooner rolled violently during the four days we were there. It was very uncomfortable, but the ship's work went on as usual, Bill fully occupied in the cabin and galley, the motorman servicing and polishing in his engine-room and the mate and boy sujiing paintwork. Well muffled-up, the two children spent most of their time fishing over the half-round.

We were all impatient to be on our way. The motorman and boy had short memories and still hadn't learnt their lesson, for I overheard them making snide remarks about the steamer we'd seen in the North Channel, saying she'd have reached Glasgow, turned round and would be back in Belfast while we were still at anchor.

We got under way immediately the wind eased enough for us to make the Cumbraes, but it was a slow uncomfortable passage up the Firth. Between Bute and Little Cumbrae, I sighted a recent wreck at the foot of Garroch Head and she was easily recognisable as the steamer we'd seen in the North Channel four days earlier. She appeared to be a total loss; badly battered, with her bottom plates gaping where the jagged rocks had torn them asunder. There was a shocked silence from all aboard the *Nellie Bywater* as we gazed at the pathetic, salt-stained hulk of a fine steamer, and I was thankful I'd been prudent enough to seek shelter.

Under all plain sail, we made excellent time up the smooth waters of the Clyde to Gourock, where the river pilot boarded us. In spite of a fair wind, he immediately ordered the canvas to be taken in and we crawled the remainder of the way to Bowling with our small auxiliary motor.

When I 'phoned the Glasgow merchants to inform them of our arrival, a bewildered voice answered me: 'But, Cap'n,' it said, 'We'd given our prams up as lost. We heard a small ship had been wrecked on Bute during the gale and naturally thought it was the *Nellie Bywater* as she's only a sailing vessel.'

I assured the speaker that his goods were safe and sound, if a few days late in delivery, and we were anxious to discharge as soon as his transport was available.

A fleet of vans arrived shortly afterwards. I was below when the man in charge came aboard and he tackled Bill in the galley.

'You've been the hell of a time getting here, Missus!' he said.

'Reckon you've had enough time to have filled one of the prams yourself!'

It only took a couple of hours to land the cargo with our motor winch and when light, we were off again down the Clyde, Belfast bound.

17

The Human Element

The final repercussion of our early visit to Annalong hit us just as the severe winter ended. Until then, we'd held our own. Arriving in Belfast, light, on an early morning tide, I was so tired that after mooring up, I fell asleep, fully dressed, on the cabin settee. A knock on the companionway roused me.

The caller announced that he was the Admiralty Marshal and he was arresting the *Nellie Bywater* under the instructions of lawyers acting for our absent partner. I was so stupefied by lack of sleep I could scarcely comprehend what was happening. But not so Bill, who'd followed me on deck.

As the Marshal attached the writ to our mainmast, she tried to tear it down. When I restrained her from committing this unlawful act, she turned like a tigress on the lawman and it took all my strength to stop her doing him serious harm. My placid little wife was desperately angry.

The writ was so ambiguously worded it made little sense. The purpose of it will always remain a mystery to us. We offered personally and through lawyers to return our partner's total investment but the offers were refused.

We found ourselves embroiled in a legal battle as unexpected as it was unnecessary. To our amazement and dismay, our erstwhile trusted friend had mustered such a formidable array of legal strength against us that we couldn't afford to match it. Nevertheless we were determined to fight to the last for the little schooner which had brought us safely through that awful winter.

I remembered as a small boy, seeing a big four-masted schooner under arrest in the Liverpool docks. I'd been shocked by her forlorn, neglected appearance; her topsides an ugly rash of dirty white peeling paintwork, her brasswork green with verdigris and her spacious decks foul with uncollected refuse. She'd such an air of shame about her, I couldn't get away fast enough, but she haunted me long afterwards. I vowed this shouldn't happen to the *Nellie Bywater*.

Unlike other schooners, the *Nellie Bywater* was our home as well as our means of livelihood. When she was arrested, the children cried.

Day after day, we confronted the lawyers in their musty, depressing chambers but got nowhere. The case wasn't to be heard in court for nine months.

To keep up our morale, between legal commitments we beautified the schooner until she was as trim as a yacht, with spotless deck and paintwork, burnished brass and Flemish coiled gear. It helped to work off our frustrations.

When everything else failed to break the deadlock, I paid a visit to the Law Courts. I'd been brought up with a high regard for British justice and my faith was justified. A very high person of the Admiralty Division gave me a hearing and intervened. His mere voice scattered the lawyers like chaff before a wind and in less than twelve hours the schooner was freed of all legal and financial encumbrances. We'd bought the interest of our former partner and now owned the full sixty-four shares of the *Nellie Bywater*. It was my first glimmer of hope that integrity hadn't entirely disappeared from the post-war scene.

The unpleasant business had been a shock, particularly the loss of a valued friendship, but our troubles had their bright side. Our new Belfast friends had stood by us throughout our difficulties. Outstanding was a young businessman and all-round sportsman Vic, who gave us the most practical help. What you lose on the swings, you gain on the roundabouts!

During the lay-up we kept our crew intact, but the boy began to lose interest so I shipped him back home. Jack, the motorman, had been planning to start his own foyboat business and when Robertson's, the collier owners, offered him a good contract we gave him every encouragement. He'd transformed our engine-room into the cleanest and smartest I'd ever seen in a schooner. The motor looked really handsome; crankcase and cylinders enamelled Gardner grey, fuel, oil and air lines in separate colours and the brass, copper and steel brightwork gleaming. I don't personally care for machinery but I was quite proud of our 'iron tops'l'.

Jack refused to leave us until we'd found a suitable replacement.

Frank, the new motorman, came from a small River Lagan motor barge and was in poor physical shape when he joined us. He admitted he was a hard drinker, so I told him what would happen if he ever became a nuisance in front of Bill or the children. We found him to be a typical Ulsterman; fearless, unpredictable, a hard worker, generous to a fault, with a complete disregard for the laws of the Establishment. He had a permanent limp from an accident, and had been awarded £2,000 compensation which he and his friends drank away in a few months, he proudly informed us. For a time his behaviour in the *Nellie Bywater* was exemplary and, one day, he told Bill that the schooner was the first real home he'd ever had; that he'd never eaten so well before.

I fully anticipated trouble from his drinking but I only once saw him drunk. It was on a summer's evening in Belfast when I was alone in the schooner, doing something or other in the wheelhouse. I espied Frank weaving down the dockside, obviously the worse for drink. He stopped at the schooner's rail, swaying about with a look of great concentration on his flushed face. I could read his thoughts . . . 'if I go aboard like this, the old man'll crown me. Better sober up a bit, somewhere!' He staggered away behind some timber stacks for about an hour and when he returned, he boarded the *Nellie Bywater*, making a comparatively straight course for his quarters.

So far, I'd kept well out of his sight but after allowing him a breather, I followed. He'd passed-out at the foot of the fo'c'sle ladder, so I removed his shoes and outer garments, hoisted him into his bunk and left him to sleep it off. It reminded me of the many times I'd assisted fuddled shipmates in a similar way during my early seafaring.

Next morning, Frank was going about his work with a very anxious expression on his face. At length, he blurted out: 'Did I make a nuisance o' meself last night, Cap'n? I feigned surprise at the question, as if unaware of his lapse and for some reason this had him really worried. Whatever was on his mind, it effectively stopped any reoccurrence of his drunkenness aboard the *Nellie Bywater*.

About this time, we began to have difficulties in keeping our ship's boys. I was annoyed by the frequent changes as we provided excellent food and conditions for the lads although the work was hard. At first, I thought the boys were soft and work-shy when they left but, later, I became suspicious of our motorman. From the mate I learned that Frank was a practical joker with a most peculiar macabre sense of humour. In his native village on the shores of Loch Neagh, he'd become adept at playing on the nerves and superstitions of simple countryfolk by attending every possible 'wake' and contriving a variety of weird, supernatural happenings to alarm the mourners. Soon after joining us he got up to his tricks with our naive boys. One lad was frequently disturbed in his sleep by a cold, clammy hand touching his face and Frank convinced him that the schooner was haunted by the ghosts of long-dead seamen. The terrified boy left us without an explanation, following an incident at sea, when the motorman, enveloped in a sheet, had appeared from behind the heads on a wild, dark night.

Our next boy had another heartless joke played on him. We were homeward bound for Belfast with a fresh, favourable wind and the *Nellie Bywater* was snoring along with an impressive bow wave. It was a bright moonlight night and a big school of porpoises gambolled in the foam and spray from the cutwater. Some of the creatures must have been well over twelve feet in length.

According to the mate, after sighting the big mammals Frank went below and seeing the youngster dead to the world in his bunk he couldn't resist having some fun at his expense. He apparently hissed in the sleeping boy's ear: 'Wake up. Wake up, ye little so-an'-so! The sharks have come t'make a meal of ye!'

He propelled the only half-awakened boy on deck and pushed him close to the rail so that he'd have a good view of the playful sea monsters. The ignorant lad truly believed the sea was full of man-eating sharks and was so frightened that he left us as soon as we'd berthed in Belfast.

He was followed by a tall, thin, gangling youth with little aptitude for seafaring but the most voracious appetite I've ever encountered. He had Bill in despair. At considerable expense, she fed the crew with good-quality, well-cooked food, as if they were her own kith and kin. On full seamen's rations they ate their fill but that boy's stomach was bottomless. Victualling costs soared and I was seriously considering 'firing' him, when to our great relief, he left of his own accord. It was, of course, Frank's doing.

He'd thought out another gag for his new victim. During the dark nights when on passage, he'd wait for the boy to finish his watch on deck and turn in. As soon as the tired youngster was sound asleep, Frank crept stealthily down to the fo'c'sle and altered the hands of the clock to 'one bell', the end of the lad's off-duty period. He then roused the boy, who'd only been ten to fifteen minutes in his bunk, and sent him back on deck. The poor kid was too drowsy to realise he was being tricked and was soon in a most exhausted state. It was a stupid prank, like all the others, and when I discovered what the motorman was doing, I put a stop to his crude japes, although in this particular instance, he'd done us a service.

Crews we could cope with but dockers were another matter. **Their** dilatory loading and discharging neutralised all our efforts. In Belfast, the slow discharge of the brick and tile cargoes made them unprofitable, so, with the mate's assistance, we devised a simple conveyor belt worked off our motor winch to cut the handling of the cargo to a minimum. There was consternation when we rigged it.

'Glory be t'God!' exclaimed the hatchman, regarding the belt with alarm and suspicion. 'An' what's that bloody contraption, may I ask?'

I explained that the conveyor would do away with the long chain of men laboriously throwing up the cargo by hand. It only needed feeding in the hold and emptying on the quay and should cut the work time by half.

There were cries of anger from the gang gathered round to hear my explanation.

'It'll do us all out of a bloody job!' shouted one.

'Aye, let's call the whole port out on strike, starting with Harland and Wolfe's!' yelled another.

'There ye are, Cap'n,' said the hatchman. 'The lads won't wear it. It'll mean a strike if you insist on using that thing!'

I told him I could no longer stand a week for discharging. 'How would you lot like to sail in a schooner and have nothing at the end of it?' I asked. 'Is that the best a great crowd of strong fellows like you can do? . . . A week to clear a little schooner? . . . Shame on you! Me and my three lads could do it in three days.'

'That you couldn't!' asserted the hatchman. 'You won't find better lads than mine, anywhere. If you take that bloody thing away, maybe we cud knock a bit of time off for you, Cap'n.'

'Right! Every man gets a pint from me each time you clear us under three days,' I answered.

That did the trick. Their anger turned to smiles. We removed the offending conveyer belt and the dockers turned to with a will, discharging us in two and a half days. They earned their pints. Ever afterwards they cleared us in the same good time, though they still took a week for other ships. As their hatchman had said, they were grand workers; the best we ever had in any port and as tough as they were efficient.

Once, when they were working us, I happened to look into the hold and saw the gang was smaller than usual. Many of the men had minor injuries which were bandaged and some had black eyes, yet there was such hilarity among them that it aroused my curiosity.

'Looks as if they've been in a battle! Where are your other lads?' I asked the hatchman.

He chuckled. 'Battle's the right word for it, Cap'n. My lads all come from the same street and, last night, one half of the street took on the other half . . . one crowd wid hammers, the others wid axes. Three of the lads are now up at the police barracks and a few're in hospital.'

I called down the hatch, 'Who won?', which brought up-roarious laughter and typically Irish quips from the men below. In spite of the many injured it was obvious there were no hard feelings and they were all the best of mates again.

Rough and tough as they were, they always showed the greatest respect for Bill and the children. If my wife or the kids were about the hatchman would immediately sing out: 'Pipe down, lads! The Cap'n's missus' or 'kids are on deck.' . . . and the bad language ceased at once.

The best incident I can recall was when Bill—all five feet of her—took on the eighteen-stone boss stevedore.

The dockers were about to use a big grab in our small after hatch. Operated carelessly, it could severely damage the hatch coamings and side decking, so I stood by to overlook things as the mate was ashore. Just as work began, I was called away to the

Custom House and left Bill with strict instructions to stop discharging if it was being done without proper care.

I was barely out of sight when the grab hit the wooden coamings with a terrific bang, stripping away some of the metal bindings. Bill immediately stopped the dockers who sent for their boss. He arrived in a very ugly mood, using the most hair-raising language to my wife. Bill stood her ground and refused to allow the work to continue until I returned. From those who were present I was given various accounts of what had occurred but I couldn't believe the claim that she'd out-cussed their boss.

Her own version, however, was obviously an understatement: that she'd had a bit of a row with the stevedore; her face was very flushed when she spoke of it, but the important point was that she'd prevented further damage to our schooner.

The stevedore had gone after the 'row' and I didn't meet him until the job was completed. I expected trouble when he hove in sight, but instead his tough face was wreathed in smiles and he'd nothing but praise for Bill.

'Tis a fine woman ye have, Cap'n!' he exclaimed admiringly. 'A wife who looks after her man's property in his absence is indeed a treasure. If it's any help you and your missus need at any time, you can depend on me.'

A situation which reminded me of an early Wallace Beery-Marie Dresler film had made us yet another friend on the Belfast waterfront. In fact, the boss stevedore bore a remarkable likeness to film actor Beery.

We were always happy to be in Belfast for it was a most friendly port, though no better than anywhere else when chartering the *Nellie Bywater*. Brokers and merchants gave us a very rough ride and we'd little to thank them for. We kept our heads above water solely by our own initiative.

Repeated applications to the Food Ministry for a licence to carry potatoes all received the same parrot-like reply: 'the *Nellie Bywater* is too difficult to load and discharge and too slow'. When I appealed to the British Legion to press my case, the decision remained unaltered.

The Fuel Ministry were more subtle about a coal licence. I was invited to meet their official and he produced a bulky list of places

202

needing coal supplies, ticking off with a pencil a dozen of these on the typewritten sheets.

'There you are, Cap'n!' he said with an insincere smile. 'You can carry to all those places.'

The spots he'd assigned us were, without exception, tiny towns and villages situated on the west coast of Ireland and not one of them had a safe harbour. They were wide open to the Atlantic and for much of the year would be unapproachable.

Hiding my disgust with difficulty, I told him we'd take half of these dangerous places if he'd allocate us an equal number of sheltered ports.

'Sorry, but those are all fixed,' was his reply; a faintly veiled 'brush-off'.

It was perfectly clear that our two main trades were permanently closed to us by the bureaucrats. We fared poorly at the various brokers as they had little interest in an out-dated sailing vessel when there was modern tonnage available. I had to make a tiresome walk into the city each time I deposited the ship's papers at my agents, as their premises were a long trudge from the docks. The papers were accepted by a clerk in a bleak, functional office lacking any atmosphere of the sea and ships. A time when the principal of a firm personally welcomed a master was long past.

In some offices, business was transacted at a counter, but I remember one where the clerk sat at a desk and against a wall was a row of hard, wooden chairs for waiting captains. Most of the anxious-faced mariners I saw there were company captains awaiting their owner's orders. Looking ill-at-ease in their shore rig, they resembled patients in a doctor's or dentist's waiting room rather than commanders of merchant vessels, responsible for valuable ships' cargoes and the safety of their crews. The supercilious clerk, juggling with two telephones, wasted little time with any of us. When I was offered a 'fix' it was rarely worth having; generally an unprofitable cargo rejected by other shipowners. We'd have starved if we'd depended on agents so I was continually searching for new sources of employment for the schooner, or trying to re-open old trades independently. It was clear that the days of the master-owner were nearly finished.

Our efforts with the *Nellie Bywater* didn't go un-noticed by

203

seafarers, however. One summer evening in Belfast, some unexpected visitors arrived.

The dockers had cleared us early in the day and the *Nellie Bywater* was good to look at after her usual scrub down and brass polishing.

In the cool of the evening, I was having a quiet pipe of baccy on deck when I noticed a group of elderly men approaching the schooner. They bore the unmistakeable stamp of the older generation of shipmasters, soberly dressed for the shore.

Abreast of me they stopped and one of them addressed me most courteously: 'Good evening, Cap'n. May my friends and I come aboard?'

'Certainly,' I replied, very curious to know the reason for their visit.

Solemnly they filed aboard the *Nellie Bywater*, looking like a deputation, which was just what it turned out to be.

'We're all masters of ships lying in the port,' explained a grizzled old mariner. 'As senior, my friends have asked me to be their spokesman. We were having a drink together this evening and we were discussing you and your smart little schooner. It was unanimously agreed that we should pay you a visit before returning to our ships, to meet you personally and congratulate you on the way you sail and maintain your vessel. We're glad to meet a man who keeps alive the old traditional ways of seafaring.'

One by one they shook my hand, murmuring gruff compliments, then filed ashore.

Unaccustomed to praise, I was frankly very embarrassed by the commendations of such old and experienced masters, but, looking back, I think it was about the nicest and kindest action I've ever met with in the course of my life.

18

Tramping

When scrap metal and bricks and tiles failed to give us a fair return, we decided to go 'seeking'.

We began tramping with a cargo of moulding sand for the railway foundry, Dublin. When loading finished, our nine-year-old daughter Inga climbed into a filled hatchway with her bucket and spade and began making sandcastles. To our amusement, Jo, her elder sister, joined her when she discovered the remarkable modelling qualities of the sand. Hitherto, she'd been behaving in a very grown-up manner for a thirteen-year-old. It was nice to see her drop her adult pose and enjoy playing in the sand with her sister until we covered up.

It was a pleasant sail to Dublin with fine sunny weather and light to moderate winds.

For the first time, I'd given up trying to find a ship's boy who would stay and profit from a period in sail. In the meantime, the children kept the brasswork bright and helped their mother in the galley. They were natural little sailors, deserving their nickname, 'the *Bywater* kids.' Healthier or happier children couldn't have been found anywhere and their pride in the schooner equalled our own.

We made a few basic rules for their safety; they had to keep off the deck when we were loading or discharging and during bad weather at sea; the rigging, engine-room and winch-house were out-of-bounds. They obeyed unfailingly.

Inga, an agile climber, must have been sorely tempted by the rigging. In her inimitable fashion she found a way to abide by the rules yet satisfy her longings for heights. Whenever her best friend the mate climbed aloft to do his periodic inspections, she was on his back, clinging there like a little monkey. Jo disapproved of such bending of the rule but was very tolerant with her extrovert sister.

Both children enjoyed helping with the daily early morning deck scrubbing when the weather was fine, as it was on passage to Dublin. If warm enough, they turned out in swim suits and the mate from time to time would purposely misdirect the contents of his drawbucket so the water splashed over them instead of the deck, causing squeals of alarm and laughter. The children thrived on the clean, unpolluted salt air and the uncomplicated life in a schooner.

We berthed alongside the North Wall in the Liffey and our cargo was speedily discharged. It was a pleasure to find that Betson, our Dublin broker, still carried out his business with the same friendly courtesies of the old days. He fixed us with River Plate wheat to Waterford.

Dublin, always a city of contrasts, appeared startlingly different to us as we'd become accustomed to the bleak austerity of post-war Britain. The smart stores, tea-shops and restaurants of Grafton and O'Connell Streets and the city centre were crammed with luxury goods and expensive foods we'd nearly forgotten ever existed. Bill and the children had a wonderful time window-shopping.

But not far from this state of affluence, there was unbelievable poverty and misery.

Just up-river of our berth stood the historic Custom House, its south façade a vast stone-stepped Doric colonnade. Every evening just after dusk, the homeless of the city gathered there to find a space on the steps for a night's sleep. Human derelicts of both sexes, young and old, huddled together, occupying every inch of the classic portico. We were shocked, especially the children, by such large-scale distress.

Our few days in Dublin were very pleasant but we couldn't afford to linger. When the wheat cargo was available we loaded in the Alexandra Basin and immediately sailed for Waterford. It was a slow, wet uncomfortable passage with strong unfavourable winds and grey sea and sky. As soon as we were in Waterford, the sun reappeared and the weather was perfect during our stay there.

The brokers received me cordially and I asked them to try to fix us with pit-props, Youghal to Garston, when we were clear of the wheat. They promised to do their best. As bread was rationed in Eire, I enquired about permits for the schooner.

'Bread permits for ships are issued by the Civic Guard. I'll ring them to say you're coming, Cap'n,' said the broker helpfully.

As I entered the Civic Guard barracks, a burly sergeant, with his back to me, was speaking into a telephone.

'No, no. I won't let the furriners have any! Coming here an' taking' the very bread out of our people's mouths!' I heard him say.

He turned and saw me standing there. Knowing I'd overheard this ridiculous outburst, he looked very abashed and in some confusion made out the necessary cards.

Powerful suckers cleared the *Nellie Bywater* of her grain cargo in a day, but we remained in Waterford hopefully awaiting news of the Youghal pit-props.

There was an air of lethargy about the little port that reminded me of Spain, as we found it difficult to pin anyone down to a definite time for anything. Our water tank needed refilling, but each time we arranged to move across the harbour to its only water point, we were informed the berth had already been taken. In the end, we were obliged to bucket a few days' supply from a tap nearly a quarter of a mile away. It was a case of no water at Waterford!

To curb our impatience when waiting, we took the children for a days outing to Tramore and one evening paid a visit to the local cinema. Part of the programme consisted of Nazi war films and included one of Hitler's rallies at Nuremburg which was enthusiastically received by the audience. There was prolonged applause as it ended and Bill's face was a study when the lights went up. From that moment it dawned on me why we were getting such poor co-operation and I realised we were wasting time hoping for the Youghal cargo. We wouldn't get pit-props or anything else in this part of Eire.

A phone call secured us a brick and tile cargo, Liverpool to Belfast, loading in a week's time, so we decided to call in at Holyhead, on our way to Liverpool, to see if there was any possibility of re-opening the once brisk schooner trade in Welsh slates from Port Dinorwic.

On the point of leaving Waterford, a young man begged me to give him a job. He told me he was from Cheek Point, a tiny village on a bend of the River Suir and had been working in their pulling fishing boats. He was a strong-looking lad of eighteen years but was very ragged and dirty. I liked him immediately despite his poverty-stricken condition and offered him the 'boy's' job which he gladly accepted. Before allowing him below, I ordered him to strip and have a thorough scrub down with hot water and carbolic soap. His filthy rags were dumped overboard and Bill rigged him out with some of my clean working clothes. Cleaned up, he was handsome and even his mop of curly, dark hair had changed to a beautiful red gold after washing, to the surprise and delight of the womenfolk.

We dropped down the Suir, with the local pilot, after dark. As we rounded Cheek Point, the shore was ablaze with bonfires and waving torches. The pilot explained it was a send-off for Michael, our new lad. It was an old custom to do this when Cheek Point boys first left home to become seafarers. Nearly all the young men of the tiny village became merchant seamen. Shouts of farewell and good wishes followed us until we were out of earshot.

We crossed the Irish Sea with light southerlies, in warm sunshine. Two new sails were given their first airing, a maintops'l and a triatic stays'l. It was part of our plans for restoring the *Nellie Bywater* to full rig as funds allowed. Our next targets were yards, square sails and gear for the foremast, but it was several months before we could afford these.

With perfect weather, I allowed the children to steer for a time. Both knew the compass and were natural helmswomen. Jo had a very sensitive touch on the wheel and, but for her lack of strength, could have taken a trick at any time. Her young sister had to stand on a box to see over the binnacle rim and look up at the sails, but she corrected her course with the confident air of an old shellback. I realised for the first time how the children were growing up.

Anchoring in the famous harbour of refuge, Holyhead, I was reminded of the changed times, for we were the only vessel brought up in the fine spacious outer harbour.

To explore the possibilities of slate cargoes, Bill and I were landed with the schooner's boat and travelled by train to Port Dinorwic, but it was a wild goose chase. The once lucrative slate trade was completely finished. During our journey, the weather had broken and we lost no time in getting back to Holyhead, to find conditions in the harbour so bad that the R.N.L.I. lifeboat had to ferry us out to the *Nellie Bywater*.

Although it was only August, we'd seen the last of the summer weather. Strong to gale force nor'-easters made it difficult for us to reach the Mersey in time for our charter. We battled against high winds and sea until in sight of the Bar lightship, only to be driven back to Point Lynas where we ran back for the shelter of Holyhead.

At a second attempt a tide later, we succeeded in reaching the Mersey but were unable to dock owing to the gale's severity. From our anchorage in the Sloyne we watched a big tanker, on her way to the Dingle Oil Jetties, blow ashore on a sandbank in spite of the frantic efforts of four tugs which were attending her. It required eight tugs to refloat her when conditions had improved. The wind eased and we berthed in the Canning Dock just on time for loading.

Although there were sufficient dockers in our hold for a thousand-tonner, work proceeded at a snail's pace. Instead of working outwards from the mainhatch, they began loading through the afterhatch so that the *Nellie Bywater* developed a big list to starboard and was well down by the stern.

Looking into the hold to find the cause of a long pause in the loading, I was horrified to see half the gang lying in the straw dunnage, smoking. The fire risk was so great, I lost my last shreds of patience and dressed them down in the language they would understand. The cigarettes were extinguished.

Still fuming at the men's stupidity, I turned to find my old father on the dockside. He'd always strongly disapproved of swearing and from the expression of agony on his face it was obvious he'd heard my choice epithets. It was a bad beginning to his unexpected, ill-timed visit.

I helped him aboard the schooner and across the straw-strewn deck to the cabin companionway. Below, in the uncomfortably canted cabin, he'd little to say to me, being too shocked by the bad language and my rough appearance. I was unable to spare him much of my time during his short stay, but Bill and the children did their best to entertain him. He told Bill he could scarcely recognise me I was so changed and he didn't know how she and the children could put up with such a terrible life.

A schooner being worked by dockers was no place for social calls and this visit fully confirmed my father's opinion that seafaring was a dog's life. He was so ill-at-ease and out of his element aboard the *Nellie Bywater* that it was a relief when he departed.

Before leaving the Mersey, our Liverpool agent offered us a

series of scrap metal cargoes from Douglas, Isle of Man, to Chester River, with bricks and tiles back. As most of the scrap would have to be loaded with the schooner dried out I refused it but said I'd accept the bricks and tiles. I was told I couldn't have the one without the other, so we lost the lot. I wasn't prepared to risk loading the scrap when on the ground as it was punishing enough for a wooden vessel even when she was afloat.

About six weeks later, the Norwegian master-owner of the schooner *Ellie Park* took up the charter I'd turned down but he loaded only one scrap cargo. We were in Belfast when we heard the tragic sequel.

On 11 November 1947, the packet steamer *King Orry*, Douglas to Liverpool, sighted a raft about twenty-six miles off Douglas Head. Two men were rescued from it and they proved to be the survivors of the crew of four of the schooner *Ellie Park* which had foundered. News of her sinking was a great shock to all of us in the *Nellie Bywater*.

Previously, the schooner *Volant* had been purchased by a young Australian film producer named Cross who intended sailing her to Sydney. She left Belfast when we were trading to Chester River, but her voyage was abandoned at Falmouth where she was stripped to a hulk and left on the mud near Penryn to rot.

With the loss of the *Ellie Park*, the *Nellie Bywater* remained as the sole survivor of the former fine County Down schooner fleet.

Our round voyage in quest of more profitable employment had not been very successful and we were again stuck with the meagrely paid trades of scrap and bricks and tiles. We could have had a better return from this business by cutting down on wages and food but to do so was against our principles.

Since Michael had joined us, we'd had a good crew. He and Frank got on famously although the boy was Catholic and the motorman a staunch Orangeman. This happy state was ended one day in Belfast, when a black-garbed priest arrived to enquire for the Cheek Point boy. He was closeted in the fo'c'sle with Michael for some time and I knew he was up to no good. Shortly after the priest's departure, a very upset lad asked me for his discharge. The interfering cleric lost us the best boy we ever had, solely on religious grounds. Such petty acts of religious intolerance have always been the seeds of Ireland's troubles. I was able to put a good word in for the lad with the master of a Coast Lines ship and we eventually heard he did very well in that company, being a natural born sailor.

During our next visit to Belfast we nearly lost Colin, our mate, in chilling circumstances. The dockers were discharging us as usual in the Clarendon Dock and before I left for the agents, Colin told me that he was setting the new boy on scraping down the maintopmast. I agreed to his suggestion that part of a new, unopened coil of manila rope in our half-deck should be used for the bosun's chair gantlines. I returned to the schooner at midday. The dockers had knocked off for their break and I noticed the new rope stretched along the deck ready for reeving aloft. After a meal, I returned to the agents where I was detained for some time. When I finally got back to the *Nellie Bywater* both the mate and the boy were aloft in separate chairs and they'd already scraped down two thirds of the spar. It struck me that it was typical of Colin to go up with the new lad to give him confidence.

Sorting some papers in the cabin, I heard a horrible thump on deck and instinctively knew someone had fallen from aloft. I moved fast and reached Colin—for it was he who had fallen—before anyone else. He was lying across the coaming of the open mainhatch, still conscious after his seventy-foot drop.

The hatchman phoned for an ambulance and Bill arrived unbidden with an armful of pillows and blankets. We carefully eased the injured mate onto the pillows and covered him with blankets. He asked me for a cigarette, so I lit one and put it in his mouth and he puffed away quite calmly until the ambulance arrived to take him to hospital.

When he'd gone, I remembered that the boy was still aloft and lowered a very shaken youngster to the deck. My most urgent task was to investigate the cause of the accident as it was inconceivable that a careful and experienced sailorman like Colin could have been at fault. I was shocked to find that the new manila rope had parted just above the chair and each side of the break its fibres were powdered for a few inches. Immediately I realised what had happened. Astern of the *Nellie Bywater* lay a ship which had been discharging a deck-cargo of carboys of acid, and one of the glass containers had broken during the morning, spilling acid on the quayside. Someone, probably a docker returning to the schooner after his lunch break, had stepped in the acid and then walked over the new rope stretched on the deck. The acid must have been gradually burning through the rope just above the mate's head the whole time he was aloft.

We cancelled all commitments for the schooner so as to be on hand if needed at the hospital. Colin's injuries were a broken pelvis, and several fractured ribs. He also had pneumonia, resulting from shock.

The accident brought home to us how attached we'd all become to our quiet, capable mate. When he'd first joined us, his taciturn undemonstrative manner worried us until we realised he enjoyed his own privacy and was perfectly happy with us. He modestly accustomed himself to my ways, then anticipated every need of the schooner. Within a few weeks, we had such a complete understanding that speech was unnecessary when working ship; a minimum of hand signals sufficed. Calm and dependable in difficult situations, he was a natural sailorman, highly skilled in the arts of the sailing ship and a craftsman with rope, wire, canvas, metal or wood.

Only occasionally communicative, his yarns were worth listening to as he'd had a full adventurous life, voyaging around the world in sail, spells in lifeboats after torpedoings during the War and an eventful period as mate of the ketch *St Helens* under the command of Captain Arthur, explorer and treasure hunter. He buried his captain in Curacao, returning to the U.K. as a D.B.S. just before coming to us.

He'd become like one of the family and the kids loved him. We were deeply concerned for him and it was an immense relief when he was off the danger list. Possessed of an iron constitution and an indomitable will, he made an amazing recovery. In under six weeks he was back with us aboard the *Nellie Bywater* to convalesce, but within days, he was carrying out his normal duties including climbing about aloft as if nothing had ever happened, and we were unable to stop him.

During the long lay-up, I approached the importers of the bricks and tiles to request a modest increase in their rates for the cargoes. They refused to allow me a penny more so I was obliged to look elsewhere for business. I visited every possible source for charters in the city which involved a considerable amount of walking. Returning to the schooner from one of these attempts to drum up business, I was met by a radiant wife. She told me the children had seen me from a distance in the city, walking with scarcely a trace of a limp. For a short time I relapsed into my dragging gait but the war-damaged leg was just beginning to work normally, although still weak.

First Colin's incredible cure and then mine . . . our cup of happiness was indeed full!

19

Oil Strike

Our long lay-up had drained our slender resources until they were at danger level and we urgently needed profitable employment for our schooner if we were to survive. By telephone, I succeeded in fixing a brick cargo at a good rate, Bowling to Belfast, quite independent of brokers; the only snag was the light passage to the Clyde at our expense.

When I collected the ship's papers before leaving Belfast, my agent suggested it would be greatly to our advantage if we had an agent in Glasgow and offered to arrange for one of his 'friends' in the port to act for us.

Some instinct warned me not to accept his proposal, especially as the firm he named owned some small ships which occasionally loaded brick cargoes for Belfast. As I demurred, the broker insisted that his 'friends' would look after us well, so unwisely I gave in.

Arriving in the Clyde, I sadly discovered my instinct had been correct, for the Scottish agent received me with the utmost rudeness and informed me there was no brick cargo for the *Nellie Bywater*. He said: 'My advice to you, Cap'n, is to cut your losses and return to Belfast immediately for you'll get no cargo for your schooner in the Clyde . . . that I can promise you!'

A visit to the brickworks had no better result—our promised cargo had vanished into thin air, for we'd been double-crossed. Bitterly I thought of the shipbrokers proud motto: 'Our word, our bond'. It apparently no longer applied. But the spiteful words and the duplicity of our so-called Glasgow agent thoroughly aroused Bill and me, and we were determined not to leave the Clyde until we'd loaded a paying cargo. When faced with such deceit, we can be a very stubborn pair.

The Oil Pool's bunkering jetty and filling station were adjacent to Bowling Harbour. From there, the lubricating oil quota for the whole of Ulster was despatched in forty-gallon drums, first by road to Glasgow, then by passenger ferry to Belfast.

A plan rapidly formed in my head and I sought and was granted an interview with a highly placed Pool official. My luck was in, for he was an ex-serviceman who gave me a sympathetic hearing. I outlined to him a scheme for cutting down the transport costs of the oil by half; with the motor winch, we could load the oil ourselves into the *Nellie Bywater* direct from their jetty, thus cutting out double handling and road haulage. After delivering the oil to Belfast, I guaranteed to bring back all their empty drums at a rate just covering our expenses. The empties were my trump card, for they were in very short supply and nearly impossible to replace at this time. They were cluttering up the Belfast docksides and other valuable storage spaces as it was uneconomical for other ships to carry them, but without drums, the traffic in oil would halt. I asked for a trial cargo to prove my words and this was granted.

Within hours of being warned to 'cut our losses and clear out of the Clyde', we were loading a cargo of lubricating oils into the *Nellie Bywater* which the Customs' manifests valued at a staggering figure. It was the most valuable cargo the schooner had ever carried during her long life.

Later, at the schooner's wheel as she dropped down the Clyde, Belfast bound, I could scarcely credit our good fortune, but our luck held throughout the trial period. We found a brave, fair wind below the Cumbraes and as if aware of the urgency, the *Nellie Bywater* sailed as I'd never seen her sail before.

Old shellbacks held a belief that a liquid cargo in a sailing vessel had some strange affinity with the salt sea, assisting the sailing qualities of the vessel. Whatever the cause, laden to her marks with oil, our schooner was at her best for both speed and seaworthiness. Our time to Belfast couldn't have been bettered by a steam or motor ship.

The oil importer and a gang of dockers awaited us on the quay as we docked in Belfast and discharging commenced as soon as we were alongside. Our hold was cleared in about six hours.

The importer, a very influential figure in the city, seemed suitably impressed by the performance of the *Nellie Bywater*, for he instructed us to make a fast turn-around with the empties and bring another cargo of oil. In less than thirty hours, we were outward for Bowling, the hold crammed with empty oil drums.

The schooner was practically 'light'; the empties making little difference to her draught, so she was in poor trim for sailing in bad weather and we had plenty of that, for it was late autumn when we began the trade. Returning the empties proved to be the most difficult part of my plan.

Berthing at Bowling Oil Jetty, we immediately commenced discharging the empty drums, a dirty job, for many of the containers leaked sufficient oil to soak us thoroughly. Meanwhile, oil company staff were building up our next consignment of filled drums on the jetty. We loaded these as soon as the hold was clear. Berthing space for bunkering the big ships was in constant demand, so there was no lingering at the jetty for a 'breather' before sailing. As we battened down, the Clyde pilot was aboard, ready to take us to Gourock.

This was the constant, unvaried routine of our oil trade. Throughout the long winter we battled to and fro between Belfast and Bowling, delivering our oil cargoes on time and never once letting our charterers down, though we encountered the usual gales, snow and dense fogs. We averaged a round voyage a week, even in severe weather or delayed by berthing difficulties at the oil jetty.

Loading the oil at Bowling was the worst part of the job, for with the motorman driving the winch, this left only the mate, the boy and myself to stow the hundreds of heavy drums in the hold. We soon began to hate the difficult and sometimes dangerous passages to Bowling with the empties, with nothing but discharging and loading without a proper rest, at the end of them.

Homeward to Belfast was a different story. Filled to capacity with oil, the *Nellie Bywater* never failed to amaze us with her ability to carry sail and her fine turn of speed, whatever the weather, as hitherto we'd only experienced her performance when laden with stiff, inflexible cargoes.

During her period in the oil trade, we enjoyed many fast and stirring sails down the Firth of Clyde and across the narrow but often turbulent North Channel. Speed is a vexed subject with sailormen and it tends to become exaggerated. But on two noteworthy winter passages from the Clyde to Belfast, the *Nellie Bywater* must surely have reached her maximum rate.

The first occasion was on a bright, cold, moonlit night in late December. The wind was nor'-nor'-east, strong but steady. We'd passed Garroch Head and were on course for the Holy Island light, off Arran, with every sail set to a grand quartering wind. As the Firth widened and we lost the lee of the land, the wind freshened considerably, driving the schooner along in fine style. Closing Holy Island, I was standing to wind'ard on the listing deck, anxiously judging the increase in the wind strength, when Colin, from the wheel, drew my attention to the lights of a big ship astern of us. She was on the same course as ourselves and soon overhauled us, passing under our lee. Through my binoculars I saw she was a big Norwegian tanker. From her bridge wing several of her officers were inspecting us and the *Nellie Bywater* must have been a fine sight to them as she drove headlong through the seas, the spray flying in sheets from her bows and every sail a graceful, curved, black silhouette against the moonlit sky.

I expected the tanker to quickly drop us astern but she remained with her quarter just off our lee bow. Clearing Arran and getting the full benefit of the wind, the schooner settled down to really sail, listing over until the lee waterways were flooding.

Relieving the tired mate at the wheel, I soon began sweating profusely, although it was a chilly night. It was tricky steering, requiring all my strength, and I could feel the immense power of the wind through the wheel spokes.

Throughout the night, the schooner raced on, snoring through the seas and unbelievably maintaining her station on the tanker's weather quarter. It was as if she were attached to the big ship with an invisible towline and we remained in this position, past Ailsa Craig and into the North Channel where, at length, our courses differed, the tanker going north about whilst we continued across to the Copelands.

The second occasion when the *Nellie Bywater* showed her remarkable speed and seaworthiness, the circumstances were quite different, for under great stress, I was driving the schooner recklessly through weather which would normally have obliged us to seek shelter.

After a winter in the trade, all aboard the schooner began to feel the strain. We could never have kept up the pace without Bill's nourishing food, and undoubtedly her duties were the hardest in the schooner, for in addition to her victualling, cooking, cleaning and washing, she cared for the two children as if ashore. The anxious War years, the shock of my 'demob' in a crippled state

217

and her valiant efforts to assist in my recovery and rehabilitation had all taken their toll. She was constantly overtaxing her strength in the *Nellie Bywater*, especially since we'd been carrying oil. She became very ill and a Belfast specialist diagnosed a condition that required immediate surgery. On hearing the medico's verdict, I thought of paying-off the crew and laying-up the schooner.

Our Belfast friends rallied round us when they heard of my wife's illness. The oil importer was kindness itself. He pointed out to me that I couldn't do any good by taking this course; that it would be more sensible to keep earning for the family whilst the doctors did their work. He and his good lady promised to visit the hospital regularly, see to Bill's needs and keep me fully informed of her condition by telephone. Others volunteered to look after the children. The advice of these kind people was sound, and I accepted it and their practical assistance, though very reluctantly.

With Bill in hospital, we sailed from Belfast with the usual 'empties' and made a fair passage. The strenuous work at Bowling was made even harder, for we missed the regular, appetising meals which Bill had always prepared. The schooner wasn't the same without her.

We were loaded and ready for sea when I received a message via the Pool office, to say my wife had received her operation and 'she was as well as could be expected', the standard hospital bulletin.

I was worried sick and knew I'd never forgive myself if things went wrong in my absence. The weather was bad, with severe gales forecast for most areas but I was so anxious to reach Belfast that I ignored the warnings. As we passed the obvious shelter of Gourock Bay, the wind was fairly piping through the rigging and I guessed the pilot thought me crazy when we dropped him off at the pilot station and set all plain sail, including the full main.

We swept down-river and passed Garroch Head in record time with the schooner palpably over-canvassed, but I refused to reef until it was too late. To start the bar-taut main halyards would lose us the sail so we let everything stand and prayed that nothing would carry away. The strains on the little ship made her shiver like a living thing as she leaped through the seas.

Below Arran, the wind was about west-sou'-west—a full gale— and close-hauled, the schooner lay over like a racing yacht, with the foam hissing loudly along her sides and the spray flying foreyard-high, striking the wheelhouse with the force of buck-shot.

Colin and I did alternate hourly tricks at the wheel: even that was too long for the schooner needed very careful nursing in the big breakers. It was difficult to anticipate their run in the pitch darkness and the violent movement and noise tended to dull the senses, when alertness was most necessary. It only needed a single rope yarn to part to bring the whole of our vessel's tophamper tumbling about our heads and we all were aware of it. Even our phlegmatic mate was apprehensive and showed it for the first time.

We tore past Ailsa Craig as dawn was breaking and in the cold, grey light the North Channel was a daunting sight, a maelstrom of very confused seas whipped up by the strong wind warring with a very high Spring tide. We hadn't seen a single ship all night and the North Channel appeared deserted. The *Nellie Bywater* sailed across this desolate strait at what was undoubtedly her greatest speed, breasting the whitecaps magnificently, her stout Irish flax canvas stretched to bursting point, her lee coverboard awash and a broad, white frothing wake swirling astern.

Her average speed from Garroch Head to the Copelands was twelve knots.

I sighed with relief as we opened up the entrance of Belfast Lough but our worries weren't over even when we were inside. The Lough was comparatively smooth but the force of the wind unchanged. Our problem was getting the canvas off the schooner, for in that wind, a single slat could lose us a sail. This was the kind of situation where our mate showed his mettle. Patiently waiting for the right moment, he let the main halyards go with a run, then jumped to lend his enormous strength to the others on the down-haul. The big sail came down without a hitch and was gathered in and roughly furled. The other sails weren't so difficult but we were up to the Pilot Lightvessel before they were all secured.

While anxiously concentrating on the sail drill and assisting it with my steering, out of the corner of my eyes I'd noticed unusual activity about us in the Lough. Several big tugs and other vessels had scurried past us at top speed, all bound outwards for the North Channel.

When the pilot boarded us, he told us that a motorvessel,

loaded with steel rods, had sent out a 'Mayday' on the distress frequency, saying her cargo had shifted and she was on her beam ends in the North Channel. The tugs and other vessels were on their way to her assistance.

Later, we learnt that their missions were unsuccessful, for by the time they'd reached the last named position of the stricken vessel, she'd disappeared with all hands.

Immediately we were docked, I hastened to the hospital and was met at the ward door by the sister-in-charge.

'Thank God you've come, Captain!' she exclaimed. 'We've had a terrible time with your wife. The storm blew the glass out of the ward skylight during the night and she said you'd be drowned trying to get here to be with her. Nothing we did could calm her down!'

It was typical of Bill . . . even when in pain and acute discomfort, all she could think of was my safety. I was glad I'd not let her down.

She made a full and rapid recovery from her operation but it was several weeks before she was able to return aboard the *Nellie Bywater* and resume her former duties. In her absence, the smooth running of the schooner was badly upset. Our tight schedule allowed us little time for the preparation of meals and most of the time we were too exhausted to do any cooking. None of our ship's boys could do the simplest task in the galley and they arrived and departed with such frequency that I gave up carrying them. Then to add to my difficulties, the mate was suddenly called home to attend to urgent family matters, and I was obliged to work the schooner for a round voyage or two with only our motorman and an ex-fighter pilot.

The airman, who was a wealthy young man, had plans for buying and operating two or three small motorvessels in the Home Trade, and he joined us to get some first-hand knowledge, which he did. Day and night I galloped from one end of the *Nellie Bywater* to the other, as neither of my lads had sufficient experience to do the simplest task without supervision. They did their best, but were both sadly lacking in strength. It was hard enough for them when making sail or working anchors, but the loading of the oil at Bowling quickly finished the would-be shipowner. Completely demoralised, he discharged himself just as

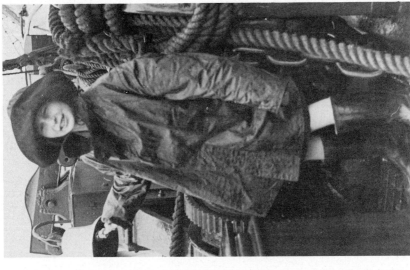

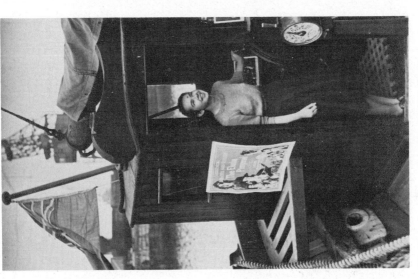

23. Daughter Jo at the wheel of *Nellie Bywater*.
A film publicity photo. (*J. Holman, Plymouth*)

24. Inga, youngest of the 'Bywater kids'.
(*News Chronicle*)

25. *The Elusive Pimpernel*. The Pimpernel's *Daydream* creeps into a secluded inlet to embark the rescued Comtesse de Tournai and her children.
(*Michael Powell, London*)

26. *The Elusive Pimpernel*. Danielle Godet, Edmond Audran, the author,
Arlette Marchal. (*Michael Powell, London*)

Colin providentially returned. It was a happy day when Bill and the children rejoined us and life in the schooner became normal again. Thanks to our wonderful Belfast friends we'd managed to keep to our charter obligations throughout a trying period.

For the next few months we ploughed the same furrows between Belfast and the Clyde without untoward incidents. The winter weather behind us, our lot was much easier and we sailed with the regularity of a packet, being in Belfast most weekends. I allowed the motorman Frank weekend leave to go home, but it was only granted on the strict understanding that he was back by eight on Monday. He returned on time in a very good humour, so the leave became a regular thing. Eventually, it was his undoing.

We were now enjoying a settled phase and everything pointed to a brighter future. The oil trade gave us a satisfactory return although we earned every penny.

Colin was popular with everyone he met, but one trip he won the everlasting admiration of the Belfast dockers with a feat of strength I've never seen equalled. Schooner men, of necessity, have to be well muscled but the immense power hidden in our mate's large and lanky body was unbelievable.

We docked in Belfast with a full cargo of oil plus forty or fifty drums carried as deck cargo to cope with a last minute order. Two of these extra drums of oil were a nuisance to the dockers when they began discharging, so a couple of hefty fellows were manhandling them, one at a time, out of the way.

Colin noticed how they were struggling with the first drum and nonchalantly strolled up to them and said: 'Are they in your way, lads? Here! I'll shift them for you.'

He coiled his extremely long arms about both the heavy forty-gallon drums, with one lift picked them up and casually walked away with one under each arm.

'Holy Mother of God!' exclaimed the burly, bullnecked hatchman, his eyes nearly popping out of his head at the feat. 'I wouldn't care to fall out wid that mate o' yours, Cap'n.'

I assured him there was no danger of that happening, as Colin was the most even-tempered man I'd ever met.

It's impossible to ignore religion in Ulster, for it keeps cropping up in every aspect of life. We were surprised to find in our business relations in Belfast, that besides the two main warring Faiths and the Nonconformists, many other lesser denominations were well represented. Whatever the beliefs, they were practised by their followers with the same fiery zeal. We found it necessary to tread warily and remain neutral in the midst of so much fervour but in spite of our precautions, on one occasion we became reluctant evangelists.

I was about to collect my papers from the agents before leaving for Bowling when I was accosted on the dockside by a seedy, cadaverous man with matted long hair and the staring eyes of a fanatic.

'Would ye be doin' me a great favour now, Cap'n?' he enquired in an unctious voice, then launched into a tirade about spreading the Gospel, bottle messages, the works of God and how I could further them. The gist of his rambling discourse was simply this; I was being requested to take a few bottles containing religious pamphlets to sea and drop them overboard—a novel way of distributing tracts.

I hastily checked the flood of religious fervour, assured the speaker I'd do as he requested if he'd leave his bottle messages with our mate, and then made my escape.

Returning to the *Nellie Bywater* after completing my business, I found my crew gazing open-mouthed at a big stack of beer crates on the deck. It looked as if we'd taken a delivery from a brewery. There must have been about a hundred crates, all filled with Guinness bottles neatly sealed with red sealing wax. I just couldn't believe that the most ardent gospellers would go to such lengths.

I felt very uneasy about the contents of these expensively pre-pared bottles, so took half a dozen from random crates to see what was in them. Opening the first bottle and taking out the literature it contained, I read the tracts, one after the other. They were all naive and innocuous, especially the long sermon de-nouncing drinking which seemed very inept coming from a Guin-ness bottle. All six bottles had identical contents.

I left it to Colin to stow them below and promptly forgot them with the arrival of the pilot.

It wasn't until we were bound back to Belfast with oil that I was reminded of the bottle messages. In the middle of a dark, fresh night, the motorman poked his head into the wheelhouse and asked if he should sling some of the bottles overboard. I nodded assent and again dismissed them from my mind. Steering needed my full attention as the schooner was sailing fast on a broad reach over a rough sea.

In daylight next morning, as we closed the Copelands, I noticed two or three Guinness bottles rolling about in the lee waterways. I called to the 'boy' to throw them overside. I asked him how many of the bottles remained aboard.

'They're all gone, Sorr. Frank slung 'em at the porpoises that were round *Nellie* last night . . . never missed, he didn't!'

I experienced a sudden chill at the thought of our crazy motorman flinging bottles at the inoffensive porpoises, though it was very unlikely that he'd injured any of them. I share the old mariner's loathing for those who, without cause, needlessly inflict suffering on the creatures of the deep, and I'd a strange premonition that bad luck would follow.

A few weeks later we lost the oil trade. It wasn't entirely unexpected. From the moment we'd wrested it from the giant shipping combine, we knew they'd sooner or later take it back. So, when I heard through the 'grapevine' that one of their motor-vessels was going to Bowling to continue the operations we'd initiated, I wasn't surprised, although nothing had been said to me about it either at Bowling or Belfast.

The first positive intimation we received was when the Belfast importer drove up to the schooner in his limousine. Instead of giving me the usual instructions regarding the next oil shipment, he informed me that no oil cargoes were immediately available at Bowling but said he'd let me know if the situation changed. Our conversation took place on deck, near the galley.

When the businessman had gone, Bill emerged from the galley, bristling with indignation and anger.

'Why couldn't he tell us straight out that another ship has gone to Bowling to load the oil?' she demanded, her eyes blazing. 'They haven't the guts to tell us that they've finished with the *Nellie Bywater*. Oh! I hope the bunkering jetty falls down on the bloody ship they've sent to load our cargo!'

She expressed my own feelings exactly, as it was the perfidious manner in which the businessmen were terminating our trade that really hurt. So we were back to seeking the few cargoes still free of Ministry restrictions.

But we hadn't heard the last of the oil trade. Next morning we were again visited by the importer, this time in a very distressed and excited condition. We met at the selfsame spot where we'd talked the previous day.

'It's a good thing I didn't send you to Bowling for another cargo, Cap'n!' he blurted out. 'Both the filling station and the jetty have collapsed into the river and I very much doubt if any more oil will ever be shipped to us from there.'

There was an odd choking sound from the galley which made us swivel our heads. We were just in time to see Bill hastily retreating aft, with her hands over her mouth and her shoulders shaking convulsively. Although obviously puzzled by my wife's strange behaviour, our visitor was too well-mannered to comment, and left soon afterwards.

There was a simple explanation for what had happened at Bowling. The waters of the Clyde must have been scouring and eroding the foundations of the installation for years and, of course, it was sheer coincidence that the structures collapsed when they did. But when I gave my opinion to Bill, she wasn't entirely convinced, and still clung to the extraordinary notion that it was her angry words of the previous day that had precipitated the disaster. Since then, she's been very careful not to wish ill to anything or anyone.

We were glad to know, however, that others wouldn't profit from our loss of the oil trade.

20

Film Ship

Dockers foiled all our efforts to earn a modest living carrying bricks and tile cargoes. The record for time-wasting was our loading at Ellesmere Port where twenty dockers took a full week to load 150 tons.

In the hopes of obtaining something better, we did an outside broadcast from the *Nellie Bywater* for the B.B.C. Belfast and were featured in their 'Ulster Mirror' magazine programme. This brief excursion into the strange world of entertainment provided us with a little light relief; the children thoroughly enjoyed the new experience. From the 'play-backs', they undoubtedly stole the show with their unscripted, inimitable backchat, but we never heard the actual broadcast as, at the time, we were at sea in bad weather with our small radio out of action. We heard later that the programme aroused great interest with the general public, but in spite of a most generous 'plug' from the B.B.C., it failed to bring us any business from the hard-headed merchants of the port.

The entertainment value of the broadcast set me thinking of a new role for the *Nellie Bywater*. Surely the booming film industry could find employment for a picturesque, romantic-looking schooner? Without contacts or any knowledge of the motion picture business, I didn't know how to begin. Then, ironically, a cable arrived for Colin, our mate, offering a job of sailing one of the replicas of Columbus's ships in the West Indies for the filming of the Gainsborough picture, *Christopher Columbus*. The appeal of working a medieval ship proved irresistible to our adventurous, itinerant mate and he was Barbados bound within a few hours. It was like losing my right arm when he left.

In his place, I engaged an aged former schooner captain widely known as 'Old Bones', but it was an unhappy choice. The first meal he had aboard the *Nellie Bywater* brought him into conflict with Bill. He'd watched her dishing out the lads' dinners at the galley before joining us in the cabin and when she set our food on the table, he remarked: 'No wonder your husband's always hard up, feeding the crew like this. All they need is a few bones in the pot with lashings of spuds and vegetables.'

Bill fixed him with an icy stare. 'Does the food suit you?' she demanded.

'Oh aye! It's fine for us in the cabin, Missus,' he replied.

'Then eat up and shut up and don't interfere with what is my business. When my husband was a boy, he sailed under men like you and went hungry, but nobody's going to do that in the *Nellie Bywater* while we have her.'

We were about to sail light for Irvine to load bricks for Belfast when a telegram arrived to say that London Films were interested in the *Nellie Bywater* for one of their forthcoming productions. I wired back saying that we'd call in at Stranraer to meet their representative, on our way to Irvine.

We anchored in Loch Ryan and picked up the film man with the dinghy. Our talk aboard the schooner was satisfactory on both sides. The small, sandy-haired film executive was an amusing character, with terrific energy and enthusiasm, emphasising his fast talking with extravagant gestures. He assured me that the film charter would be just a well-paid holiday for us all and we'd personally meet some of the world's top screen stars and see them at work.

'All we need,' he said, 'is a few shots of your ship sailing off the Breton coast and off Dover. You'll have a marvellous time!'

'Cocky' Mills, as he was affectionately known in the film world, certainly knew his job. Before we put him ashore, I'd agreed to his proposals. 'Old Bones' and the crew were almost bursting with curiosity and were all ears during the film man's inspection of the schooner.

After 'Cocky's' departure, something made me phone the brickworks at Irvine to confirm that we'd soon be there. They replied with the disconcerting news that, owing to a sudden strike at the works, no brick cargoes would be available until it was settled. 'Cocky' Mills' visit had been providential.

We immediately returned to Belfast to take in ballast and prepare our vessel for her glamorous new employment. A few days later the charter party was signed for the *Nellie Bywater* to appear as Sir Percy Blakeney's *Daydream* in a Technicolor version of Baroness Orczy's romantic novel of the French Revolution, *The Elusive Pimpernel*.

The film was to be produced and directed by independent

producer Michael Powell for London Films. He'd just completed a ballet film, *The Red Shoes* and was utilizing the same cameramen and technicians for making the *Pimpernel*.

It was to have a dazzling cast: David Niven in the lead as Sir Percy Blakeney, with Margaret Leighton as his wife. Jack Hawkins was playing the Prince Regent and Cyril Cusack the villainous Chauvelin. They were to be supported by a fine Anglo-French company.

Although duly impressed by our famous charterers and their glittering array of stars, my natural caution warned me not to be too optimistic about our new venture. The terms of the charter were straightforward and included a clause I'd requested: that my powers as master embraced all film personnel once they were embarked in the schooner, and my decisions were to be final regarding the working and safe navigation of the vessel. The charter rate was not over-generous, but if all went well, we should be slightly better off than we were in the oil trade. It was a modest beginning in a new sphere of work and I was more than satisfied. As usual, Bill was non-committal. Inveterate cinema fans, the children were thrilled by the thought of meeting some of their screen idols and the prospect of seeing a big feature film being made.

The reactions of the mate and crew, once we were fully committed, were a mixture of ignorance and greed. They believed in the Hollywood myth that all connected with 'movies' were rolling in money and wrongly assumed that Bill and I were on the road to untold riches. Inadvertently I'd let slip to Old Bones that our contract was null and void if we failed to reach Falmouth at a stated time. They waited until we were about to leave Belfast for Falmouth, then struck for more pay. Absolutely disgusted by their conduct, I nevertheless patiently explained the uncertainties of the film charter to them and promised them generous bonuses at the successful conclusion of the work. But I'd wasted my breath, for their attitude was unchanged so, to their utter consternation, I immediately paid them all off. On the eve of our venture, we were crewless.

But the incident really got our danders up and within hours we'd gathered together a scratch crew and sailed at the appointed time—right into a sou'-westerly gale which obliged us to return to

Belfast Lough. We brought up with two anchors and a full scope at what I believed to be a safe distance from the Pilot Lightvessel. Just after dawn, the wind suddenly backed northerly and blew even harder and I felt the first ominous shudders of dragging anchors. Rearing and plunging, with the wind shrieking through the rigging, the *Nellie Bywater* began to blow down on the lightship although the auxiliary was at 'full ahead'. My green crew hove up the port anchor but it seemed certain we should foul the lightship before we could weigh the other one. Those on the lightship had the same fears, for they were frantically indicating the positions of their four moorings. With little time to spare before there was a disastrous collision, we changed our tactics. Instead of trying to stem the wind, under backed stays'l and with the Widdop full astern, we dredged in a semi-circle around the lightship, the starboard anchor just on the ground. We brought up safely again on a shoaling bank. I offered up a silent prayer to the old bargeman who'd introduced me to the finer points of dredging, many years before.

It was a tough beginning for the new motorman and boy, as it was their first time at sea, and particularly for our yachtsman mate, but they'd all done well.

Twenty-four hours later the wind took off and we enjoyed light to moderate nor'-westerlies all the way to Falmouth, arriving on time.

From the moment we anchored in the Carrick Roads, we discovered our humble little trading schooner had already changed her character to those on the waterfront. There was great competition amongst the quaypunt men to wait upon the 'film ship' and we were charged the most exorbitant prices for everything we needed.

The call at Falmouth was for loading film company stores. A fortuitous delay in the arrival of a mobile generator allowed me sufficient time to engage George Cort as mate for the duration of the filming. One of the most experienced schoonermen left on the coast, he'd found himself a shore job with the China Clay Co. at the end of the War and married a widow with six children. I practically 'shanghaied' him. Knowing his weakness for the sea stories of Captain Marryat, I suggested he could be one of his pigtailed heroes of olden times by shipping with me in the *Nellie*

Bywater. Unable to resist such an appeal, George did a pierhead jump aboard us as we were leaving for St Malo, which was to be our base for the filming. As the Lizard faded astern, I casually asked my new second-in-command if his good wife had objected to him coming with us.

'Oh!' replied our bluff Cornishman, 'I daresn't tell my ol' woman 'bout coming. I'll drop her a card from St Malo.'

Which led me to suspect that his true reason for joining us was his need for a short respite from the cares of fathering his big, ready-made family. But it was a marvellous stroke of luck securing him as mate and he, in turn looked happy and contented, back in his old familiar surroundings of a schooner. There was just time for him to lick our greenhorns into shape before we began the filming.·

We docked the following day in the Bassin Vauban, under the picturesque walls of the ancient, war-scarred city of St Malo. 'Cocky' Mills and some of his company's executives were waiting to welcome us, bursting with enthusiasm for the sea sequences we were to do. The little location manager arranged to pick me up next morning for some undisclosed assignment.

'Cocky' duly arrived in a taxi and we were driven through the quiet Breton countryside with my companion chattering away non-stop. When the car finally pulled up, the scene before me took my breath away.

We were on the shores of a vast, dried-out bay, the sea invisible beyond the horizon. The exposed mud, shingle and sand were in nightmare contours. Out of this tortured seabed rose a small, high, granite islet, completely built-up with a huddled, wall-encircled medieval town, crowned at its summit by a fairy-tale castle and abbey.

'Cocky' threw his arms apart in an ecstatic, theatrical gesture. 'There! What d'you think of Mont St Michel as a set for our picture?' he enthused. 'Wait till you've seen it from the abbey gallery, four hundred feet up! But, come on. I'm going to take you first to lunch at the famous Hotel Poularde to sample one of their superb omelettes.'

In a daze, I followed him across the shingle causeway and through the turreted gateway of Mont St Michel.

From the instant I'd seen the sinister bay, I'd known what was in store for us. The expensive lunch in the exquisite little hostelry was only a softening-up for the shocks to come.

During the meal, my companion kept surreptitiously glancing at his watch and we'd scarcely finished eating when he abruptly stood up, saying: 'Follow me, Cap'n!' then bolted out of the hotel.

Close on the heels of the eccentric film man, I almost ran up the steep incline of the Grand Rue which degenerated into a seemingly endless stairway of granite steps. We were both completely out of breath by the time we'd reached the high ramparts on the seaward side of the island. Gasping for breath, I surveyed the fantastic seascape for the second time. From our lofty vantage point, the silvery gleam of the sea was just visible in the distance; the dried-out bay appeared even more menacing.

'Cocky' again consulted his watch.

'Now, Cap'n!' he announced, dramatically. 'Watch carefully, for in a few minutes you're going to see something really spectacular.'

Gazing intently across the bay, I noticed a narrow ribbon of white appear, extending the full width of the inlet. It began travelling towards us at an incredible speed, a monstrous, foam-topped tidal wave. Soon it was audible as a low murmur which rapidly increased to a roar. Sweeping forward at a devastating rate, the huge wave struck the island with an explosive boom, dissolving in spray on the rocks below us. Mont St Michel was again a true islet of the sea.

Statistics of the remarkable phenomena I'd just witnessed state that the sea withdraws as far as ten miles at certain periods, leaving some 100,000 acres of the bay dry, sometimes for as long as two weeks. When the tide again covers the seabed, it races in at the extraordinary speed of 210 metres a minute.

On our return journey to St Malo, I'd plenty to worry about. 'Cocky' didn't dare hint at it but I'd guessed the next move—a request from his company for me to sail the *Nellie Bywater* into that deathtrap of a bay. I recalled his words at Stranraer: 'It'll be a paid holiday and you'll have a marvellous time!' Like hell we would!

My surmise proved correct. At a conference with the film executives aboard the schooner, I was told the highlight of the filmscript was a rescue of the Scarlet Pimpernel from Mont St

Michel by his schooner *Daydream*. Scenes were to be filmed of the Pimpernel escaping from the clutches of his arch enemy Chauvelin in the authentic setting of the abbey, which had been looted and turned into a prison during the French Revolution. He was to be picked up by his schooner which had dared the perils of the bay to the consternation of Chauvelin. It was all exciting costume drama in a breathtaking, historically correct location but unfortunately, the script writers had been too accurate in one respect. The perils of the bay were so real, the waters were un-navigable.

I bluntly pointed this out to the film men, reminding them that both my charter and my cover with Lloyds were for sailing in 'safe navigable waters'.

Somebody said: 'If you can't do this, then there's no sense in having your ship in the picture!' Ignoring the remark, I explained that the only period when there would be sufficient depth of water in the bay for a vessel of our draught was on the highest tide of the year in October; it was then early September. Providing the weather was favourable, I'd make an attempt then, if they were prepared to wait until the big tide and insure me for the risky venture. They seemed reasonably happy with my proposals and agreed to them.

We were taking a big gamble but it was an excellent opportunity to become 'known' in film circles. And it was a terrific challenge.

The long wait in St Malo posed unexpected problems. At Falmouth Bill had been allowed victuals for only the estimated ten-day stay in French waters. The food situation was far worse in France than in Britain and the procedures for obtaining merchant-ship provisions were denied us as none of my 'pierhead jump' crew had either seamen's documents or passports. When our food ran out, Bill concocted an ingenious method of obtaining the necessary stores, helped by a friendly old French yachtsman. Her reward from our crew was angry complaints about the French food which had cost her dearly in time, worry and money. But the worst of all, she had to listen every mealtime to our mate dolefully moaning: 'Oh! What I'd give for one of me ol'woman's Cornish pasties.'

I read the riot act to my crew about behaving themselves when ashore, but our dim boy nearly involved us in serious trouble.

A French Navy frigate on a training cruise docked opposite to us in the Bassin Vauban. Our boy was so impressed by the tricolour vests worn by her conscript ratings that, after dark, he helped himself to one from a washing line strung up aboard the warship.

We caught him in the act as he climbed aboard the *Nellie Bywater* with his prize. In his alarm at being discovered, he dropped the newly washed vest into the filthy dock water and it was sadly grimed when it was recovered. It was scarcely daylight when two very trucculent French matelots, breathing fire and brimstone, boarded us.

I marched the quaking boy, carrying the dirty sopping vest, around to the frigate, where he had to run the gauntlet through the grim-faced crew.

The vest was returned, with apologies, to its rightful owner, in the presence of the frigate's captain. One good thing came out of the incident: my crew daren't venture ashore until the training ship had departed.

As the big October tides began to make, we changed our schooner's identity for filming to *Daydream* of Newhaven by screwing plywood nameboards over her cut-in names and registration. The French waterguard combed the docks looking for the *Nellie Bywater* but she'd vanished and in her place they found a vessel of which they'd no record. It required the invaluable help of a few cognacs to sort out the resulting confusion.

Two days before the peak of the big Springs, 'Cocky' and I again journeyed to Mont St Michel armed with the only published chart of the area and it was instructive to read on it the date of the bay's last survey: 1800.

From the abbey, at low water, I studied the shape of the seabed. When the tide made, from a hired motor launch we sounded the most likely approaches to the island on the top of high water, marking the depths on the chart and taking shore features in transit as leading marks. Having taken every possible precaution, I prayed the weather would remain settled over the filming so that the seabed stayed unaltered.

I'd heard somewhere that films were the most expensive of all art forms. The following evening I was reminded of this when the *Nellie Bywater* was invaded by a horde of film technicians: cam-

232

eramen, electricians, wardrobe, continuity and 'Cocky'. Members of the film's cast were entirely absent.

'Cocky' was accompanied by a short, tough-looking Frenchman, whom he introduced to me as a pilot.

'He's been born and bred on the shores of Mont St Michel and knows every inch of the bay,' he explained.

After loading stacks of equipment, we left St Malo bound for our dangerous location.

Under the auxiliary and easy canvas we sailed down the Breton coast, arriving off Cancale at daybreak. Here, a large open motor fishing boat, crowded with men, came alongside and we transhipped into the boat cameras and other equipment. Some of the people in her were in costume and 'Cocky' pointed out to me a villainous character, wearing a red nightcap ornamented with a tricolour cockade and said: 'That's Cyril Cusack. He's the up and coming actor of today. Sometime in the future he's going to be a great star!' . . . a prophecy which proved to be correct.

Filming was to be done from the fishing boat, so I arranged through 'Cocky', for the cameramen to hoist a flag on her stumpy mast immediately their work was completed and strongly emphasised the dangers of even a few minutes delay. They pushed off as the light strengthened and the tide neared high water.

We'd all changed into 'period' seamen's costumes, supplied by Wardrobe. I felt slightly ridiculous in the inaccurate rig, but at a distance, my crew had the authentic appearance of old time pig-tailed 'tars', as they loosed and set the tops'ls.

Weather conditions were perfect as I laid the schooner on the pre-established leading marks and under full sail headed into the bay. A steady, light offshore breeze ruffled the surface of the innocent looking waters, just sufficient to give us good steerage way. The only ones aboard who were aware of the dangers beneath the sea were the pilot, 'Cocky' and myself. The Frenchman had been very quiet when we entered the shoals but as the island loomed larger, he suddenly panicked.

'Retour. Retour, Capitaine!' he pleaded urgently. 'Retour, or I'm ruined, for I've never before lost a ship. Retour, for I've a wife and six children!'

In the strongest terms I told him to 'get lost' and it was the last I saw of him for several hours.

It was an anxious time for me with only a few inches of water below the schooner's keel and I could feel her smelling the bottom. To ground on the highest tide of the year could be the end of the *Nellie Bywater*. The island was now very close and I wondered how much longer the filming would take. It seemed an age before the 'Filming ended' flag fluttered from the camera launch. Coming about, we retraced our hazardous course through the seven miles of treacherous shoals and I sighed with relief when we finally reached deep water. My instincts told me we were uninsured when sailing in the bay, for no mention had been made beforehand about the sum to be covered. We'd more than earned our charter money in the bay of Mont St Michel.

The French pilot had drowned his worries in cognac thoughtfully provided by the film unit, but by the time we'd arrived back at St Malo he'd regained his aplomb. As the schooner entered the lockpit the dockmaster hailed him: 'Where have you been filming, Pilot?'

The little man drew himself up to his full five feet and struck an attitude. 'It is a triumph . . . a great triumph!' he shouted back. 'We sailed right to the walls of Mont St Michel.'

They were speaking in their own language, but I easily understood the dockmaster's scornful reply: 'Do you think I'm such a bloody fool as to believe that nonsense? It can't be done and well you know it. You're nothing but a bloody liar, Pilot!'

The remainder of our work on the French coast was simple; the schooner was just a 'set' for shipboard scenes. Actors and actresses in period dress and an army of technicians crowded our deck, making it difficult to work ship. We were continually required to alter course for correct lighting or backgrounds for the cameramen so I wasn't surprised when the mate complained about our overlarge company being in his way.

'Ask them politely to move,' I advised him, soothingly. 'If they don't . . . just barge them out of the way.'

From the look on the Cornishman's rugged face, I could see he considered the mild request a waste of breath. But I was a bit shocked when I saw him putting his broad shoulders into all and sundry during our constant manoeuvres. There were no complaints, for in the freshening winds and lumpy seas, most of the film unit suffered severely from seasickness and neither knew nor cared what happened to them. The weather became worse and filming was very trying for the actors and actresses in their flimsy period costumes. Cold and wet, they succumbed to seasickness in such numbers that our deck was sometimes covered with their prone bodies. Some were so ill, I was very concerned for them. One white-haired old French actress was so bad that I assisted her into the shelter of the wheelhouse and with my arms about her murmured sympathy and encouragement.

In spite of the *mal de mer*, out of sequence and with tiresome waits between, the various scenes were shot. I marvelled at the way the players acted under such unfavourable conditions and decided they must be dedicated to their art.

Our two children were overjoyed when offered small parts as the young daughters of a French nobleman, who'd been rescued by the Scarlet Pimpernel. But, after hours of waiting on the cold, damp deck in costume, they found there was little glamour in filming on location and weren't so keen on becoming 'film stars'.

One of the few hardy souls unaffected by our heaving deck was the film's director, Michael Powell. About forty years of age and at the peak of his fame as a director and independent producer, he was a well proportioned man of medium height, who gave the impression of being much taller. His tanned, out-of-doors complexion and trim toothbrush moustache suggested an army officer in mufti, for unlike many British film men who copied the extravagant outfits of Hollywood, he was always faultlessly clad in immaculate, well tailored casual wear on location.

In action he was a hard taskmaster, a perfectionist demanding the utmost from his unit and accepting no excuses. I saw an example of this as a romantic scene was being filmed in the schooner's bows. The light was perfect, the camera readied, with the young actor in position . . . but his screen sweetheart—a pretty French starlet—was stretched out on a hatch, violently seasick.

'Take that girl's cloak and hat, put them on and stand in for her' the director commanded the wardrobe mistress, in a voice everyone could hear.

As she felt the wardrobe mistress unfastening her outer garments, the seasick actress sprang to her feet, tottered into position and played the love scene very convincingly. Her work done, she again collapsed to the deck in utter misery.

Michael Powell was as hard with himself as he was with others. One dark night, off a desolate, steep-to coast, he requested us to anchor. The soundings indicated that we should need a scope of five or six shackles of cable out, which takes some heaving up with only two men and a boy on the windlass. My small crew had a strenuous day in front of them so to conserve their energy for later, I suggested to the director that he and his ample team of husky young men should do the heaving up for us. He agreed to this and at the beginning there were plenty of volunteers to man the windlass brakes, but by the time three shackles of cable were in, most of the film men had collapsed from exhaustion. My crew hove up the two remaining shackles with Michael Powell assisting doggedly to the bitter end.

Our work on the French coast completed, we were ordered to Dover. Under ideal conditions, we made a quick passage there and, in the Granville Dock the film unit shot scenes of the French émigrés landing from *Daydream*.

For the time of the year, the weather had been remarkably kind to the film men, but with only a few shots of the *Daydream* approaching the white cliffs of Dover needed to complete the sea sequences, the weather finally broke. It blew hard from the sou'west—a typical autumn gale and we spent a sleepless night in the Camber tending doubled-up moorings and fenders. Morning came with no change in the bad weather.

The gale unheeded, Michael Powell and his unit arrived on time and were very put out when I advised them that the weather was too severe for filming. I explained that once we were outside the eastern entrance, we'd be unable to return until the gale abated and his people and equipment would be in some danger. The director seemed unconvinced so I didn't persist but got under way, motoring to the lee of the breakwater, where we began to make sail. The thunder of flogging canvas plainly demonstrated the wind strength and, without further ado, Michael Powell said: 'Return to the Camber, Captain!' I could sense his frustration. A hold-up on location could mean a serious added expense for his company. We landed the glum-faced film people and as I watched them return to their hotel it was obvious that none of them had an inkling of what they'd narrowly missed. A gale against the strong Spring tides in Dover Strait was most unpleasant.

I thought Michael Powell had given in gracefully to the weather but I was wrong. Within the hour, he sent a taxi to the Camber to pick me up. He joined me in the vehicle at the White Cliffs Hotel, silent and morose. When next the taxi stopped, we were on the Prince of Wales pier, alongside the *Lady Brassey*, one of the largest and most powerful rescue tugs under British registry. She was in full readiness for sailing. In a flash, I read the director's intentions. From the huge, powerful *Lady Brassey*, I was to be shown that I'd exaggerated the weather conditions outside the harbour. But I kept quiet. The sea would do the talking.

Immediately we were aboard, the tug cast off and surged away from the pier, throbbing and pulsing with latent power. Her master tipped me a humorous wink as we joined him in his splendidly equipped wheelhouse, for he evidently knew what was going on.

The *Lady Brassey* steamed purposefully across the outer harbour and poked her massive bows through the eastern entrance. We were barely clear of the piers when a big, snarling white-capped sea struck the tug, burying her forward deck and flying right over the wheelhouse top. In spite of her 4,000 h.p. engines, it nearly stopped her. Shaking violently, she wallowed out of the trough and with the sea clearing from her deck, battled up the next giant roller. The 'clear-views' only allowed us a brief look ahead before they were obscured by another breaker hitting with the force of an avalanche.

'Turn back, Captain!' said a defeated Michael Powell, quite calmly. A stubborn man but philosophical.

'Thought you should take 'em filming in this weather?' grinned the *Brassey*'s master, knowingly, when we were alone for a few moments. 'Shows they don't understand the sea. But, you'll have a bit of peace now, Cap'n.'

For three days the gale persisted then blew itself out. In good weather we completed our work in the Straits of Dover, then returned to the Camber to disembark the film unit and their equipment for the last time.

As Michael Powell and his London Films crew left the schooner, they were passed by two Gainsborough Pictures executives arriving for preliminary talks about another film charter for the

Nellie Bywater. Our future prospects in the film industry seemed assured.

George Cort, his work well done and happy with his filming adventures, returned home to face an irate wife. Our efficient though gloomy motorman left, hoping to obtain an engineer fitter's job ashore. The gullible boy we tried to keep for his own sake but he insisted on being paid off. The film extra's pay he'd received for donning a costume had gone to his head so he already considered himself a movie actor. Some humorists in the film crew had egged him on, assuring him he'd the makings of a star, and he set off for the film studios, determined to act in movies. The ragged, penniless youth who'd joined us in Belfast had earned enough in the schooner to fit himself out with a good suit, shoes and underclothing, a suitcase containing a complete change of clothes and, in addition, I'd saved him some of his pay to provide him with a nice little nest-egg.

But it was all wasted on the gormless lad for, as I expected, he eventually returned to his native Belfast as poverty stricken as before.

We'd not entirely finished with the *Elusive Pimpernel* filming, for we received a kind invitation from Michael Powell to visit the National Film Studios, Boreham Wood, to see some of the indoor scenes being made and to view the 'rushes' of our own efforts. National Studios were very impressive; the huge, hangar-like buildings housed some of the best and largest sound stages in Britain.

An essential part of a 'costume' film was a ballroom scene, and film makers always vied with one another to produce the most sumptuous on record. Michael Powell had planned a super spectacle for Lord Grenville's Ball.

It was inevitably 'Cocky' Mills who escorted us to the ballroom 'set'. We followed him down a long echoing passageway, through a soundproofed door and halted, spellbound.

The vast stage was crowded with players and extras attired in beautiful and colourful Regency costumes. Never before had we seen such a gorgeous array of rich and costly silks, satins, velvets, brocades and lace. It must have cost a fortune to dress this one scene. At last we were seeing the glamorous side of films.

High in the roof, Michael Powell and his cameraman were

setting the cameras to record the brilliant assembly and their reflected image on the highly polished floor.

Work ceased at our arrival and the director and his entire cast gave us the warmest welcome. We were overwhelmed by their kindness. As the French contingent greeted us, a beautiful young blonde stepped forward, saying: ''ow are you, Capitaine?'

It was the 'old' woman I'd comforted when she was prostrate with seasickness off the Breton coast. Her effective make-up and the *mal de mer* together had completely fooled me even at close quarters. Bill's twinkling eyes caught mine as she thoroughly enjoyed my momentary confusion.

The showing of the 'rushes' was the climax to a memorable day at National Studios. To see our work on the cinema screen was very rewarding and reminded us of the difficulties and hazards we'd overcome.

Twelve months later, at a showing of the complete *Elusive Pimpernel* film at a Plymouth theatre, we discovered that the whole of our hard-won Mont St Michel sequences had been 'cut' from the picture. Such are the strange ways of the motion picture industry.

21

The Bubble Bursts

Gainsborough Pictures required the *Nellie Bywater* for their film adaptation of Winston Graham's novel *The Forgotten Story*.

Deeply involved with schooners and sailormen at the turn of the century, the plot was made for our vessel and the scope for us in the filming had me very excited. My hard-won knowledge of out-dated schooner customs and practices could now be put to good use.

Negotiations began at Gainsborough's headquarters, Shepherds Bush Studios, a unique film complex in the heart of London. It took several visits to the 'Bush' to hammer out details of the charter. Much of our work would be just patient routine but shipwreck scenes, the climax of the story, were to be shot in a new, original way that demanded a high degree of skilful, daring seamanship. The accuracy of the seafaring sequences were to be my responsibility as the company's nautical adviser. Once the technical problems had been solved, the financial terms were quickly settled in a most businesslike way. There was only one obstacle in all our dealings, when I insisted that my name should appear on the film credits. It required a special meeting of Gainsborough's 'top brass' before they acquiesced most reluctantly. Our business ended in mutual verbal agreement, the Gainsborough executives assuring me that their legal department would have the written contract ready for signatures within ten days.

Before leaving the 'Bush', I was taken on a tour of the various stages to see the filming of their current productions and on the set of *Diamond City* I met Alex McKendrick, their top director, who had been allocated to *The Forgotten Story*.

My contract never arrived, nor was *The Forgotten Story* ever filmed. A week after my last visit, Shepherd's Bush Studios closed down and the famous Gainsborough Lady faded for ever from the silver screen.

The sudden and unexpected collapse of this major British film company was just the beginning of a bad recession from which the industry never fully recovered.

For us, the loss of a professionally satisfying and lucrative charter as it was about to be ratified was both tantalising and disappointing; a sad blow, indeed, for we'd expended both money and effort to obtain it. In retrospect, it was a deciding factor in future events.

My first natural reaction to this set-back was to forget about the film industry and return to normal trading, but I soon found that the Home Trade was equally depressed. Even the most modern Dutch motorvessels were having great difficulty in finding business, so there was little hope for us in trade with our out-dated sailer.

American film producers were still making films in Britain with 'frozen' assets. Walt Disney proposed filming R. L. Stevenson's *Treasure Island* in this country. I contacted him in Hollywood, offering to do the *Hispaniola* sequences authentically with my schooner, and his reply was encouraging. He informed me that his manager and art director were sailing to Britain in the *Queen Mary* and would contact me upon arrival. The meeting with Disney's executives aboard the *Nellie Bywater* at Dover began very well. Then the period of the story needed confirmation and my eldest daughter's nicely illustrated copy of *Treasure Island*— her primer when I first taught her to read—was produced, with disastrous results. Thumbing through its pages, the art director's expression changed and so did his manner. It was plain to see that in some way the book had offended him, and from that moment our prospects of a contract had vanished. Many months later, the sudden change of attitude was explained: Jo's book had been illustrated by the art director's most hated rival!

The *Nellie Bywater* attracted so many admirers wherever she berthed, we'd long since ceased to notice them. So I doubt if I'd have been aware of yet another one on the Granville dockside, at Dover, if it hadn't been for his strange, colourful garb of white baseball cap, blue and white striped T shirt, red hipsters and fancy red and white kid shoes. He was the most obvious American I'd ever seen—a tourist doing the usual sight-seeing, I assumed. Leaning on the taffrail, I watched the quaint character complete a thorough, open-mouthed inspection of the schooner and then head my way.

'Say, Bud,' he addressed me, in the nasal accent of the Bronx. 'Y'don't happen to be the captain of this ol' timer?'

I admitted to being that person.

'She sure is a cute bit o' wood, Cap!' he enthused. 'Didn't catch y'r name?'

I told him, with startling results.

'Jeez!' he gasped, excitedly. 'Y're not kidding, Cap? . . . England-France. France-England. Oh, boy! Wait 'til I tell 'em. England-France . . . France-England. Here's my card, Cap. Give us a call at the White Cliffs Hotel . . . eleven in the mornin'.'

Still repeating ecstatically to himself 'England-France' . . . 'France-England', the odd American walked away.

Thoroughly amused by his eccentric behaviour and mystified by his reiteration of 'England-France . . . France-England' I examined his business card, hoping for a clue. As near as I can remember, it read:

TED WARNER. N.Y.

AGENCY. CASTING. PUBLICITY. PRODUCTION.

FILMS. THEATRE. VAUDEVILLE. RADIO.

His connection with show business explained some of his peculiarities but I had to wait until the next morning before my curiosity was satisfied. At the White Cliffs Hotel, Ted Warner told me that he'd brought over from the States a young Massachusetts girl who was a brilliant long-distance swimmer. On condition that she successfully swam the English Channel, he'd promised her a Hollywood film contract, with the publicity and grooming to make her into a successor to Esther Williams, the swimming movie star. I was then introduced to the beautiful sixteen-year-old girl and Warner's hysterical utterances of the previous evening made sense, for her name was Shirley May France. As publicity, the coupling of our two names for a crossing of the Channel was heaven-sent to the American impresario.

Shirley was accompanied by her father, a trainer and a school-mistress chaperon; all quiet, charming people and I couldn't help wondering how they ever got mixed up with their brash show-man, Ted Warner. I supposed he'd talked them into it just as he talked me into accompanying the cross-channel swim with the *Nellie Bywater*.

'Only a day's work, Cap, with me an' a few good friends with you to watch Shirley. Y'r picture'll be in all the papers with Shirley and you'll be known from coast to coast in the States.'

His ingenuous, boyish enthusiasm and his funny appearance were very disarming but behind the naiveté lurked a ruthless, needlesharp business brain. Under the spell of Shirley and her attractive party, I made a loose, unbusinesslike 'gentlemen's agreement' for a day's charter of the *Nellie Bywater* at a rock-bottom rate.

Believing the swim to be imminent, I wired Colin, just back from the Caribbean, to return as mate, engaged a local crew and had the schooner ready for sea within forty-eight hours. Our haste was needless. Day after day, Warner wobbled down to the schooner on a borrowed bicycle with excuses for delaying the swim. The weather wasn't right or the tides were unsuitable, although to me, conditions appeared to be ideal.

We became increasingly annoyed and frustrated by the hold-ups for our expenses soon exceeded the amount we were to receive for the charter. The only person in the *Nellie Bywater* who thoroughly enjoyed the long wait was our youngest daughter, Inga. Right from the start she'd chummed up with Shirley and spent every available moment with her. She accompanied the American girl during training sessions and received instruction and coaching from the experts. Between them, Shirley and her trainer turned the little girl who could only swim a few hesitant strokes, into a strong and confident swimmer. Subsequently, in terrifying circumstances, the friendly tuition from the two American swimmers undoubtedly saved our daughter's life. If we'd been able to see into the future, instead of fretting and fuming at the many postponements of the swim, we'd have been thankful for Ted Warner's machinations.

The hitherto fine weather became very unsettled and, oddly enough, it was then that Warner announced that the swim was definitely 'on'. We moved the schooner round to the Camber and, at midnight, embarked his 'few friends'. The *Nellie Bywater*'s deck was packed with newsmen from many countries, cameramen from all the leading newsreels, film company executives and technicians. In the hold, the B.B.C. had set up a broadcasting station to relay a live commentary of the swim to America. All these people had paid Ted Warner handsomely for the privilege of being aboard the schooner. It must have taken a great deal of scheming and haggling to assemble such a gathering for the event, and it was now obvious why there had been so many previous postponements.

As we left Dover, with our strange assortment of sensation-mongers bedded down on every available inch of deck, the sky was a threatening mass of low, black thunderheads and visibility so poor that we were half-way across Dover Strait before we picked up the white flashing light on Cap Gris-Nez where we were to rendevous with Shirley's party.

Ted Warner was in a very nervous and excited state. He couldn't understand why I wasn't heading directly for the light, unaware that I was making an allowance for the very strong tidal set. He became such a nuisance I sent him packing with a flea in his ear as I needed all my wits to handle the schooner during the several severe squalls we encountered.

The first streaks of dawn lightened the sky. We sighted the small launch carrying the swim's pilot bobbing about on the edge of the shoal water bordered with a wide, white margin of heavy surf. Another sharp squall struck us, hiding the boat from view and whipping the sea into a lather of foam. When the sky cleared, through my binoculars I again picked up the pilot launch with the indistinct head of a swimmer near it. Shirley must have commenced her swim at the height of the squall and battled through the rough breakers into deep water. I couldn't imagine a more unfavourable time to start the girl on her difficult undertaking.

The weather having done its damndest—Shirley's protective grease had been washed off during the squall—the sky cleared, the sun came out and the leaden sea became a tropical blue for the remainder of the day.

Aboard the *Nellie Bywater* it was bedlam. A rough, rude, jostling throng of over-excited newshounds milled about the deck. Cameramen perched on the deckhouses, the lifeboat and aloft in the rigging, reminding me of a flock of vultures awaiting a kill. In the galley, a distraught father clumsily prepared soup for the brave little swimmer, refusing Bill's proffered aid, and he poured the boiling liquid into a glass milk bottle which immediately burst into fragments. Below, in the hold, Stephen Grenfell kept up a racy, highly coloured, minute-to-minute commentary of events. The gabble was completely drowned by the noise of the two giant-size Tannoy speakers at full volume, blaring out a never-ending repetition of Shirley's favourite pop record, 'On a slow boat to China'.

The fantastic proceedings were further enlivened by the arrivals of a positive armada of small craft. Motor yachts and speed boats surrounded us and overhead, two or three chartered aircraft circled and dived over the struggling swimmer.

Bill and I were frankly sickened by the whole, bizarre set-up. All we could think of was the courageous young girl in the sea, fighting desperately against the fierce Channel tides, until it became too painful to watch her. Hour after hour she gallantly battled towards the Kentish coastline, her progress seemingly a snail's pace. When more than three parts of the swim had been accomplished, Shirley's unprotected body and limbs became affected by the extremely cold sea. But she still fought on.

Finally, the adverse tide began to set her offshore and with the cold paralyzing her, the gallant little Shirley was defeated. Her pilot, Temme, Junior, forcibly took her from the water, fighting and begging him to allow her to continue with her swim, for her spirit was still unbeaten. It was a sad end to a very brave effort.

For a few seconds Ted Warner gazed in stunned disbelief at the drama in the pilot launch and then went crazy, nearly tearing his hair out in handfulls, moaning: 'Jeez. Oh Jesus Christ!'

Frantically signalling to a waiting speedboat to come alongside, he leapt into her and streaked away at top speed in the direction of Dover. His departure triggered off a general exodus of his 'friends' for they had news deadlines to meet. We were left, in blissful peace, with a few executives and technicians. It was well after midnight before we landed them and their equipment at the Camber.

The most publicised and adroitly stage-managed Channel swim of all times had a depressing sequel at the White Cliffs Hotel the following morning.

I'd called to collect my charter money from Warner and met Shirley's father and trainer in the otherwise deserted lounge. They were a picture of gloom and despondency which wasn't improved by my arrival. When I asked for Warner, they said he was already on a plane winging its way back to America, but he'd left an envelope for them to deliver to me.

I examined the contents of the envelope . . . half the agreed charter fee that was owing. Absolutely furious, I turned on the two Americans and gave them my candid opinion of Yanks. In the middle of a juicy sentence I was shocked into silence when a door opened and Shirley entered the room. I could scarcely recognise her. Previously, except when swimming, she'd always been groomed and gowned to perfection. Now she was in an old dressing-gown with her hair in dank rats-tails. Her eyes were swollen and dark ringed with fatigue; her cheeks stained with tears. She'd heard my angry remarks and broke into a fit of sobbing.

With the girl's plucky efforts still on my mind, it was all too much for me. I did my best to console her and told her she would have succeeded with her swim if she'd been given a fair start. Seeing her in such a state, I couldn't help thinking that it was just as well she'd failed before her exploiters took further advantage of her.

I left a message for Warner with the Americans. 'If you ever see him again, tell him from me that if I ever catch up with him, I'll see that he swims the Channel next time!'

We held a post-mortem in the cabin when I returned to the *Nellie Bywater*. Bill's comment was philosophical: 'We're lucky to get half the money. Warner could easily have gone without leaving us a penny!' When I suggested that I may have been taken for a 'sucker', that the scene in the hotel could have been acted for my benefit, Inga was very indignant, for her friend and idol, Shirley, was beyond reproach. To this day, she remembers her American swimmer friend with the greatest affection. Colin, still chuckling at the extraordinary events of the previous twenty-four hours, summed it up by saying: 'I've seen some odd things in my time but nothing to beat that swim!'

The newspapers had a field day, plastering accounts of the swim across their front pages. The headlines of one 'daily' read: THE BALLY-HOO SWIM, fully endorsing Colin's opinion.

We were the losers at the time but subsequently we were bountifully repaid for our brief association with Shirley May France.

* * *

In spite of our reverses, we were still determined to pursue a
course in films. With super optimism we spent money on increasing the schooner's accommodation to make her more suitable for
motion picture work. We were bottom cleaning at Newhaven
when we were approached by Coronado Films of Hollywood,
who were making *Circle of Danger* in this country with frozen
dollars. The film was about a hard-up American captain of a
South Sea schooner who became suddenly wealthy by recovering
the valuable cargo of a freighter sunk by enemy action during the
War. By coincidence, I'd just returned from working a wrecked
liberty ship also sunk by enemy action in the War but, in my case,
my earnings for a very hazardous, successful salvage operation
were only sufficient to tide us over a lean period. And, the rate
offered by Coronado Films to do their work wouldn't improve
our finances very much, but I was still glad to accept their charter.

The schooner's bottom cleaning was finished and we were
about to begin topside painting but the film people stopped us.
'Oh, no, don't do that. The captain in the film is supposed to be
broke, so we want your schooner to look run-down and weather-
worn,' they said. It was closer to reality than I cared for; our
painting and maintenance of the *Nellie Bywater* was now being
done at the expense of necessities for the family.

The filming was to be done off Plymouth and we had a hard
beat down Channel against strong sou'-westerlies to reach our
location, but arrived twenty-four hours ahead of time. The Coronado unit was already assembled on the quayside as we tied up in
the Millbay Dock. They were real hustlers; even as I conferred
with their executives, their technicians were building camera
towers on the *Nellie Bywater*'s topsides and bow, and loading
diving equipment, cameras and props of every description on our
deck. Within a few hours we were ready to sail for the filming.

Jacques Cartier was directing and Ray Milland starring as the
schooner captain. A more professional pair couldn't be found in
the whole film industry. Without a single 'retake', the sea sequences, with the Mewstone in the background, were shot in the
record time of two days. This was greatly to our disadvantage as
we were on time charter, but we used all our seamanship to
expedite the work and avoid hold-ups.

The additional accommodation below was a great success,

providing actors and executives with comfortable quarters to relax in between filming. During one of his waiting periods below, Ray Milland asked our forthright daughter Jo for a 'cawfee', strongly accenting his American speech.

'Mr Milland,' she said, severely. 'I'll not make you a coffee unless you ask for it in plain English. You're no more an American than I am!'

Contritely, but with twinkling eyes, the great star rephrased his request in 'plain English' and duly received his coffee. A thoroughly nice man, Ray Milland, entirely unspoilt by his long term of success.

Forewarned by previous experiences, immediately our work was finished and before the Coronado unit moved to its next location, I presented them with my account through our Plymouth agent. They rewarded our herculean efforts by drastically trimming our modest claim. But I'd learnt my lesson. I instructed the agent to inform the company 'moneybags' that I'd have their cameras and equipment held in Plymouth unless the account was settled in full that very day. They paid up without further delay or argument.

It was the last film work we ever did with the *Nellie Bywater*. The elusive, dangerously attractive bubble we'd been chasing had finally burst. Throughout the world, the empires of the great film moguls were crumbling.

But, far more serious than that, revolutionary changes in transport were decimating the Home Trade fleet of small ships. It was obvious that there was no future for us in Britain with an obsolete sailing vessel.

Schooners were still fully employed in the inter-island trades of the West Indies, so after long deliberation we decided to try our luck in the Caribbean.

22

A Brave Little Ship

Bill and I have a deep-rooted love for the land of our birth. The decision to leave Britain was no light-hearted matter, as those who've been faced by the same situation will appreciate. And, of course, it wasn't all that easy to leave the country.

Our first step was a thorough refit of the *Nellie Bywater*, which was a very expensive business. At Plymouth we renewed all the running rigging, footropes and ratlines as the auxiliary was being overhauled. It was a problem to find a dry dock where the schooner's hull and bottom could be attended to at a reasonable cost, but after many exasperating delays, the Ponsharden Shipyard, Penryn, Falmouth gave us every facility at the most moderate charges. It was the beginning of December before refitting finished and we were able to undock and haul out to the buoys in the Carrick Roads.

Bill had a headache with the victualling, for everything, even flour, was still strictly rationed. She had a tough duel with the Customs before she obtained the necessary permit for adequate food for the Atlantic crossing. Traditional staple items of sailing ship fare were unobtainable in Falmouth and our 'cabin' hard tack biscuit had to be specially ordered from Liverpool. Monsen, the Falmouth chandler, provisioned us and did a capital job.

The hold-ups over victualling were only the beginning, for little men with ambiguous titles delayed us and kept us at the buoys with an amazing variety of pretexts. They destroyed our last hopes of a quiet crossing of Biscay. The weather became progressively worse, gale following gale. As an extra precaution, I had Penrose, the Truro sailmaker, make me the strongest possible flax trysail with an all-round wire boltrope.

When we were finally given clearance in ballast for Port Castries, St Lucia, we had the worst of the winter weather ahead.

The *Nellie Bywater* was in fine seagoing order after her extensive refit. We carried supplies of ropes, wires, paints, bottom compositions and other stores sufficient for two years. In addition to the sails bent, we had a full spare suit of stout flax working canvas and a reserve topmast.

Five tough young men had joined us as crew for the adventure of sailing-ship life. Unfortunately, they were none of them schoonermen. We'd hoped to have Colin with us as mate, but a sick and aged father kept him at home. Our new mate had served in sail but was an unknown quantity. At his request we took as a supernumerary a young nursing sister who was travelling to St Lucia to take up a hospital appointment. With the children, our total complement was eleven.

The evening before we left Falmouth, all our young people had shore leave for a farewell drink with friends. It was the first time for weeks that Bill and I had been alone with the children. Now that our preparations were complete and all difficulties overcome, we tried to relax but were unable to do so.

Our living quarters had never looked more snug and inviting, with a cheerful fire glowing in the stove and the cabin brightly lit by the gently gyrating lamp. Despite this, I felt terribly depressed and could sense that Bill shared my low spirits. I attributed this to the pressures we'd been under for so long; also we were already missing Colin as we always did when we were without him, for no-one else had his understanding of the *Nellie Bywater* or his sympathetic insight into our personal problems.

Our spirits were not improved by a curious remark made by Jo, our daughter. Curled up in her favourite corner of the settee with a book, she suddenly said: 'Daddy! I've been trying to picture what my life will be in the West Indies, but all I can see is a complete blank!'

The whole family was in the grip of a disturbing malaise on the eve of our most ambitious venture with the *Nellie Bywater*. We'd no illusions about what we were doing; exchanging the familiar problems of home waters for unpredictable ones in the Caribbean. Already we'd suffered our first set-back, for a film company were vacillating about a contract they'd promised us in St Lucia. Hitherto, a new challenge with fresh horizons had always refreshed and stimulated us, now it was quite different. Without any valid reason, every sense warned me against sailing on the morrow and I was sorely tempted to remain in Falmouth over Christmas which was only four days distant, but pressures on us to leave were too great to be ignored.

Saturday, 22 December, 1951

The gales had abated and the day began with light variable winds and an overcast sky. The shipping forecast gave moderate winds in Biscay, the first time for several weeks.

A powerful Dutch deepsea tug bound for Genoa with a difficult tow of two new engineless merchant ships had been sheltering for two or three weeks near to us in the Carrick Roads. I noticed her crew were preparing the tow for sea.

Jo, our self-appointed 'boatman' during our long stay at the buoys, ferried me ashore to collect the ship's papers from our agents. In Arwenack Street I met the Harbour Master and he greeted me with: 'Thought you'd be well on your way by now, Cap'n! The Dutchman's gone, so the weather must be good in the Bay.'

The mood I was in, his remarks irritated me, and I felt like telling him to mind his own bloody business, but instead made a suitable jocular reply.

At midday we unmoored from the buoys and headed for the sea under the auxiliary. The day matched my mood; grey sky weeping a drizzle of rain over a sullen, slate-coloured sea. Our rain-soaked flax canvas when hoisted was the same depressing shade and the brightly coloured signal flags, spelling out the compliments of the season to friends ashore, were the only relief to the sombre scene.

Under plain sail and triatic stays'l we passed St Anthony lighthouse, listing gently to the light, damp, westerly breeze which just allowed us to lay our course for Ushant.

Once clear of the land, watches were chosen and set. Our most promising lads were the Divers brothers, Peter and John. Tall, lean and tough, they'd both worked as yacht hands and John had served his time as a shipwright. Peter was in my watch, John in the mate's. The boy in my watch was Michael Goddard, who'd had some previous sea service in freighters. The mate had a quiet, stocky, ex-Trinity House light-keeper, Allan Davies, and a bewildered seventeen-year-old beginner to seafaring, David Wheeler, to complete his watch. As usual, Bill presided over the galley. Given a fair spell of weather to settle down, the young men had the makings of a good crew.

With gradually freshening westerly wind, the *Nellie Bywater* ploughed her way towards Ushant, the loom of the powerful Lizard light still visible astern until dawn.

Sunday, 23 December

The wind backed to west-sou'-west and increased to Force 7–8. By midday the schooner was snoring over a rough, white-capped sea, close-hauled on the starboard tack, spray flying in sheets over her bows as she smashed into the steep, hissing rollers. Reluctantly, we were obliged to take in the small triangle of triatic stays'l as it was almost at bursting point.

Twenty-four hours from the Lizard we passed Ushant and I was very pleased with our progress. Unfortunately, the force of the wind was steadily increasing, building up a very big sea. A reading of the barometer shocked me for I'd never seen a glass so low. Before darkness set in I took a careful appraisal of the weather. The *Nellie Bywater* was buoyantly riding the steep rollers though, from the sharply inclined deck, I could see she was being over-pressed. On the crests of the seas, the schooner was beginning to stagger in the fiercest gusts. It was time to get the big mains'l off her. At the change of watches I ordered the sail to be taken in. Under the rough conditions it was a tricky job for an inexperienced crew but they managed it without mishap after a hard struggle.

With the main snugly furled and double gasketted and the brand new trys'l set in its place, the schooner rode the big breakers with ease. It was fortunate we'd made the sail reduction before dark, as the wind velocity soon reached Force 10.

Although we were in one of the busiest of sea lanes, we'd only sighted one ship since leaving Falmouth. Off Ushant, in the fading twilight, a grey and white Norwegian tanker of some 10,000 tons, on the same course as ourselves, overhauled and passed us about two cables distant. Her size scaled down the big seas until they seemed insignificant. She appeared to be impregnable as she vanished into the night.

To my dismay, after dark the weather deteriorated still further until wind and sea were the worst I'd ever encountered. To increase my anxiety, the wind backed to the sou'-west, so that we were gradually closing the land. By midnight, the sea was so bad we were making no headway; the schooner just rode up and down

27. *Nellie Bywater* arriving in port. (*Western Morning News, Plymouth*)

28. On a grey December day, under rain-soaked canvas, *Nellie Bywater* begins her last voyage. (*Mr Morris-Pugh, Falmouth*)

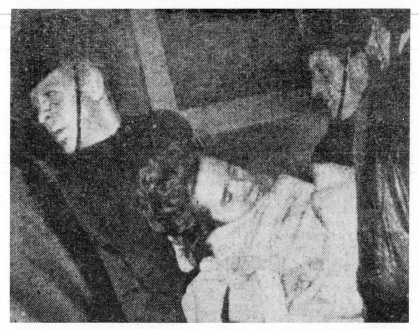

29. The tragic end to *Nellie Bywater*'s last voyage. Bill is carried ashore from H.M.T. *Careful*. (*Western Morning News, Plymouth*)

30. Recognition of a young girl's courage by master and crew of H.M.T. *Careful* in Devonport Dockyard. (*Western Morning News, Plymouth*)

the great rollers with considerable leeway. In the spume-filled blackness to loo'ard lay the dreaded 'Saints' and the reefs and rocks of the Armen. Unless the wind changed to our advantage, we would soon be obliged to put the schooner on the other tack to stand away from a most perilous stretch of Breton Coast.

Monday, 24 December

The wind had reached a monstrous force, greatly exceeding anything I'd experienced. Charged with salt water snatched from the wave crests, it roared over our little vessel, intent on destroying her. We were choked, blinded and deafened by its ferocity. It stunned the senses until simple thought or action became a great effort. I marvelled that the *Nellie Bywater*'s fabric could withstand such an onslaught. Unable to see more than a few feet, I could nevertheless gauge from her violent movements that she was soaring dizzily over the steep whitecaps with the buoyancy of a gull, though listed far over by the blast. If nothing carried away and given sufficient searoom, she inspired confidence in her ability to survive even this great storm, if left to ride it out on the same course. I was most apprehensive of attempting to wear her round in such terrible conditions with an untried crew and for over two hours delayed the inevitable orders in the faint hopes of a lull.

Our leeway towards the land was of such a rate that by 2 a.m. I knew we could wait no longer. There wasn't the slightest easing of the weather. The hands were mustered and in the shelter of the wheelhouse I did my best to convey to the mate the need for skill and caution when rounding to. 'See the sheets don't take charge!' was my final warning. I instructed him to send a lad aft to let me know when he was ready for the dangerous manoeuvre, as I'd be unable to see or hear anything of actions in the eyes of the schooner.

Receiving the mate's message that he was prepared, I let the schooner's head gradually fall off the wind. My only guides to what was happening were the swinging compass card and our change of motion. We were before the wind. Another spoke of the wheel and from the compass heading I knew we were around on the new tack, apparently unharmed by wind and sea. On a heading of nor'-west, away from the land, the schooner was riding as well as before. My relief at the successful change of course was

253

premature. The dripping form of Peter Divers burst into the wheelhouse, yelling into my ear: 'Quick, Sir! The mate wants you. The forestay's gone!' It was the hell of a shock.

Giving the lad strict orders to 'nurse her', I turned the wheel over to him, grabbed a torch and clawed my way for'ard.

The light from the powerful torch was pitifully inadequate but it was sufficient to see the extent of the storm damage. All the headgear, including the massive forestay, had carried away. Without longitudinal support, the lofty masts would lean aft, slackening shrouds and backstays until they were virtually unstayed. I was unable to see this with visibility nil but knew we would soon be completely dismasted unless we quickly secured the badly working 'sticks'.

The crew were just hanging on out of range of a madly thrashing tangle of wire, rope and canvas until I took charge.

Heavy wire strops were brought from the half-deck and shackled on the windlass. To these we secured the fish tackle and two burtons, setting them up as taut as possible as jury forestays. We next cleared and lashed down the flailing raffle of loose rigging and canvas. It required several hours of desperate effort before we were finished as we were working blindly by touch, under a constant avalanche of salt water, with our vessel's bows soaring and plunging dizzily and the roaring wind making movement and communication very difficult. Two hands were sent to man the pumps but the suctions were unable to reach the bilgewater properly owing to the schooner's heavy list. At length we completed all that could be done for the safety of our vessel until daylight, so I sent the mate's watch below on stand-by. Nagged by thoughts of unseen damage to our vessel, the remaining hours of darkness seemed never-ending.

I've always been depressed by a dawn and as the eastern sky lightened to a new day my heart truly sank as I saw the havoc inflicted on the schooner by the raging wind.

The foretopmast, snapped off at the lowermast cap, hung insecurely by a tangle of wires and ropes at the foremast head. Fortunately, it had jammed itself between the foreyard lifts and the cap backstay. The tops'l yard, sprung at the slings, drooped forlornly across the foreyard. A few wildly slatting pennants of canvas were all that remained of the furled triatic stays'l. The canvas lifeboat cover had been torn to shreds. Lifebuoy cleats had been ripped away from their fastenings and the buoys, splintered woodwork and a litter of wire and cordage washed about in the lee waterways. It was hard to believe that our trim vessel could have been so badly mauled in just a few hours.

We were surrounded by high, vicious, whitecapped rollers, their sides marbled with foam and their size made the *Nellie Bywater* seem very small and vulnerable although she was riding them magnificently, shipping very little solid water.

As the daylight strengthened, I noticed a slight veering and lessening of the wind. Its roar had become a whistle and there was less spume in the air.

Fortified by a good breakfast, prepared by Bill in a galley that looked as if it had been bombed, we turned-to, under greatly improved conditions, clearing and repairing the wreckage. We began by sending down the broken spars and their gear from aloft as they were the most immediate hazard. The headstays were our next task. These had all parted at their chain pennants and we were able to set up the forestay and standing jibstay until they were as strong as ever.

A thorough examination of mast partners, wedges and coats revealed no damage in spite of the violent workings of the spars when they were unsupported. The schooner was making the normal amount of water for a wooden ship in heavy weather and short spells of pumping each watch were sufficient to contain it. By midday, with the wind reduced to between Force 8 and 9 and much of the viciousness gone out of the sea, we bent and set two new headsails, a forestays'l and standing jib.

Except for being baldheaded on the foremast, the *Nellie Bywater* was now as shipshape and seaworthy as before. The crew, although exhausted, were in good spirits. Through the binoculars the Bishop Rock lighthouse was just discernible on the starboard bow. In a Force 8 westerly, we wore ship and continued our voyage.

I was very proud of our little schooner's behaviour and hoped this westerly wind would take us across Biscay to the finer weather beyond Finisterre. I was already planning to send up the spare topmast and fish and recross the tops'l yard when we reached the better weather. But I was being far too optimistic. The 'ship swallower', as early mariners so aptly named the ocean, was just playing with us as a cat plays with a mouse.

Lloyds of London were receiving disturbing news of severe storms in the Eastern Atlantic, Biscay and the Western Approaches. Reports of many casualties were coming in. A Dutch motorvessel had driven ashore near Biarritz with the loss of all hands; the tanker *Maetra* was drifting helplessly with her steering gear broken; the bridge of the Norwegian *Strix* had been swept away by a tremendous wave, with the loss of her captain and third officer.

All Biscay and Breton ports reported being battered by hurricane-force winds and mountainous seas, which were causing extensive damage afloat and ashore.

With our small radio out of action from the previous night and no further sightings of shipping since the tanker off Ushant, we were unaware of the serious weather conditions. Surrounding our small pocket of gale force winds raged one of the worst storms of the century, already claiming its grim toll of ships and seamen's lives.

Until darkness closed down, the schooner made surprisingly good progress over the steep seas, then the wind followed the pattern of the previous night; backing slowly to the sou'-west and its whistle changing into an ear-splitting roar. By 9 p.m. it was gusting up to 100 knots with a mountainous sea running. A mighty blast struck the *Nellie Bywater*, pinning her down on her beam ends and again carrying away her headstays. The powerful leverage of the unstayed masts was noticeably buckling the deck. In less than twenty-four hours the setting up of jury stays began all over again, but this time with a very tired crew and conditions far worse than before. It was heartbreaking. Desperately, we forced our numbed senses and leaden limbs to function, breathing with the utmost difficulty. With the last of our strength we succeeded in securing the masts.

Christmas Day, Tuesday, 25 December
The hours of darkness were a nightmare; a continuous roar of wind like an express train travelling through a tunnel, and it was nerve-shattering. For the first time I began to wonder if we could

survive. Most of the wheelhouse windows blew in, showering me with glass.

With the coming of dawn, the sea was a frightening sight: more white than grey, the air full of spume whipped from the yeasty wave crests.

Through a curtain of spray, I could see the dim, humped forms of Peter and Michael rising and falling as they laboured at the pumps. Bent double, Michael fought his way to the wheelhouse and shouted in my ear: 'Shall I hoist the Christmas tree, Cap'n?'

It was my first intimation that it was Christmas Day—and that my young crew hadn't yet realised our desperate plight. So far, it was just an adventure to them, which would end safely and happily. They would need this spirit in plenty if we were all to survive.

At my nodded assent, the lad dragged the little fir tree out of the cabin companionway but it was instantly stripped of its needles by the wind. In spite of this he persisted and after a hard struggle, succeeded in hoisting a pathetic, bare stick to the maintruck. Apparently satisfied, he returned to his duties on the pumps.

When it was sufficiently light, I made a survey of our further storm damage. This time the headgear had gone due to the shearing of the massive Swedish iron stemhead roller straps. The breaks were clean, straight and bright, as if cut with a power hacksaw. I supposed they were caused by what the 'boffins' call metal fatigue. Nothing could withstand such a wind indefinitely. The heavy wooden door had been wrenched off the heads and had disappeared. During the night, I'd glimpsed it fluttering in the air like a piece of cardboard and wondered what it was. The outside skin of the tightly furled mains'l looked as if it had been clawed by a wild animal. The schooner was now leaking badly and required continuous pumping.

Throughout the day there was no relief from the hurricane. Pressed far over by the savage wind, the *Nellie Bywater* rode the furious seas superbly but was gradually being driven back to Ushant.

Since encountering the storm, I'd seen little of my wife and children. The crew were being fed and, somehow, Bill had even managed to bake an enormous, though grossly misshapened mincepie.

The violent movement and racket below were very trying for the women and children and Bill had to lash little Inga in her bunk to prevent her from being thrown out.

The Ushant light showed up on our port quarter at about 8 p.m.

Reports of further casualties were pouring into Lloyds. The Panamanian steamer *Buccaneer*, 7,256 tons, had lost her propeller 150 miles west of Brest and needed immediate assistance; the American steamer *Flying Enterprise*, 6,711 tons, had split her deck and topsides and was listing over to 30 degrees, west of Brest; the Panamanian *Panamante*, 7,176 tons, was in severe weather sou'-west of Ushant, with her steering gear out of action. . . .

Wednesday, 26 December

There was no change in the weather, except for variations in the wind directions from sou'-west to west and back again. Occasional slight lulls were followed by even more furious blasts. We were losing ground and being driven back into the English Channel.

About 9 a.m., with Ushant on our lee about 12 miles distant, we wore ship during a lull. She required a scrap of headsail to help her round and two sails blew to shreds before we could get one to stand. In coming to the port tack, this one also blew away but we were on the desired tack heading about nor' by west in an effort to reach a West Country port.

The pumps were still containing the leaks, though the lads were now in poor shape with the continuous pump drill. After dark, the tough nurse Anne had a brief attack of panic but I calmed her down. The last pane of glass in the wheelhouse was shattered.

The schooner was riding well under the magnificent boom fores'l of Ulster flax made by Tedfords and the new trys'l.

All our willpower was needed to ward off a dangerous lethargy induced by the constant battering of the wind.

Thursday, 27 December

Veering westerly, the wind was worse and so was the sea. The trys'l, new in Falmouth, was showing signs of the terrific strain with some of the treble stitching at the seams parting. During the afternoon, the maintopmast backstays slackened. The metal pole-band to which they were shackled had split, opened and slid down the spar. From then onwards, the long topmast was completely unstayed.

The state of my crew was causing me great concern. Through exhaustion, their reactions had become very slow and they moved like sleepwalkers. The vital pumping had become sporadic. Knowing that their strength depended on a regular supply of hot food and drink, Bill stoically did her job in the galley, for she fully appreciated our perilous situation. Her working conditions were well nigh impossible.

By 6 p.m. the leaks began to gain on us. Removing a section of the cabin airport, I discovered that the schooner was taking water through seams immediately below the coverboard where the caulking must have spewed out when the masts were adrift. We prepared for emergencies. Lifejackets were issued, the ship's papers, instruments and extra food were stowed in the lifeboat lockers and the women and children evacuated to the after cabin.

Friday, 28 December
Estimating that we should be closing the land, with great difficulty I climbed the main rigging, pinned to the shrouds by the wind so that I could scarcely move or breathe. From aloft I sighted the flash of the Eddystone light, about ten miles away on our port quarter. At 2 a.m. we saw the lights of a ship, our first sighting since the 23rd. In the hopes that her captain would either stand by us or alert the shore by radio-telephone, we fired off two distress rockets, no mean feat from the violently moving deck of a storm-wracked schooner. Seen through spume and spray, their signals were pathetically feeble so I doubt if the crew of the neighbouring ship saw them. There were no acknowledgements. From the wildly arcing lights of the other ship it was possible her crew had their own problems.

By dawn, the wind had eased off a great deal until it was about Force 8 and the sea wasn't nearly so bad. Prawle Point and the Start were ahead and for a time I hoped we could round these headlands to find a lee. But, the wind backed quickly to sou'-sou'-west, preventing us weathering them. At last, the cunning, treacherous sea had trapped the crippled *Nellie Bywater* on a dangerous lee shore, a situation I'd been dreading. We altered course for Plymouth as there was still a faint possibility of scraping past Bolt Head and Tail. Salcombe lay tantalisingly off our starboard beam, yet inaccessible owing to the state of the bar.

Coming up to Bolt Head, the wind again flew round to the west, heading us and freshening fast. We successfully weathered the promontory, but so close that we could plainly see the great rollers thundering against the high cliffs and leaping almost to their summits.

We hoisted the NC code flags and ungriped our lifeboat. Shortly afterwards a large tanker came up astern and by semaphore, we requested her master to radio Plymouth for a tug and in the meantime stand by us. The time was 9 a.m. The vessel was the British Tanker Company's M.T. *British Birch* of 8,000 tons, light and rolling heavily in the big sea.

At 11 o'clock we were joined by the French fishing trawler, *Jacques Cartier*. Bobbing like a cork, she manoeuvred round our stern close enough for us to get a weighted heaving line across to her. We passed her our best hawser and at midday, she took us in tow. A few minutes later a huge sea surged the towrope and, as it snapped tight again, it parted. In rapidly deteriorating weather the trawler steamed away, probably to seek shelter.

We weathered Bolt Tail but were setting down on the land. The *British Birch* signalled he would try to tow us. I instructed the mate to reply: 'Keep away or you'll sink us!'

I was unable to read what was sent but the tanker continued to close our lee side. Thoroughly alarmed, I yelled to the mate to repeat his warning signal.

The tanker still approached us, enormous and lethal, rolling like a cockleshell. She was being magnificently handled but in the heavy sea anything could happen.

Bill and little Inga were with me in the wheelhouse and Jo was a few yards away in the shelter of the cabin companionway. They watched the tanker closing us, wide-eyed and apprehensive.

Dangerously near and parallel to the battered, jury-rigged little schooner, the *British Birch* fired her line-throwing gun. A rocket with its attached line arced over the *Nellie Bywater*'s after deck. The tanker steamed clear and lay hove-to, blowing to loo'ard and paying out a very big new hawser which my crew hauled aboard the schooner.

It was now 1.30 p.m. Hopes of assistance from Plymouth had faded with just two hours of daylight remaining. The weather was hourly getting worse and there was every sign of another night of hurricane-force wind. It was a miracle our sails had lasted, but the trys'l was nearly done for. Also my crew were at their last gasp. Against my judgement, I allowed the desperate expedient of towing a trial—a decision I'll regret to my dying day.

The *British Birch* steamed to wind'ard across our bows, in an attempt to straighten the towrope which lay as a great semi-circle in the sea off our lee bow. I stationed the mate with a sharp axe near the taut hawser, ready to cut it adrift if necessary.

The towrope resisted the efforts to straighten it but the immense power of the tanker was transmitted through the hawser, listing our little vessel over in the most alarming way; the strain was too much for any wooden ship. I signalled the mate to cut but before he could do so, the hawser apparently parted. With incredible speed, the *Nellie Bywater* rolled over to port, throwing me over the wheel and dipping the weather foreyardarm into the sea. Then, even more violently, she rolled back to starboard and I felt a dreadful shudder passing through her timbers—the convulsive paroxysm of a stricken ship as the holding-down bolts of engines, water and fuel tanks sheared and everything, including the ballast, thundered to starboard.

The wheelhouse was instantly submerged, trapping all inside below the sea. Swirled about like a chip of wood, my sense of direction gone, I tried desperately to find my wife and daughter. With lungs nearly bursting, I touched someone's clothing and instinctively knew it was little Inga. Groping blindly, I found a window opening and pushed the child through it. I was nearly done for but the fear of losing my wife spurred me on. With a last frantic effort, I found her trapped under the wheel spindle and, with difficulty, got her through the window, her lifejacket nearly foiling me.

It was my last recollection of being in the submerged wheelhouse. I must have lost consciousness and the structure, battered by the seas, probably broke up and released me, for when I came to again I was on the surface.

The *Nellie Bywater* lay capsized on her starboard side, the masts level with the water. The crew were perched along the high, exposed port topside, looking like seabirds on a dead whale. Two of the lads were hauling the tiny figure of Inga over the slippery, curved bilge planking and two others were attempting to reach Bill who was rising and falling in the big waves near the schooner's stern. With my help they managed to grab her and lift her onto the half-round. From the wave crests, I scanned the huddled figures on the wreck looking for Jo and I believe I saw her with the others. Using the chain rudder kicking strop for a handhold, I was half way up the stern overhang when the schooner righted herself with a vicious jerk, throwing us all back into the sea. The steep breakers rapidly swept us away from the wreck and I lost sight of Bill.

Frantically I searched for her in the mighty undulations of a storm-swept ocean. Battered, frozen and barely conscious, it was only the determination to find her that kept me alive.

By God's grace, I miraculously succeeded. From the hissing crest of a mountainous comber, I caught a glimpse of her orange lifejacket in a flotsam-littered trough. Somehow I reached her. She was unconscious and face down in the water but I turned her on her back and tried to keep her head as high as possible. The giant wave tops kept breaking over us, forcing us deep below the surface so that it was impossible to keep the water out of almost bursting lungs.

From the wave crests, I could see the *Nellie Bywater* from time to time. The upper halves of her masts were above water, perfectly upright. Then, very slowly and poignantly they sank and the last I saw of our very gallant little schooner was the maintopmast truck, still bearing the remnants of the Christmas tree, dipping from sight.

I was rapidly weakening and being without a lifejacket myself, my heavy clothing and seaboots were weighing us down. Several times I'd struggled to rid myself of the boots and outer garments but was unable to do so. Gradually my lungs were being clogged with choking brine. Numbed by exposure and exhaustion, we were both immune to further suffering and it seemed best to let the sea take us. On the point of giving up, I saw a big, ocean-going tug not more than fifty yards away and summoned up a final effort.

The tug was rolling violently, alternately exposing her bottom to the keel and then plunging her heavy beltings below the waves.

A line of lifebuoys hung along her side. Reaching the vessel, I waited for the dangerous belting to hit the water and then thrust my free arm through one of the buoys. The tug rolled away from us, nearly pulling my arm from its socket and I blacked out.

I came to briefly aboard the tug. I was lying on her saloon sole, two burly seamen pumping salt water out of me. Around me were members of my crew, huddled in blankets.

Struggling to a sitting position, I asked for my wife. Someone said she was in the Chief Engineer's quarters with Inga and the nurse. Still in the throes of a nightmare, I checked the survivors. John Divers and my eldest daughter Jo were not with them.

Fearfully, I asked where they were, although I already knew the answer. The silence confirmed that they were both lost.

The shock was too much to bear and, mercifully, I lost consciousness again and knew nothing for several hours.

Subsequently, I received the following letter from the master of the *British Birch*:

B. T. C.

M.V. 'British Birch'

at River Humber . . . *Date* 21st January . . . 1952

To Captain T England.
Late Master Schooner 'Nellie Bywater'
c/o Mr. H. Rockey,
Pleasant View,
Yelverton. Devon.

FROM MASTER

Dear Captain England,

On our arrival from Trondheim, I received from my Owners a copy of your letter of the 4th inst.

The 'Nellie Bywater' was a brave little ship and had undoubtedly taken a severe beating.

I had hoped the trawler, being so much smaller than myself, could have towed you until the tug arrived, but when I saw he was unable to do this, my next thought was to hold you off the land until the tug reached us. I had just signalled

H.M.T. 'Careful' to take over when the tragedy occurred.
We chopped our towline at once when we saw you were
sinking and prepared our No 4 boat to pick up survivors.
The tug signalled 'Survivors picked up, returning to
Plymouth', which gave me to understand all had been saved,
and it was in that vein I reported to Lands End Radio.
So it was a great shock to us, when we heard the 6 o'clock
news broadcast, that two of your gallant company had been
lost.

Please accept the deep sympathy of myself and all on
board my ship for your wife and yourself in your great loss.

Yours very sincerely,

Master. M. V. 'British Birch'

EPILOGUE

The rescue vessel, H.M.T. *Careful* of Devonport, A. J. Phillips, Master, landed the nine survivors of the *Nellie Bywater* at Plymouth.

The Admiralty duly recognised the skilful seamanship and initiative of Captain Phillips and his crew, awarding the master a parchment and A. B. Harry Willis the British Empire Medal. I'd let go of my wife when I'd blacked-out alongside the tug and as she was swept away, Harry Willis, a non-swimmer, had instantly dived overboard with a line and saved her. He also assisted thirteen-year-old Inga, who was still bravely swimming in the furious sea although nearly finished.

These fine men insisted that the rescue was just part of their normal duties but we shall never forget their understanding and kindness aboard the *Careful* and after we were landed. They fully shared our grief at the two lost lives.

The unpretentious but invaluable Shipwrecked Mariner's Society cared for my crew and returned them to their homes. They clothed me so that I could attend to the duties still required of me as master/owner of the lost schooner.

Of the many kind people who rallied round us after our tragic loss, those in the small Dartmoor village of Yelverton deserve a special mention. They heartened us in the most difficult period of our lives.

Writing this book has vividly brought back to me my life in schooners. Except for the last chapter which I found very difficult to set down and caused me distress even with time's healing, I have enjoyed reliving the past, remembering old ships, old shipmates and the many interesting people I've been privileged to meet in the course of my seafaring.

Schoonering was a hard life but one that suited me. Apart from my tragic loss, I have no regrets. Aboard those lovely little wooden sailing vessels I was happy and found complete fulfilment.

Sic transit gloria mundi.

GLOSSARY

Abaft. Towards the stern.

Abeam. In a direction 90° from the ship's heading.

About (Go). Change from one tack to the other.

Adze. A shipwright's tool for chipping, with an arching blade at right angles to its handle.

Aft. Stern part of vessel.

Airport. A removable, narrow plank of the hold lining (ceiling) which is taken out to ventilate between a vessel's ceiling and skin planking.

Alee. On the side opposite to the wind.

Arming. Tallow placed in a cavity at the bottom of the sounding lead, to pick up samples from the seabed.

Athwart. Across a ship; from side to side.

Auger. A shipwright's tool for boring holes.

Back. Of the wind, when it changes direction anti-clockwise. Of the sails, when the wind fills the wrong side of sails, impeding a vessel's forward motion or driving her astern.

Backstay. A wire supporting a mast against forward pull. See Profile and Sail Plan, p. 283.

Bag-O-Wrinkle. Material made of ropeyarn and used in the rigging to prevent chafe to sails—i.e., chafing gear.

Baldheaded. A sailorman's description of a vessel that is normally rigged with topmast(s), when she is without such spar(s).

Barque. A sailing vessel with three or more masts, the aftermost fore-and-aft rigged and the others square rigged.

Barquentine. A sailing vessel with three or more masts, the foremost square rigged and the others fore-and-aft rigged.

Barratry. An illegal or fraudulent act committed by a shipmaster or his crew—i.e. fraudulent dealing with a ship's cargo.

Batten Down. Securing canvas cloths over the hatches with wedged battens to make them watertight.

Beam Ends. A vessel is on her beam ends when lying on her side.

266

Bearing. The direction, by compass or relative to a ship's head, of any object.

Beat. To make progress against the wind by sailing a zigzag course with the wind first on one bow and then on the other.

Belting. A protruding guard around a vessel's topsides to protect them from damage when going alongside.

Bend. To fasten with a knot; to secure sails to spars or stays.

Bight. A loop, a bend, a curve.

Bilge. The spaces in the bottom of a ship, underneath the ceiling and between the frame timbers. These spaces are connected by limber holes bored through the floor timbers to allow bilge water to drain to the pump suctions. The rounded 'shoulders' of a ship's midship sections formed by the futtocks. Sharply turned futtocks form a 'hard' bilge.

Billboard. A stout timber guard covered with sheet iron, on the outside of a ship's bows to prevent the anchor bills from doing damage.

Billet-Head. An ornament at the extremity of a ship's curved stem.

Bill of Lading. A document acknowledging receipt on board of cargo as described in the bill.

Binnacle. A stand for a compass, its cover, lighting and correctors.

Bitt. A strong post to which moorings or cables are secured. A supporting part of a windlass.

Blackwall Hitch. A suitable knot for attaching a rope to a hook.

Block. Pulley with one or more sheaves.

Bogey. A small, iron, solid-fuel heating stove.

Bolt. A roll of canvas containing approximately 40 yards.

Boltrope. The strengthening rope along the edges of sails.

Boom Fores'l. See Profile and Sail Plan, p. 283.

Bosun's Chair. A wooden seat with rope slings, on which a sailor sits when hoisted aloft to do work to a ship's spars or rigging.

B.O.T. Board of Trade.

Bower. The heaviest anchors, two of which are kept ready for instant use.

Bowsprit. Spar projecting over the ship's bows to carry the headsails. See Profile and Sail Plan, p. 283.

Box. The compass. Name the points of the mariner's compass.

Braces. Tackles for swinging the yards. See Profile and Sail Plan, p. 283.

Break Sheer. When an anchored vessel lies at a dangerous angle to her cable.

Breakers. Seas so steep, the tops curl over and break.

Brig. A sailing vessel with two square rigged masts.

Bulkhead. A partition.

Bullseye. A hardwood ring, grooved around the edges for a strop.

Bulwarks. A stout barrier, for protection against boarding seas, around a ship's deck.

Bunt. Of a sail. The middle of a squaresail.

Buntline. Line for hauling up the middle of a squaresail. See Profile and Sail Plan, p. 283.

Burton. A type of tackle. Schooners had burtons rigged each side of their masts for general lifting and for launching work boats.

By-The-Wind. Steering close to the wind but keeping the sails drawing.

Cant. With a vessel head to wind, to steer so the wind comes on the desired bow.

Capping. The rounded finishing pieces on top of wooden bulwarks.

Cast. Throwing a sounding lead into the sea to take a depth of the water.

Cathead. A wooden or iron fitting extending outboard over each bow from which the anchors are hung from their rings. See Deck Plan, p. 285

Catstopper. A chain securing the ring of an anchor to the outward end of a cathead. See Deck Plan, p. 285.

Caulking. Driving oakum into the seams of a wooden ship to make her watertight. The seams are then finished off with boiling pitch. The materials in a seam.

Ceiling. The inside planking forming the lining of a ship's hold.

Chafing Gear. Bag-o-wrinkle or other such material used to protect the sails from chafe.

Chandler. A dealer in ship's stores.

Characteristic. Of seamarks, such as buoys, lighthouses, lightships, beacons, etc. Their shape, colour, lighting, sound signals, topmarks, etc.

Charter. To agree to a contract for a ship to carry goods, or for her hire. The actual agreement is called a charter party.

Checkrope. A rope made fast ashore for the purpose of controlling a ship's movements in a restricted area—i.e. when docking.

Chocks. Shaped wooden supports for a ship's boat to rest on.

Claw Off. Sailor's term for battling off a lee shore.

Claw Stopper. A short length of chain with one end secured in the ship's bows and at the other end an iron claw-shaped fitting which slips between the links of an anchor cable. The fitting is commonly termed a dog.

Clearance. The authority for the departure of a ship from port.

Clew up. To haul up a sail with clewlines and buntlines ready for furling.

Close-Hauled. When the sails are sheeted in to sail as close to the wind as possible.

Coaming. The raised edging to a hatchway or other deck opening.

Cod End. The pointed extremity of the conical trawl fishing net.

Companionway. A raised shelter covering over stairs leading from the deck to below.

Con. To direct the steering of a ship.

Correctors. Magnets, spheres and Flinder's bar used for compass adjusting.

Counter. A type of ship's stern which extends beyond the sternpost.

Coverboard. The timber covering the frame heads in a wooden ship.

Cowhitch. The traditional two half-hitches used for knotting rigging lanyards to a shroud or stay.

Cringle. Rope eye on boltrope of sail.

Crook. A naturally curved log of wood.

Cross. (A yard) Hoisting a yard aloft and securing it with parrel or truss.

Crown. The bottom of an anchor at the junction of the shank and the arms.

Cuddy. A small cabin.

Cutter. A single masted, fore-and-aft rigged sailing vessel with a bowsprit.

Dan. A mark buoy used by fishermen.

D.B.S. Distressed British Seaman.

Deadeye. A circular hardwood fitting, pierced with three holes and scored around its edges, used for tautening ship's rigging.

Dead Muzzler. Head wind.

Deadrise. The angle of the ship's bottom with the keel.

Deckhead. The underside of a deck when viewed from below.

Deepwaterman. A vessel engaged on ocean-going voyages.

Dog. The claw-like fitting on a cable stopper.

Dolly. A small hand-winch.

Dolphin Striker. A vertical spreader under a bowsprit for the jibboom rigging.

Donkey's Breakfast. Seamen's term for a straw mattress.

Draught. The measurements taken from the bottom of the keel to water-level of a ship afloat, read off markings on stem and stern.

Draw Bucket. A bucket with a rope lanyard, used for drawing water from overside.

Dredge. Manoeuvring a ship astern with an anchor just on the ground.

Dried-Out. When a tide has withdrawn from an object.

Dumb Block. A plain sheaved block.

Dunnage. Material used as packing for the prevention of damage to cargo in a ship's hold, from either water or movement.

Fall. The rope in a tackle or purchase.

Fathom. Six feet.

Fid. A tapered hardwood tool used for splicing and sailmaking.

Fiddle. The curved extension at the top of a vessel's stem.

F.I.O. Free in and out. A charter term meaning that loading and discharging costs are to the charterer's account.

Fish. (A spar) A method of repairing it when sprung. (An anchor) Hoisting the anchor flukes onto the ship's bow.

Fix. Charter.

Flake. Loosely spiral running gear on the deck before working ship, so that it will render through blocks without jamming.

Flattie. A seaman's term for a barge-like, shallow-draught steamer used in the River Mersey.

Fleet. Move along.

Flemish Coil. An ornamental way of coiling ropes for extra smartness, the turns lying flat on the deck alongside one another, looking something like a mat.

Floor. A structural timber of a ship's bottom, running athwartships of the keel.

Flotsam. Goods floating on the water after a shipwreck.

Flying Angel. The device of the Missions to Seamen; a white angel on a blue ground.

Flying Jib. The foremost headsail when four headsails are used.

F.O.B. Free on board. A charter term meaning that the cost of cargo handling and stowage inboard from the ship's rail is to the ship's account.

Fo'c'sle. Forecastle. The crew's living quarters, below deck in the bows.

Footropes. Wires slung below a ship's yards for men to stand on when loosing or furling the sails.

For'ard. Forward. The fore part of a ship.

Fore-an'-After. The rig of a sailing vessel without square sails.

Forefoot. The rounded intersection of the stem with the keel.

Forepeak. The space between the stem and the foremost bulkhead underneath the fo'c'sle, part of which is the chain locker in a schooner.

Forestay. Of schooners. A massive wire from the foremast hounds to the stemhead, longitudinally supporting the foremast, also the other masts. See Profile and Sail Plan, p. 283.

Forestays'l. Forestaysail. See Profile and Sail Plan, p. 283.

271

Freeboard. The vertical distance between the water level and the upper level of the deck measured on a ship's sides amidships.

Freight. Money payable to shipowner for the carriage of cargo.

Freight Rate. The amount payable per ton or for any given quantity.

Founder. To sink.

Foyboat. A boat employed on assisting ships in and around harbours.

Full-Rigged Ship. A sailing vessel with three or more masts, all square rigged.

Furl. To fold in a sail and secure it on its spar or stay with gaskets.

Futtock. An upward curving extension of the floor timber of a wooden ship; two futtocks generally form the turn of the bilge.

Galliot. A small traditional Dutch sailing vessel with blunt, round bows.

Gantline. A line used for hoisting something aloft.

Garboards. The skin planks immediately adjacent to the keel.

Gaskets. Short lengths of rope used for securing furled sails.

Gin Block. A steel cargo block with a single large sheave in a skeleton frame.

Grommet. A rope, wire or metal ring.

Ground Tackle. Anchors and cables.

Gunnel. Gunwale. Upper edge of a boat's sides.

Guy. A steadying or controlling rope or wire.

Half-Deck. In the *Nellie Bywater*, a small tween-deck bosun's store.
Apprentices' living quarters.

Half-Round. The semi-circular taffrail timbers at a schooner's stern.

Halyard. A rope or combinations of rope, wire and blocks, used for hoisting and lowering spars, sails, flags, etc.

Harbour Stow. An extra neat furl of a sail when going into port.

Harden-up. Of a seam. To drive the existing oakum caulking tighter into the seam.

Harness cask. An upright, tapered cask used for salt meat.

Hawse Pipe. The iron lead for an anchor cable at a ship's bow.

Headgear. The rigging at a ship's stem, bowsprit and jibboom.

Heads. The lavatory.

Headsails. Forestaysail and jibs. See Profile and Sail Plan, p. 283.

Heave-Up. To raise the anchor cable and anchor with the windlass.

Heaving Line. A light line with a turk's head or monkey's fist at one end, thrown to make contact with ship or shore and then used to pull over heavy moorings, etc.

Home Trade. Trading between ports of the U.K., Eire, Isle of Man, Channel Islands and the Continent between Ushant and the Elbe.

Horse. In a schooner, the wire or iron rod on which the fore-staysail sheet traveller slides; in a sailing barge the beam serving the same purpose.

Hoveller. A local unlicensed pilot.

Inset. The tidal stream into a bay or inlet.

Irish Pennants. Untidy rope ends, tatters of canvas or parted rigging aloft.

Jibboom. A spar extending beyond the bowsprit.

Jibing. Allowing the sails of a fore-and-after to swing from one tack to the other.

Jury Rigged. A temporary rig used after suffering damage aloft.

Keelson. A massive longitudinal timber over a wooden ship's floors and keel, through-bolted to the keel.

Ketch. A two-masted fore-and-aft rigged sailing vessel, the mizzen mast, stepped forward of the sternpost, being shorter than the main.

Kicking Strop. A chain from the rudder to a ship's quarter, which is tightened to prevent the rudder swinging about when at anchor.

Kingplank. The extra thick planking down the centre of a ship's deck.

Knee. A wooden or iron reinforcement at angles in a ship's framing.

Knightheads. Two strong vertical timbers in the bows of a wooden sailing vessel between which the squared heel of the bowsprit is shipped.

Knuckle. The rounded stonework either side of a dock or harbour entrance.

Lands. Parts of a ship's structure where the skin planking and ceiling make contact with the framing.

Lanyard. A short length of rope for securing something—i.e. rigging lanyards for securing the rigging.

Leadline. A marked line with a lead weight at the end, used for measuring the depths of water. There are two leadlines, the hand leadline and the deepsea leadline.

Lee. The side opposite to the wind.

Lee-Ho. The order for the helmsman to put the helm alee.

Leeway. The off course movement of a ship, due to the wind pressures.

Legs. Vertical timbers fixed temporarily each side of a ship to keep her upright when dried out.

Lemster. A type of Dutch galliot.

Let-Go. The order for dropping anchor or releasing moorings.

Lifeline. A line fixed in bights around a lifeboat or lifesaving apparatus for persons in the water to grab.

Lift. Rigging for topping up the ends of spars. See Profile and Sail Plan, p. 283.

Light. A ship is 'light' when she is without cargo.

Light List. A list of the seamarks of a coastline with their full characteristics, in the order they occur.

Limber Boards. Removable ceiling boards either side of a vessel's keelson.

Lines. A sailor's term for ropes in general.

Lining. The hold 'ceiling'.

Log. Instrument for measuring the distance a ship sails. To enter something in a ship's logbook.

Log Fender. A timber spar with rope lanyards at either end, used as a fender.

Longshoreman. A person employed on or about the waterside.

Loo'ard. Leeward. Down wind.

Loom. The reflection of a seamark's light in the sky. The handle of an oar.

Lowers. The sails below the topsails—i.e. boom foresail and mainsail.

Lug. A simple fore-and-aft sail, popular for ship's boats. It is set on a yard which extends forward of the mast.

Main Gaff. Spar at head of mainsail. See Profile and Sail Plan, p. 283.

Mains'l. Mainsail. See Profile and Sail Plan, p. 283.

Manger. An open-ended trough with a grated bottom, for containing spare anchor cable abaft the windlass. See Deck Plan, p. 285.

Marks. A ship's loading marks of Plimsoll and draught markings.

Marline. A two-stranded cord, usually dressed with Stockholm tar, used for servings, seizings, etc.

Marline Spike. A tapered, pointed steel tool for opening the strands of wires or ropes when they are being spliced.

Mast Coat. A canvas cover at deck level around a mast for keeping out water.

Mast Partners. Supports in the deck framing for the masts.

Mast Wedges. Shaped wooden wedges driven around a mast to secure it in the deck aperture.

Messenger. A connecting rope or tackle from a winch or capstan to transmit power to something needing it—i.e. cable messenger.

M.O.T. Ministry of Transport.

Muzzle. Gather in billowing canvas, sails, etc.

Nickey. A type of lug-rigged Irish fishing boat.

Nip. The point where a mooring passes through a fairlead and can easily chafe.

Offing. A ship's distance off shore.

Old Man. A sailor's term for the Captain.

One Bell. Fifteen minutes before a change of watches, when the watch below is called.

Outward. Going from a port.

Overfall. The confused sea over shoals or caused by strong tidal actions.

Overhaul. Extending the distance between the blocks of a tackle. To overtake. To inspect or examine.

Palm. A sailmaker's hand-guard with thimble, used when hand-sewing.

Parcel. Winding strips of canvas or other material around a wire or rope.

Parrel Bead. A hardwood ball with a hole through it for threading it on wire or rope parrels.

Patent Sheave. A sheave fitted with ball-bearings.

Pawl. A metal catch which engages on a ratchet. A stout mooring post.

Pawlbitt. A strong wooden post on the fore side of the windlass to which the pawlplate and rockerarm are bolted. See Deck Plan, p. 285.

Peak. The outer end of a gaff. The uppermost outer corner of a gaff sail. A compartment in a ship's bows.

Peak Downhaul. A rope for hauling down the peak of a gaff. See Profile and Sail Plan, p. 283.

Pennant. A length of wire, rope or chain from a block to adjust its position.

Pinrail. A wooden rail bored with holes to take belaying pins. See Deck Plan. p. 285.

Point. To head in a certain direction. To taper the end of a rope.

Pole-Band. The metal band at the pole of a topmast with eyes to shackle on its stays.

Poop. A ship's raised after deck.

Pully-Hauly. The toil of manually working a sailing vessel.

Punt. A schooner's work boat.

Purchase. Using systems of pulley blocks to gain mechanical advantage.

Quarter. The ship's side, from the centre of the stern to about 45° degrees forward.

Quay Punt. A Falmouth Harbour boat primarily designed for waiting on ships.

Rails. A loose sailor term for the bulwarks, which consist of a topgallant rail, a pinrail, etc.

Range. Laying a long cable or hawser on the deck in an up-and-down pattern so that it will run out freely.

Ratch. Reach.

Ratline. Rope steps in the rigging. The three-strand tarred hemp used for these 'rungs'.

Reach. To sail with the wind abeam.

Reef. Reducing the area of a sail.

Render. Pass through a block or deadeye.

Ring Netter. A fishing boat working a ring net.

Round-The-Land. Around Land's End.

Rovings. Short lengths of plaited ropeyarns used for bending sails.

Rubber. Rubbing strake. A protruding belt around a boat for protecting her sides from chafe.

Run. The diminishing and hollowing of a ship's underwater sections towards her stern.

Running Gear. Blocks and tackle used for working a sailing vessel.

Running Rigging. The moveable parts of rigging. See Profile and Sail Plan, p. 283.

Saddle. A shoulder built around a mast for supporting the inboard end of a boom.

Sailhook. A steel hook for holding canvas when it is being handsewn.

Scantlings. The sizes of a ship's timbers.

Scarf. A lapped joint for timber.

Schooner. A fore-and-aft rigged sailing vessel with two or more masts. A 'topsail' schooner also sets squaresails on her foremast and foretopmast.

Scope. The length of cable to which a vessel rides when at anchor, measured from the anchor to the hawsepipe.

Scuttle. A small deck opening covered by a sliding or lifting top.

Sea-Room. The safe distance for a ship to be off the land.

Seizing. A secure fastening made with marline or seizing wire.

Sennit. A cord made of plaited rope yarns, which may be flat, square, round or corkscrewed according to the way it is plaited.

Serve. Cover a rope or wire with a binding of small stuff, such as marline, spunyarn or seizing wire.

Serving Mallet. A tool for putting a service quickly and tightly on a rope or wire.

Set. The operations of loosing, hoisting, sheeting and trimming a sail. Tightening up rigging.

Settle. To lower a little.

Shackle. A U-shaped metal fastening. A fifteen-fathom length of chain cable.

Shank Painter. A chain for securing the shank of an anchor on a ship's bulwarks.

Sheerlegs. A tripod used for lifting and stepping masts, etc.

Sheerpole. An iron rod seized at the bottom of shrouds or standing rigging to space them correctly. See Profile and Sail Plan, p. 283.

Sheet Home. To correctly tighten the sheet(s) of a sail.

Shelf. The timbers bolted along the top of a wooden ship's framing to support the ends of her deck beams.

Shellback. A nickname for an old sailorman with shoulders rounded by years of pulling and hauling.

Shorten. To reduce sail. To reduce a scope of anchor cable.

Shrouds. A set of stays laterally supporting a mast.

Slant. A term for conditions when the wind allows a sailing vessel to lie her course.

Slings. Chains or wires by which a yard is suspended or 'slung'. The centre of the yard to which the chains or wires are attached.

Smack. A small sailing fishing vessel.

Snub. The snatch of an anchored ship against her cable in a seaway.

Snug. Comfortable.

Snug Down. Reduce sail to a comfortable spread to suit weather.

Sole. The floor of a ship's living accommodation.

Soul-and-Body Lashings. Ties on wrists, waist and legs of oilskins to prevent the entry of water.

Spanker. The fore-and-aft sail on the aftermost mast of a square rigger.

Spectacle. A metal fitting, resembling three rings welded together, forming the clews (lower corners) of square sails.

Splice. Joining ropes or wires by interlacing their strands.

Spritty. A spritsail-rigged sailing vessel such as a Thames sailing barge.

Sprung. Beginning to break.

Spurling Pipe. A metal lead for a ship's cable from the deck to the chain locker.

Square Foresail. A square sail set 'flying' from a schooner's foreyard, when before the wind.

Square Rig. Rigged with yards and square sails.

Stanchion. A vertical structural timber for supporting a ship's bulwarks or deck.

Standing Jib. A sail set from the bowsprit. See Profile and Sail Plan, p. 283.

Standing Rigging. The semi-permanent staying of masts and spars and rigging not moveable when working ship.

Staysail. A sail bent on a stay. See Profile and Sail Plan, p. 283.

Stealer. A single skin plank developed from two others as they reduce in width towards the bow and stern.

Stem. The upright structural timber at the fore end of a ship's keel.

Sternpost. The upright structural timber at the after end of a ship's keel.

Stiffness. The ability to withstand strong wind pressures without excessive heeling.

Stock. The crosspiece of an anchor below its ring.

Strongback. The wooden ridgepiece supporting a canvas boat cover.

Strop. A length of wire or rope with eyes at each end. A rope or wire spliced into a circle. Both used for securing a block or tackle where needed.

Stun's'ls. Studding sails. Light-weather sails set as extensions to the square sails.

Styrman. The Chief Officer of a Scandinavian ship.

Suji. Caustic soda used for cleaning purposes.

Surge. To slip short lengths at a time—i.e. surge a cable over a windlass barrel or a rope around a belaying pin.

Sweep. A long oar.

Swig. To pull a rope sideways against its belaying pin or cleat and then take in its slack, to gain maximum tightness.

Swing Ship. Turning her to compass headings for compass adjustment.

Tabling. The doubled edging of sails and awnings.

Tack. Turning a sailing vessel into the wind until her sails fill on the opposite sides. The foremost lower corner of a sail.

Tackle. An arrangement of pulleys and rope to gain mechanical advantage.

Taffrail. The rim of a ship's stern.

T'Gallant. Topgallant. The sail immediately above the topsail.

Thimble. A metal fitting for reinforcing rope and wire eyes.

Throat Halyard. The rope or tackle for raising and lowering the inboard end of a gaff.

Ticket. Certificate of Competency for ship's officers. Originally issued by Board of Trade, then by the Ministry of Transport.

Tiller. The steering arm from the rudder head. In a schooner, this is connected to the wheel by a chain tackle.

Tops'l Yard. Topsail yard. The spar to which a topsail is bent. See Profile and Sail Plan, p. 283.

Trailboard. Ornamental boards on either side of a fiddle bow, from the billet or figure head, trailing to near the hawsepipes.

Transom. A type of ship's stern with a broad, flat finish.

Triatic Stays'l. A staysail bent to the triatic stay. See Profile and Sail Plan, p. 283.

Trick. A helmsman's two hours at the wheel.

Trim. The way a vessel floats on the water, indicated by her draught marks.

Trot. A line of mooring buoys.

Truck. A circular wooden cap at the top of a mast.

Trunnel. Treenail. A wooden dowel fastening used in wooden ships.

Trysail. A small, very strong sail for use in bad weather.

Underway. Vessel freely moving.

Up-and-Down. Of an anchor cable, when it is vertical, with its anchor under a vessel's bow.

Veer. Of the wind: when the wind changes direction clockwise. Of an anchor cable: to let out more scope. Allow to run out.

Warp. To move a ship by taking out a hawser (warp) ahead of her and securing its end to something immovable, then heaving it aboard with a winch or capstan.

Washport. An opening through a ship's bulwarks for draining heavy water off the deck.

Waterguard. The branch of H.M. Customs concerned with shipping.

Waterway. A raised timber kerb along the sides of a ship's deck, which guides deck water to the scupper pipes.

Wear. Turning a sailing vessel away from the wind until her sails fill on the opposite sides. The opposite to tacking.

Weather. To safely pass to windward. To safely ride a storm.

Whelp. A projecting rib on a windlass barrel, a capstan or winch drum, for providing a good grip for cables, warps, etc.

Wift. A windvane made of bunting, fitted above a ship's truck.

Wind'ard. Windward. The direction from which the wind blows.

Windbound. Held up by contrary winds.

Windsock. A wind vane consisting of a swivelling tapered tube of bunting.

Whip. A rope or wire through a single block.

Yard. A spar crossing a mast. See Profile and Sail Plan, p. 283.

Yardarm. The extremities of a yard.

Yaw. To swing from side to side of a ship's desired course, due to difficult weather conditions or bad steering.

Schooner Nellie Bywater of Annalong,
Port Newry 69715, Signal Letters M S F V
Built 1873 W. Thomas, Millom.
Rerigged 1946-48 by Captain England,
Master-Owner.
Gross Tonnage 115

Rig : Tops'l Schooner. Length from
knightheads to half-round, 98ft ;
between perpendiculars, 89.7ft.
Beam, 22.2ft. Depth of hold, 10.1ft.
Draught loaded, 11.5ft.

PROFILE &
SAIL PLAN

0 1 2 3 4 5 6 7 8 9 10 Feet

KEY TO PROFILE AND SAIL PLAN

SAILS

1. Boom-foresail.
2. Boom-jib.
3. Fore-staysail or,
   in schooner parlance, drummer.
4. Fore-topsail.
5. Mainsail.
6. Maintopmast-staysail or,
   in schooner parlance,
   triatic-staysail.
7. Main-topsail.
8. Standing-jib.

SPARS

9. Bowsprit.
10. Crosstrees & Spreaders.
11. Doublings.
12. Fore-boom.
13. Fore-gaff.
14. Fore-lowermast.
15. Fore-topmast.
16. Fore-topsail yard.
17. Fore-yard.
18. Hounds.
19. Jaws.
20. Main-boom.
21. Main-gaff.
22. Main-lowermast.
23. Main-topmast.
24. Parrel.
25. Pole.
26. Reefing-gear.
27. Truck.
28. Truss.

STANDING RIGGING

29. Bobstays.
30. Boom-jibstay.
31. Bowsprit-backropes.
32. Bowsprit-guys.
33. Cap-backstay.
34. Deadeyes & lanyards.
35. Footropes.
36. Forestay.
37. Foreyard-slings.
38. Lifts.
39. Ratlines.
40. Sheerpole.
41. Shrouds.
42. Standing-jibstay.
43. Topmast-backstay.

RUNNING RIGGING

44. Boom-guys.
45. Bowline.
46. Braces.
47. Buntline.
48. Burton.
49. Clewlines.
50. Downhauls.
51. Gaskets.
52. Headsail halyards.
53. Headsheets.
54. Lifts.
55. Peak halyards.
56. Sheets.
57. Signal halyards.
58. Throat halyards.
59. Topsail halyards.
60. Vang.

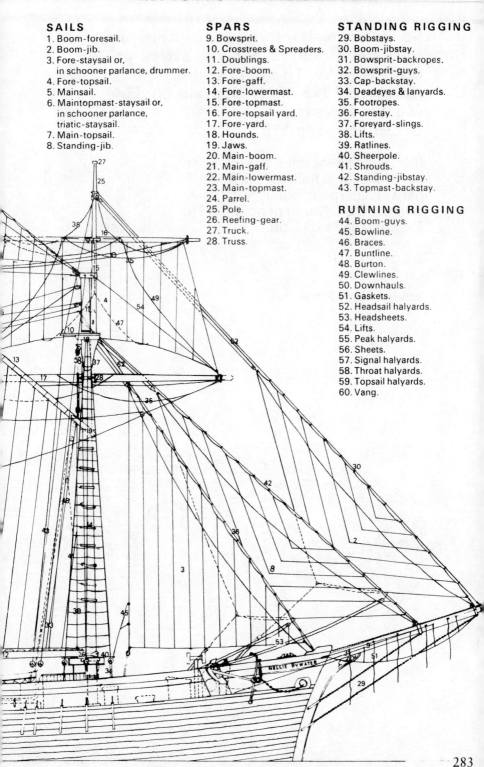

Schooner Nellie Bywater of Annalong, Port Newry 69715, Signal Letters M S F V Built 1873 W. Thomas, Millom. Rerigged 1946-48 by Captain England, Master-Owner. Gross Tonnage 115

Rig : Tops'l Schooner. Length from
knightheads to half-round, 98ft ;
between perpendiculars, 89.7ft.
Beam, 22.2ft. Depth of hold, 10.1ft.
Draught loaded, 11.5ft.

DECK PLAN

0 1 2 3 4 5 6 7 8 9 10 Feet

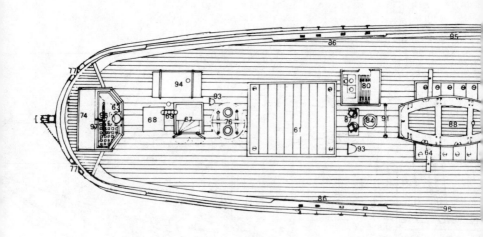

DECK PLAN KEY

61. After-hatch.
62. Bell (hung on pawlbitt).
63. Binnacle & compass.
64. Boat chocks & skids.
65. Bogey stovepipe.
66. Bower anchor.
67. Cabin companionway.
68. Cabin skylight.
69. Cabin stovepipe.
70. Cable manger.
71. Cable stopper.
72. Cathead.
73. Catstopper.
74. Chart table.
75. Compressor.
76. Engine-room skylight.
77. Fairlead or, in schooner parlance, knatch.
78. Foremast.
79. Forescuttle.
80. Galley.

81. Heads.
82. Knightheads.
83. Mainhatch.
84. Mainmast.
85. Pawlbitt & rockerarm.
86. Pinrail.
87. Pumps.
88. Punt-lifeboat.
89. Rope-rack.
90. Shankpainter.
91. Sheet-horse.
92. Spurling-pipe.
93. Ventilators.
94. Water tank.
95. Waterway.
96. Wheel.
97. Wheel-house.
98. Winch-house.
99. Windlass.

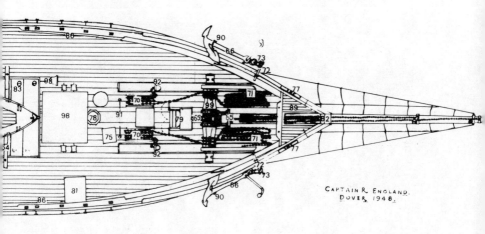

CAPTAIN R. ENGLAND.
DOVER 1948.

285

INDEX

287